Leonard
Cohen

STUDIES IN CANADIAN LITERATURE

Leonard Cohen

Stephen Scobie

Douglas & McIntyre

Vancouver

Douglas & McIntyre Ltd.
1875 Welch Street
North Vancouver, British Columbia

Canadian Cataloguing in Publication Data

Scobie, Stephen, 1943-
  Leonard Cohen
  (Studies in Canadian literature)

  ISBN 0-88894-194-3

  1. Cohen, Leonard, 1934-   -Criticism
and interpretation. I. Series.
PS8505.03Z76   C811'.5'4   C78-002033-2
PR9199.3.C57Z76

Typesetting by The Typeworks
Cover design by Nancy Legue-Grout
Printed and bound in Canada by Hunter Rose

Acknowledgements

Acknowledgements are due to many people, of whom I can mention only a few. First of all to Leonard Cohen himself, who generously made available to me an early draft of *Death of a Lady's Man*. Margaret Larock guided the manuscript through early difficulties, and thanks are due to her. Gary Geddes, my editor, has given invaluable help and advice at every stage of the enterprise. Finally, my thanks to all the friends and colleagues with whom I discussed Cohen's work over the years, especially to Lola Tostevin and Douglas Barbour.

Contents

Preface

The last time I saw Leonard Cohen, he was standing on the stage of the Olympia in Paris. He was wearing a very sober, conventional grey suit, and his face in the spotlights was pale. He could have passed as a harried business man in his mid-forties. But around him was a group of musicians with fierce electric instruments, and in front of him was an enthusiastic, almost a frenzied crowd, whose insistent applause was pulling him back onto stage for encore after encore.

Leonard Cohen has been the favourite singer of two consecutive French presidents. A German translation of his work describes him as "the incarnation of the unfulfilled wishes and unanswered questions of the young generation." Prior to this present volume, the longest published critical study of his writing was in Portuguese: *Leonard Cohen: Redescoberta da Vida e uma Alegoria a Eros,* by Manuel Cadafaz de Matos, Lisbon 1975.

These somewhat miscellaneous facts attest to the strength and extent of Leonard Cohen's reputation. He is one of the few Canadian authors whose fame is world-wide. Yet in Canada itself, Cohen's reputation, though high, is not overwhelmingly pre-eminent. Out of caution, or perhaps out of envy, Cohen's Canadian critics have always held back in their estimation of his writing, especially of *Beautiful Losers.* His books, however, continue to sell, and to sell well, whatever the fluctuations of his reputation amongst critics.

Cohen himself has never had a high opinion of his critics. "There's nobody in Canada who can judge my work," he said in a recent interview. "I'm not putting everybody down, but there's no mind that could possibly approach the work that would know what to do with it, how to incorporate it. People don't take me seriously in this country."

Part of the problem is that comparatively few writers have been interested in the work at all, whereas they have been obsessively interested in Cohen the man; he has always had more interviewers than critics. Popular Canadian magazines, from *Miss Chatelaine* to *Toronto Life,* have published dozens of interviews in which a star-struck reporter finds The Poet brooding about life, surrounded by a succession of mysterious and attractive women, and uttering gnomic sayings like, "I never really considered myself a poet. A poet is something that is dead."

In reality, the outlines of Cohen's biography are unremarkable, and notable mainly for the care with which he has detached himself from the possibilities of power, or of allying himself with movements or political parties. He was born in 1934 in the wealthy Westmount district of Montreal. His family was in the clothing business, but he never took an active role in it; *The Favourite Game* contains some dutiful satire on the stuffiness of the milieu. He went to McGill University, and when put in charge of public debates, he decreed that there would not be any public debates. In the late fifties, he spent some time doing graduate work at Columbia University in New York, but this was the extent of his involvement with academia: he has never taught at a university, nor accepted a post as writer-in-residence.

In the spring of 1961, as "the only tourist in Havana," he was in Cuba during the Bay of Pigs invasion; later in the sixties he maintained a home in Greece during the troubled years of the Colonels' rule. Yet, though his sensibilities are in some ways profoundly political, he has never joined in any major political causes, or movements, or parties.

Similarly, he has maintained an aloof position as a Canadian writer. He has a close personal friendship with Irving Layton, but does not associate himself with any of Layton's fierce public polemics. Cohen has never published any critical statement or views on Canadian literature; he has never joined any organization such as the League of Canadian Poets; in 1969 he turned down the Governor-General's Award.

Since the early sixties, he has been an occasional resident of California, where he lived in a Zen monastery; of the Greek island of Hydra; and of Montreal, to which he periodically returns in order, as he once said in a widely quoted phrase, "to renew my neurotic affiliations." He is well known for preferring cheap hotels and sparsely furnished rooms. In the midst of his growing fame as a singer, he has managed to preserve a personal anonymity, almost an absence.

For the last eight years he has been married to a woman named Suzanne (not the same Suzanne as the subject of the famous song, but, he says, perhaps "conjured" by it), and they have two children, Adam and Lorca. Having children, Cohen said recently, "is the only activity that connects you to mankind and makes a serious assault on the ego."

Yet for all the glamour and mystery, Cohen's public career, and the facts of his biography, are largely irrelevant to an understanding of his writing. Certain aspects are clearly important — his Jewish inheritance, and the pervasive atmosphere of the city of Montreal — but it would not greatly aid the reader of Cohen's work to follow all the details of his romantic entanglements (even if that were possible). What does it really add to our appreciation of "Suzanne" to know who Suzanne Vaillancourt is? Nothing at all: all that is important is there in the song itself.

Even in *The Favourite Game,* Cohen is not really an autobiographical writer (and he has usually expressed irritation with critics who have stressed this view of the novel). The facts of his life, and of all the various women he has known, are transmuted, metamorphosed, made over entirely into his personal mythology, a total world view which is present and accessible in the books alone.

This study, then, is not a biographical one. I have made little attempt to research Cohen's life; I have not interviewed him myself; and I have made only limited use of other interviews. The focus is firmly on the texts themselves. My purpose has been to re-examine the complete body of Cohen's writing, hoping to arrive at some definite conclusions about his work of the sixties and to make tentative introductions to his more recent books and recordings.

My view is a critical one, but not an unsympathetic one. I do not share Cohen's world-view, but I find much to admire in his work. Throughout his career, he has been an innovative and courageous writer, never content to rest on the laurels of his popular success but always exploring new forms and modes of expression. There is an intellectual daring to his work, a willingness to take the most outrageous risks, which I find admirable and exhilarating. Of course, these risks do not always come off, but even Cohen's failures tend to be spectacular. And his successes are magnificent. At his best, he writes with outstanding control, producing lines, passages, whole poems which resonate with meaning and beauty. His imagery is vivid and exotic in a way which few other Canadian writers have achieved, yet it can also be direct, factual, brutal, or obscene. His writing sparkles with wit and humour, yet the laughter is never far from the apocalypse. In his songs he has produced a body of work as entertaining as it is profound, as lovely as it is memorable. On that evening in Paris, I too was applauding.

CHAPTER ONE

Introduction

*I have always said that my strength is
that I have no ideas. I feel empty. I have
never dazzled myself with thought,
particularly my own thought—it is
one of the processes that my heart
doesn't leap out to.*

(*Leonard Cohen, interview, 1967*)

Although Leonard Cohen's major period of creative activity (so far) lies in the mid-sixties, his first book of poetry, *Let Us Compare Mythologies,* was published in 1956, the same year as Allen Ginsberg's *Howl.* In many ways, Cohen's work can be seen to have grown out of the atmosphere of the fifties, the social and cultural milieu which produced the early Beat poets. The opening section of *Howl* describes a world which is recognizably the world of *Beautiful Losers,* with its "ordinary eternal machinery" sought in madness and self-destruction:

> I saw the best minds of my generation destroyed by madness,
> starving hysterical naked,
> dragging themselves through the negro streets at dawn looking
> for an angry fix,
> angelheaded hipsters burning for the ancient heavenly connection
> to the starry dynamo in the machinery of night [1]

Conventional modes of morality and authority have been breaking down for a long time, at least since 1914. In his book *Bomb Culture,* the English writer Jeff Nuttall claims that this process was given a special impetus in the fifties by the general expectation of impending nuclear catastrophe. "The people who had not yet reached puberty at the time of the bomb," he writes (and Cohen was eleven in 1945), "were incapable of conceiving life with a future." The result was that:

> In the new world the light was harsh, a perpetual noon of decisions, every crucial action being possibly final. No man was certain anymore of anything but his own volition, so the only value was pragmatic. Moral values, thought absolute, were now seen to be comparative, for all social entities around which morality had revolved were now called into doubt and nothing of morality remained. [2]

Similarly, Cohen once said: "Whatever we have been told about anything, although we remember it, and sometimes operate in those patterns, we have no deep abiding faith in anything we have been told, even in the hippest things, the newest things." [3]

These comments describe a climate of thought and opinion which was prevalent in the fifties, and which was unredeemed, at that time, by any concept of united social action or political motivation. Later generations were able to rally to such causes as the Campaign for Nuclear Disarmament in Britain, and the Civil Rights movement in the United States; these in turn led to the international agitation against the Viet Nam War in the late sixties. But the fifties offered no such alternative: the only resource was the unsupported self.

The fifties mood was at worst apathetic, at best introspective. And since the moral boundaries were down, the exploration of the self led many people deeper into the underworld regions of drugs and sexuality. *Howl* is a key text, and Ginsberg's celebration of his homosexuality, together with his experiments with such drugs as LSD, set a tone for the era. Recently, Michael Gnarowski has described the characteristic attitudes of the Beat movement, in terms which are directly relevant to Cohen, as "shifty saintliness and a terribly mobile sense of the self." [4]

Of course, a preoccupation with the self has been a central theme of Western literature ever since the Romantic period, which may ultimately be seen as the beginning of the break-up of the solidity of any possible world-view. Sandra Djwa has described Cohen as a "Black Romantic" [5] and placed him in the tradition of Baudelaire and Genet. Nuttall also speaks of an artistic tradition beginning with De Sade and including Rimbaud, Lautréamont, and Apollinaire as well as the painters — Cézanne, Picasso, the Futurists, the Dadaists, the Surrealists — leading to Ginsberg, Burroughs, and the Beat writers. In a situation where all traditions are called into question, only this tradition, that of the cultural revolutionaries and anarchists, seems to remain valid.

For the Romantic artist, individual perception is more important than social consensus. He delights in the non-rational aspects of human consciousness (imagination, hallucination, vision, madness) rather than in the rational. Traditionally, he has sought his values in the world of untouched Nature rather than in the civilization of man. The position of the "Black" Romantic is to take these things to their extremes, exulting in the darkest aspects of the non-rational self in the face of the "sane" values of society. Thus Baudelaire's *Flowers of Evil*, Lautréamont's sharks, the Dadaists' destruction of form, Sartre's *Saint Genet*. The use of drugs pushes imagination through hallucination towards madness; sexuality is seen primarily in terms of cruelty, violence, and personal domination. The self defined as distinct from society becomes the self defined only at the expense of society.

The Romantic preoccupation with the isolated self has been seen by some as a kind of sickness. Cut off from social contacts and responsibilities, the self turning in on itself becomes perverse and morbid, seeking death. The High Romantic *Liebestod* is not too far removed from the ultimate diseases of Nazi atrocity; the flowers of evil become the flowers for Hitler. This view has been dramatized by such films as Luchino Visconti's *The Damned* and Liliana Cavani's *The Night Porter,* and it may also be seen in a fascinating speculation from John Glassco's "The Black Helmet."

> Could [Romanticism] not be simply a kind of disease, whose germ was first isolated and pampered by Rousseau, with his nervous disorders, his skirted Armenian costume and his famous "I am not made like any man I have ever seen"? Is it not, then, the triumph of the sick man, who becomes more than ever an individual by virtue of the malady that sets him apart and exasperates his nerves? In any case, a hundred and fifty years ago

books came to be written, for the first time in history, by men avowedly occupied by their digestion and the state of the weather — two new factors of inspiration.

And since then all art has been sick.

But if the invalid has now come into his own, it has taken the supremely sick to make any mark. These are the neurotics who, deprived of their grandiose identities by an unsympathetic world, feeling themselves thrust outside life, have projected themselves into foggy, criminal and melodramatic characters, bisexualizing themselves, seeking to feel they are alive by an exchange or duplication of gender. The romantic artist, sick unto death, has become the true psychic hermaphrodite. [6]

This passage is clearly relevant to the image of Leonard Cohen projected by his writings.

But to Cohen in the mid-fifties, such ideas would have come in severely modified forms. It is tempting, and perhaps too easy, to say that in Canada they could not possibly be found in such extreme form. Genet might be possible in France, but in Westmount? In fact, there has always been something very self-conscious about the extremity of the positions that Cohen adopts. Robertson Davies has characterized Canada as "a much softer-focussed country" than the United States: "This intellectual ferocity and sort of black/white quality is very strong there. We're fuzzier, but I think we're more humane."[7] In the same book, Robert Kroetsch describes Canadians as "fascinated with problems of equilibrium."[8] This is a tendency which Cohen has had to defy to go to the extremity of the Black Romantic, and the defiance induces a defensively ironic awareness of the pose. This is a point which is central to any consideration of Cohen: *excess*, often for its own sake, is central to his style and subject-matter.

Cohen's view would also be modified by his awareness of and deep interest in his religious tradition as a Jew, a tradition which still offers a coherent view of the world and of history. It sees in human life a continuity in which all present events have a past context. In contrast to any view which sees the present age as fundamentally *dis*continuous from any past one, Cohen collapses time, and sees past generations working within the present; Catherine Tekakwitha is alive and well in contemporary Montreal, and *Flowers for Hitler* is essentially the same book as *Sunshine for Napoleon* or *Walls for Genghis Khan.*

Even if Cohen is not an orthodox Jew, even if he is comparing mythologies rather than believing in any one, the religious sense continues to inform his work. "As I see religion," he once told an interviewer, "it's a technique for strength and for making the universe hospitable. I think there really is a power to tune in on. It's easy for me to call that power God. Some people find it difficult." [9] In this general sense, all Cohen's work is religious — but then, so is a good deal of Black Romantic writing. It is not for nothing that Sartre calls Genet a "saint," and the saint is the controlling image of *Beautiful Losers.*

Another possible context that might have modified Cohen's inheritance of the Black Romantic tradition is that of Canadian literature. The most immediate influences on Cohen in the mid-fifties were such writers as A. M. Klein and Irving Layton (most of Cohen's books contain at least one poem dedicated to Layton), writers who shared the Montreal Jewish background. Cohen owes much to the ground broken by Layton's energetic, exuberant, and frequently absurd posturings: his Romantic (but not essentially *Black* Romantic) exultation in his own poetic and sexual prowess. Although Cohen's poses are often more extreme than Layton's, he is less fully committed to them, but it is Cohen's very self-awareness, ironic and even farcical, which protects him from Layton's more naively serious absurdities. Klein's influence is evident in the attempt made by both poets to write directly out of the Jews' obsession with Hitler; in the view of the writer's position outlined in Klein's "Portrait of the Poet as Landscape" and echoed in much of Cohen's poetry, and in the preoccupation with silence and madness, which in Klein's life was tragic and all too real.

These are immediate influences; more generally, Cohen's work can be viewed within the thematic patterns of Canadian literature proposed by such writers/critics as Doug Jones and Margaret Atwood. Of such themes, the one most clearly relevant to Cohen is that of the encounter with the wilderness. This experience, while central to a great deal of Canadian literature, is usually a profoundly ambivalent one in which attraction and repulsion are uneasily balanced. Dennis Lee uses the theological term *"mysterium tremendum* — the encounter with holy otherness, most commonly approached here through encounter with the land," [10] and he attempts to define its ambivalence by saying that "we are half spooked and half at home here . . . we cannot master the space we have been thrown in, yet are claimed by it and will be at home nowhere else." [11] The wilderness is, of course, not only the physical land but also the interior wilderness of the spirit, the dark and instinctual forces of sex, madness, death; and the two wildernesses — physical and psychic — can be used almost interchangeably.

This idea of the interior wilderness may be connected with the Black Romantic ethos. Sex, madness, and death are the experiences to which a writer such as De Sade or Genet confidently turns in search of some kind of value. Canadian writers may often turn in the same direction, but generally with far less confidence: with, instead, attraction and repulsion uneasily balanced. [12]

The repulsion side of the ambivalence expresses itself through what has been described, in a much overused phrase, as "the garrison culture." [13] The garrison shuts out the wilderness; it protects itself, often violently, from contact with and contamination by the outside unknown. In social terms, this protectiveness leads to a strong insistence on conformity and moral rectitude, often reinforced by the religious traditions of the pioneers, and a strong distrust and rejection of non-conforming individuals whose behaviour suggests unusual affinity with the wilderness. Social, class, and economic sanctions support this orthodoxy.

The attraction side of the ambivalence may partly be seen in the kind of response outlined by Doug Jones in *Butterfly on Rock*. "The weakness of the colonial mentality," he writes, "is that it regards as a threat what it should regard as its salvation; it walls out or exploits what it should welcome and cultivate. . . . The only effective defence for a garrison culture is to abandon defence, to let down the walls and let the wilderness in, even to the wolves." [14]

It is this course of action which is pioneered, throughout Canadian literature, by a series of individuals whom I have described as "saints." [15] The image of the saint has been used, in various ways, by many Canadian writers, most notably Cohen, Robertson Davies, and bp Nichol. In the context of these writers' work I use the word "saint" to describe the kind of character who explores the wilderness in the way Jones outlines, who becomes an adept in its mysteries. When they appear in "realistic" fiction, they are characters who are felt to be totally exceptional by those around them, but realistic fiction is far from the best way of dealing with them. These "saints" are strongly associated with the wilderness in one or another of its manifestations, and are usually social outcasts; in their mental and spiritual experiences as well, they exist beyond the bounds and limitations of normal human experience. Yet some of them at least are capable of acting as teachers to those few who recognize and are attracted by their special qualities.

As might be expected from the ambivalence previously outlined, Canadian writers have been fascinated by the possibilities of such characters, but many (Cohen less so than most) have also regarded them with some distrust and suspicion. Most of the saints, therefore, come equipped with disciples, who express the ambivalence by being attracted to the saints but not wholly at one with them. The drama often centres more on the disciple's reaction to the saint than on the saint's experience itself. It could be argued, I suppose, that the disciple, caught in the doubts and uncertainties of having to make a decision between opposing claims, is a more typically "Canadian" figure.

The pattern of saint and disciple may, as I have suggested, be traced through many Canadian works. While the pattern remains fairly constant, the degree to which it explicitly uses the language and imagery of saints varies. In some works, such as *Fifth Business* and *Beautiful Losers,* it is a basic and pervasive image; in others it occurs only in minor ways, such as the major characters bearing relevant saints' names.

Cohen does use the terminology of saint and disciple quite extensively (most obviously in *Beautiful Losers*), but he also uses other, similar images, such as those of master and slave. "Saint and disciple" suggests a teaching relationship, with echoes of Zen, whereas "master and slave" suggests a power relationship, often seen in explicitly sexual terms.[16] Some such relationship is at the centre of most of Cohen's work.

Power takes many forms; the obvious ones of money, social class and political rule are not overlooked, but Cohen is most interested in power at a personal level, as it manifests itself through the two central (and for him interchangeable) activities of sex and religion. The close association of these activities is evident in the comment on the song by Gavin Gate and the Goddesses: "Oh God! All states of love give power!"[17]

This association of God, love, and power reverberates throughout Cohen's work. The importance, and the strength, of Cohen's religious feelings have already been described in relation to his inheritance of Jewish tradition, but their real dynamic lies in their identification with sexual energy and emotion. It is, of course, a very traditional device to talk about divine love in terms of sexual love, and vice versa; much primitive religious thought makes no distinction at all, and the imagery has been used from the *Song of Solomon* to the "Holy Sonnets" of John Donne. Cohen's only originality here lies, if at all, in the thoroughness and the explicitness with which he applies the identification of the two areas; little more than social and linguistic convention really separates *The Song of Solomon* from *Beautiful Losers'* admonition to "Fuck a saint."

In her excellent essay, "The Pornographic Imagination," Susan Sontag comments that "Despite the virtual incomprehensibility to most educated people today of the substantive experience behind religious vocabulary, there is a continuing piety towards the grandeur of emotions that went into that vocabulary. The religious imagination survives for most people today as not just the primary but virtually the only credible instance of an imagination working in a total way."[18] Cohen is concerned precisely with such a "total" experience, and to portray it he uses vocabulary drawn from the two areas in which such an intensity has always occurred: religion and sex. The mixing of the two, involving as it does a certain amount of shock, is even more potent: the religious and the sexual vocabularies work together and intensify each other.

Furthermore, the association of sex and religion with power in personal relationships leads Cohen into another area replete with taboo, and with the potentiality for profound shock. For in every power game there must be a winner and a loser, and the loser (the slave) must surrender, according to the uncompromising rules that Cohen plays by, what Western society's tradition regards as his most precious possession: his own self, the integrity of his own individuality. At the extreme points of his vision, Cohen moves towards an obliteration of the very idea of individuality, of personal character. If the Romantic movement set up the originality and uniqueness of an individual's perception as its highest value, then the Black Romantic extension must seek its highest value in the destruction of these very qualities. If the lack of social or political commitment in the fifties threw the artist back onto the naked self, then his exploration of that self might lead to its annihilation. This process, if taken seriously, can be even more deeply disturbing than the associations of religion and sex which form its vocabulary.

It is tempting, at this point, to make another link with the general background of Canadian literature by invoking Margaret Atwood's *Survival,* and her theory that Canadian literature is obsessed with victims. Cohen certainly shares this obsession, but he does not fit neatly into any of Atwood's categories, except perhaps that "mystic" position which she postulates but does not develop.[19] Underlying Atwood's schema of "Victim Positions" is the unspoken assumption that it is not a good thing to be a victim, that all the stages of effort and progressive self-awareness are directed towards the goal of ceasing to be a victim; in fact, she wishes to escape altogether from the system of winners and losers. Cohen, on the other hand, does not merely sympathize with his victims; he approves of them. His losers are beautiful *because* they are losers, not in spite of their failure; losing is morally and spiritually preferable to winning.

This is the terrible force of Cohen's destruction of individuality: that he endorses it. In the fifties, the crumbling of all kinds of authority without the alternative of meaningful political action had put all the stress back on the unsupported self. The self was the last bulwark against total nihilism, and it was defended desperately on every psychiatrist's couch in America. It was the last taboo. Cohen sets out to break it.

His saints reach their true sainthood only in destruction of themselves, when they have destroyed all vestiges of their individual will and become "disarmed and empty, an instrument of Grace"[20] (or, in the words of an older and dissimilar Canadian poet, Archibald Lampman, "A body without wish or will"[21]). This description is close to the traditional theological definition of a saint, who makes his own will utterly transparent to the

Will of God. But Cohen's saints must make their wills transparent to Nothing. The self is not sacrificed to some higher cause; the sacrifice of the self *is* the higher cause.

The obstacle is power: the saint is always as close to the role of master as he is to that of slave, and the master or teacher has a role which prevents full self-destruction. He who exerts power over others cannot himself be powerless. This is the struggle, and the tragedy, of F. in *Beautiful Losers*: a "born teacher," he is condemned to seeing his disciple transcend him, to being always a magician rather than magic itself.

Power is the obstacle; powerlessness is the hope. In Cohen's work, roles and personalities are always interchangeable. Master and slave not merely embrace but change places. Personal pronouns have no security or consistency. The merging of all the characters at the end of *Beautiful Losers* into one indistinguishable whole is only the final extension of a tendency visible throughout Cohen's work. Any securely established sense of identity must be challenged: Cohen seeks his values in flux rather than in stability, in the personality losing itself rather than finding itself.

The interchangeability of pronouns and personalities is further complicated by the fact that sexual relationships in Cohen's work are seldom confined to two people. The presence of a third party (or fourth, fifth . . .) is continually making itself felt, though not in any conventional sense of an "eternal triangle": Cohen's lovers are rarely jealous of each other. Often, a kind of master/pupil relationship exists between two of the lovers, or between all three, as in "The Master Song." They instruct each other how to love each other, and in this process the relationships and the personalities blur into each other. At times, when a poem is simply addressed to "you," the sex of the person addressed is indeterminate: Cohen does not deal with homosexuals, heterosexuals, or even bisexuals, but simply with sexuals.[22] The sexual situation, however many people of whatever genders it involves, is an area within which relationships of power and personality play their intricate games — games which, in Cohen's writing, are always "won" by the beautiful losers.

These aspects of Cohen's treatment of personal and sexual relationships go some way towards explaining (if not excusing) the blatant sexism of his work. One feminist critic of Cohen has written, "Do you have an orifice and a pair of breasts? These are the essential if not sole requirements for a female character in a Leonard Cohen novel. Smooth skin helps, too. Intelligence and personality are of no consequence."[23] It is true that Cohen seldom views a woman in any other role than as a passive fulfiller of sexual demands which are often extreme and bizarre; but it is equally true that he seldom regards other *men* in any more favourable light. Cohen's vision is so completely self-centred that there is no room in it for *any* individualized personality, male or female, other than his own. The various characters in Cohen's novels, poems and songs merge together and become indistinguishable partly because they are all, in essence, projections of aspects of his own personality or of his Black Romantic self-image.

This consideration brings us to one of the major paradoxes in Cohen's work: namely, that the theme of the loss of personality is projected in terms of what appears to be a very strong personality and ego, that of the artist himself. Perhaps the obsession with the loss of self is only the ultimate form of self-expression. But what must be kept in mind here is the distinction between the private person Leonard Cohen, who remains unknown, and outside the legitimate bounds of our literary curiosity, and the public persona of "Leonard Cohen, poet novelist and pop star" projected in his works. For certainly Cohen writes about himself a good deal in the role of artist, and the position and the function of the artist is one of his main concerns. Perhaps it is in the figure of the artist that the paradox of self/loss of self can be resolved.

Between saint and disciple, master and slave, stands the figure of the artist. "In me," wrote Layton, "nature's divided things— / tree, mold on tree— / have their fruition; / I am their core."[24] As an exceptional figure, standing apart from the ruck of society in a conventional Romantic way, Cohen's artist approaches the roles of saint and master, but in his dissolution of himself into his works, he approaches the role of slave. The artists Cohen portrays are self-destructive types, who in order to turn into gold must first turn into clay. Cohen himself, having become the "golden-boy poet" of *The Spice Box of Earth,* has made persistent attempts to turn into clay, to become the anti-poet writing anti-poems.

Cohen built up for himself a public persona, which was in many ways outrageously egotistic (and he can still play dazzling games with that image, as witness the infamous squib about 15-year-old girls in *The Energy of Slaves*). But that persona is also a mask behind which he hid and dissolved a more private, unknowable self: in this, as in other ways, he may have learned from the age's grand master of disguise, Bob Dylan. Cohen's view of the artist is to be seen more truly in his works than in his public poses, which are often outrageously Romantic more for the sake of being outrageous than for the sake of being Romantic.

In his work, Cohen often celebrates the self-destruction of his artists, his beautiful losers, in terms which come close to the conclusion of A. M. Klein's "Portrait of the Poet as Landscape":

> Meanwhile, he
> makes of his status as zero a rich garland,
> a halo of his anonymity,
> and lives alone, and in his secret shines
> like phosphorus. At the bottom of the sea.[25]

Cohen believes absolutely in that "status as zero," and he also believes in garlanding it richly. The richness of Cohen's language and the exoticism of his imagery are aspects of his belief in excess. There is no point in complaining that Cohen is excessive (or, an even stranger formulation, *too* excessive): excess is the very centre and essence of his style. I have already spoken of his love of the outrageous, and of his deeply serious commitment to total experiences. Cohen writes about extreme situations, and he writes about them in extreme ways. When it first appeared in 1966, *Beautiful Losers* was a shattering explosion of all the conventions in Canadian novel-writing; even after eleven years of further experimentation, few writers have come close to catching up with it.

Some writers believe that life can best be understood by looking at extreme, unusual situations; others, that it can best be understood by looking at everyday, run-of-the-mill occurrences. The risk of the first kind of writing is that the work will seem absurd; of the second, that it will seem dull. Cohen is clearly of the first kind: he seeks a definition of any idea by exploring its outer limits, and going beyond them. He is never dull; he is sometimes absurd, but he defends himself against that absurdity by building into his own system a measure of self-mockery.

Some of Cohen's public gestures have been deliberately absurd: for example, he used to introduce his concerts by riding onto the stage on a white stallion. The outrageousness of such behaviour constituted a criticism of the flamboyant excess of the "romantic" pop star (while at the same time allowing Cohen to indulge in it anyway).

In Cohen's work, the moments when he seems most absurd are often the moments when he is in fact most serious. In the novels especially, the moments of highest seriousness are simultaneously the moments of wildest farce; the degree of narrative or imagistic absurdity is almost an index to the degree of seriousness. As previously argued, this mockery may partly be caused by the self-consciousness of holding an extreme position in Canada, and it certainly underlines Cohen's affinity with Layton, but it is also a necessary aspect of Cohen's gospel of Excess. One of the "saints" in one of Cohen's more whimsical (and therefore more serious) songs — "One of Us Cannot Be Wrong" — teaches that "the duty of lovers / Is to tarnish the golden rule" of moderation. Cohen has long been working assiduously at this task.

I have been outlining here what appears to me to be the central vision in Cohen's work. The beauty and sensuousness of his language have tended to disguise it; it is a harsh and disturbing one. It begins in a broken world, the world of the death-camps and the slaves, and, finding no solutions in the social and political vacuum of the fifties, it proceeds to the broken self, which it celebrates with a kind of fierce and inhuman joy. This vision provides a symbolic language which creates a hermetically sealed world, a closed-system view of reality.

But not all of Cohen's work is as harsh and absolute as this. When questioned once by Sandra Djwa about his relationship to the Black Romantic writers, Cohen replied:

> The only thing that differs in those writers and myself is that I hold out the idea of ecstasy as the solution. . . . The thing about Sartre is that he's never lost his mind. . . . I know he's never going to say "and then the room turned to gold." He'll say "the room turned to shit." But the room sometimes does turn to gold and unless you mention that, your philosophy is incomplete.[26]

Sometimes the room turns gold. Cohen always retains a belief in the power and the beauty of love. But love can only enter his world once it has accepted the essential conditions of destruction and loss. Love is possible only for the broken, the maimed, the outcasts, the beautiful losers.

It is in the songs that this view can most clearly be seen, especially those of *Songs from a Room*. They deal with the victims and losers who are characteristic of Cohen's world, but instead of celebrating their loss, Cohen offers his sympathy and his love; instead of seeing pain as a method of transcendence, he sees it as something which he must helplessly share.

Cohen's finest work so far is undoubtedly *Beautiful Losers*: in it we see the full brilliance and complexity of his genius. Nevertheless, it seems to me that songs such as "Suzanne," "The Old Revolution," or "It Seems So Long Ago, Nancy" offer an emotional experience which is deeper, more humane, and ultimately more worthy of our attention and respect.

CHAPTER TWO

The Poems, 1956–1968

*He never described himself as a poet or his
work as poetry. The fact that the lines do not
come to the edge of the page is no guarantee.
Poetry is a verdict, not an occupation.*
> (*Leonard Cohen,* The Favourite Game)

(i) *Let Us Compare Mythologies* (1956)

The central complex of themes and images, as outlined in the
previous chapter, remains constant throughout Cohen's work.
Although *Let Us Compare Mythologies*[1] shows occasional signs
of being a first book, the essence of Cohen's vision is already
clearly and confidently present.

The opening poem, "Elegy" (13), announces the main
themes with a firmness of tone and richness of texture that
reverberate through to the culmination of *Beautiful Losers.* It
takes either great pretentiousness or great brilliance (or an outrageous combination of the two) for a young poet to proclaim
himself as Orpheus in the first poem of his first book.

Many of Cohen's themes cluster into this poem. There is,
first, the figure of the poet, romantically set apart and special,
rejected and destroyed by the frenzy of society, sinking into
lower and lower depths of the sea and of himself. There is the
association with religion, especially religion as a source of secret
and mysterious power, in the memory of the occult Orphic rites.
At the same time, the "soft" and "snow-bruised" body is seen
with a sensuousness whose erotic suggestion is only increased by
the idea of that soft body torn to "shreds." The death is trans-

formed into a thing of beauty, "cliffs / Of slow green water" in which the fish become lovers, kissing the bruised body. The experience of death and beauty becomes the source of poetry; as Sandra Djwa says, "From the disintegrating body of the dead god comes art: the 'secret nests' of 'hovering' fish."[2] The possible production of art, even from the dead poet, is reinforced by the memories of Orpheus as a seasonally dying god, and his associations with such gods as Atthis or Osiris who will rise again in the spring. Poetry, religion, sex, death, beauty, power: all form an interlocked pattern, heightened by the sensuousness of the language, and touched also by a slight sense of the outrageous as we think of the young Cohen already implying his own association, through the divine role of artist, with the greatest poet-god of antiquity.

The image of the poet's body stretched, like Orpheus, undersea, recurs in "These Heroics" (28); this poem also offers the alternative mythological image of Icarus: "I could ruin my feathers / in flight before the sun." In this poem it is an aspiration rather than a reality, something for which the poet would at once abandon the limiting perspectives of a single room and lover.

These perspectives are not always limiting for Cohen; indeed, it is more common for the lover to be identified with the god, to be part of the attractive and destructive force which draws the poet in. The lover is a diversion only if she remains too firmly on the level of ordinary humanity, exerting possessive claims and urging the poet to be content with something less than his destiny. In the book's other Icarus poem, "The Flier" (49), the "clinic of your thighs" is seen as an alternative to, or escape from, the terrible but beautiful demands of the self-destructive flight. The poem is in effect an appeal to the woman to cease her temptation to normality and to allow the poet to fulfill his role as Icarus.

Orpheus and Icarus were both destroyed by their vocation; whether as poet or lover, Cohen revels in images of that destruction. Pain, madness, and death are the true sources of poetry in this book: Cohen offers his own brain

> torn and stretched for the sun,
> to be used for a drum or a tambourine,

to be scratched with poetry
by Kafka's machine.

(59)

Madness is welcomed: "For a lovely instant I thought she would grow mad / and end the reason's fever" (26); it is the brain "rotting like stumps of brown teeth" onto which poetry can be "scratched" (59).

Christ's crucifixion is a central instance of images of beauty growing out of images of pain: his wounds become "velvet," his twisted feet "delicate" (14). The opening of "Ballad" (42) sets it out as clearly as a program:

> He pulled a flower
> out of the moss
> and struggled past soldiers
> to stand at the cross.
>
> He dipped the flower
> into a wound
> and hoped that a garden
> would grow in his hand.

Poetry grows from the dead body of Orpheus, and the Icarian image of "The Flier" (49) envisages cripples, "basket men and the lame," as those who can "run / And grasp at angels in their lovely flight." The wings of Icarus are seen as "stumps and hooks and artificial skin," braces which leave scars on the flier's leg. This is the first use of the scar, which will recur later as the central image of *The Favourite Game*.

The theme of beauty and poetry growing out of cruelty and death, especially the death of a lover, reaches its fullest expression in "Ballad" (46), which is also interesting as the first extended use by Cohen of the images of pop culture. The poem opens with one of Cohen's startling juxtapositions, reminiscent of Donne's opening lines: "My lady was found mutilated / in a Mountain Street boarding house." The dignified, formal associations of "My lady," reinforced by the title and by the immediately following allusion to Tennyson, are sharply contrasted to the sordid shock of "mutilated" and the matter-of-fact, police-report tone of the address.[3] The contrast is extended through the first stanza, and then the poem moves into the fantasy world of pop culture, "the adolescents / examining pocket-book covers in drugstores," and those with "the broadest smiles at torture scenes / in movie houses." The contrast between tones is, however, more apparent than real. Although Cohen frequently uses pop culture images for shock effect, as when, later in this poem, he shifts abruptly from "the Marian year" to "tooth-paste ads," he also takes them seriously. Pop culture—movies, hit-parade songs, cheap pornography—provides the images through which desperate but inarticulate passions are expressed, and they are not to be despised. If "My lady" could have inspired the articulate adoration of Tennyson, she could also have inspired the inarticulate frustration of those who read the "tabloids" and watch "the poker blacken the eyes / of the Roman prisoner."

Sexual desperation is widespread—"There are so many cities!"—so the poet is not really surprised that "The man was never discovered." As Michael Ondaatje remarks,[4] it is really a "communal" murder, in which the whole culture, including, centrally, the poet himself, takes part. After these speculations on the killer's identity, Cohen turns the poem back towards the lady herself. He presents her beauty in another series of juxtapositions—movies and art-galleries, Goldwyn and Botticelli—which are not so much contrasts as equations. Her beauty invited its own destruction: "She should not have walked so bravely / through the streets."

In the final stanzas, Cohen settles on the dignified, "ballad" tone suggested earlier, and uses this poetic device to confirm the beauty which grows out of the lady's destruction:

> The flowers they were roses
> and such sweet fragrance gave
> that all my friends were lovers
> and we danced upon her grave.

The burial takes place "in Spring-time," another suggestion of the seasons myth symbolized by Orpheus and present in other poems in the book.

The lady's beauty is, then, a function of what happens to her. It causes her death but is also caused *by* her death. Passion is conferred upon her by the frustrated longings of all the lonely men in drug-stores and movie-houses, as much as by Tennyson or Botticelli (or Cohen). The "knife slashes / across her breasts" are the wounds from which the flowers of the final stanza grow: in a strange and terrible way, they are the scars of love.

The unknown murderer of "Ballad" also functions as a third party in the love between the poet and his lady. Many of Cohen's love poems depend on the presence of such an extension beyond the couple: the relationship cannot be fulfilled without the extra presence. Indeed, the mutilation of the lady in "Ballad" may be seen as the fulfillment of the destiny not only of the lady but of the poet as well. Only with this destruction does the relationship become complete, so that then "all" his friends can become lovers.

The suggestion of the third party is present in several of the book's love poems. In "Poem" (55), Cohen waits for the man who will climb the stairs and "clear his throat outside our door." In the fantasy "The Warrior Boats" (34) Cohen tells "my enemy sailors"

> you will find my love
> Asleep and waiting
> And I cannot know how long
> She has dreamed of all of you
>
> Oh remove my coat gently
> From her shoulders.

The tone here is one that will be repeated again and again as Cohen thinks of those others who will share his love; he bequeaths her to them without jealousy or fear, but gently, tenderly, as one who passes on a gift so beautiful that he knows it can never be his alone.

The most complex treatment in this book of the shifting relationships which occur once the central love-situation has been extended beyond the couple comes in "Song of Patience" (26). There are in fact at least four people involved in this poem: the poet himself; the "you" (presumably but not necessarily female, an uncertainty common in Cohen's poems); the "he" to whom "you" is bequeathed; and the "she" of the first stanza. In the first stanza, the poet turns away from this other woman, because, despite his hopes, she will not go mad; rather, she wards off madness as if it were a vampire, holding "Christ's splinter" in her hand. For consolation the poet turns to another relationship, one already established, and recalls "your insane letters / and how you wove initials in my throat."

In the second stanza, the vampire imagery is continued as the poet's reasonable "friends" warn him of the dangers in this relationship, but he only smiles. The relationship to "you" is founded on the very things which his rational friends shy away from: on the insanity of the letters, on the violence of the stitches in the throat, on the evil of the infecting vampire.

Then in the third stanza, as a logical extension of the relationship, Cohen introduces the third party, the pupil, the initiate:

> O I will tell him to love you carefully . . .
> And when the needle grins bloodlessly in his cheek
> he will come to know how beautiful it is
> to be loved by a madwoman.

Again, the relationship is only fulfilled when it is extended, and the roles switch around; from being a branded slave to "you" Cohen becomes the teaching master of "him."

The final stanza portrays the ultimate break-up of the relationship, when the ocean will "rust your face" and make the letters rot, until "my fingernails are long enough / to tear the stitches from my throat." This is the consummation of the relationship in its destruction, and though Cohen waits for it "not gladly" (a curious inversion), he does wait for it, as the title indicates, with patience.

"Song of Patience" may not be one of Cohen's best love poems, but it is certainly typical: in its air of mystery and strangeness spiced with cruelty; in its exotic, surreal imagery; in its insistence that the third party is a necessary extension; in the shifting of roles and the ambiguity of its pronouns; in its celebration of death and destruction as the sources of beauty and love. It also, of course, comes close to mere absurdity; Cohen is taking himself very seriously, and perhaps straining too hard for effects. It is always easy to laugh at Leonard Cohen, which may be the reason why he is usually at his best when he is already laughing at himself.

Implicit in all these poems is the idea of power: the power of the lover or the murderer, the power of the god to rise again

in the spring, the power of the poet. The most explicit statement comes in "Poem" (55):

> I heard of a man
> who says words so beautifully
> that if he only speaks their name
> women give themselves to him.

Here the power of words, such as the poet may speak, becomes
absolute. The power of the poet's words binds all things to him:
in "Story" (63) the woman who has built the house has also
invented a dead child as its fictional builder. Inside this con-
struction Cohen must take his place: "It is important / to understand one's part in a legend." The beauty of the legend created
by the woman's words will in its turn be completed by "her own
traffic death."

If poetry is one source of power, religion is another, and
the book's title seems to indicate that Cohen himself regarded
the religious source as the primary one. The book's metaphors
are frequently taken from religion: not from one specific religion
such as Judaism but from the field of comparative mythology,
where Jewish and Christian images mingle with those of Greece
and Rome. In particular, there is the central twentieth-century
instance of comparative mythology, the dying vegetation god
reborn in the spring: Orpheus, Adonis, Christ.

Sandra Djwa, in writing of this pattern, points out some of
the connections between the religious poems and the poems of
destructive love:

> The structural myth is that of the death of the poet-god Orpheus
> and the possibility of his resurrection in art. Like Eliot's *Waste
> Land* the book moves through cycles of winter death followed
> by spring re-birth, and the poet-victim as a part of this cycle
> moves between the extremes of innocent and destructive love. . . .
> The poems of this cycle would seem to make a strong case for
> submission to a destructive love which . . . can lead to a new beauty
> and a new order.[5]

The gods as much as the lovers find their beauty in destruction. The wound from which the flowers grow is the lance
wound in the side of the crucified Christ; Cohen wishes to "love

the distant saint / who fed his arm to flies" (14); the new "City Christ" is "Blinded and hopelessly lame" (25) like the Icarian flier; the protagonists of "Saint Catherine Street" (44) envy the old saints their potentiality for being tortured. But out of this destruction comes power: the rebirth of Christ, the poetry of Orpheus, the strength of a religious tradition.

Cohen is greatly concerned with the ways in which he inherits a tradition by his Jewishness. The ordering of the first few poems in the book gives some indication of the ways in which this topic can be handled. After the initial "Elegy" (13), setting out what Djwa sees as "the structural myth" of the book, we move directly to "For Wilf and His House" (14), the poem containing the line which gives the whole book its title. It starts with an urgent statement: "When young the Christians told me / how we pinned Jesus / like a lovely butterfly against the wood." For a young Jew in a Christian country, comparative mythology is not an academic exercise but an immediate fact of repression and prejudice.

The first two stanzas of the poem present two possible responses to this experience. In the first stanza Cohen accepts the Jewish communal "guilt"; he "wept beside paintings of Calvary," which he sees as sources of beauty and gentleness. But in the second stanza he reacts against this sense of responsibility: Christ "could not hang softly long." As he becomes more aware of the force of his Jewish inheritance — "when I faced the Ark for counting" — he is forced to see Wilf and his Christian friends as "your fighters so proud with bugles," with the result that "the meadow of running flesh turned sour / and I kissed away my gentle teachers, / warned my younger brothers." Rejecting guilt, he chooses an aggressive, anti-Christian stance.

In the third stanza he attempts to make another choice. In Canada, a "young" nation without the weight of inheritance, he can be "innocent" of both the "spiked wish" which nailed Christ to the cross and the "bright crusade" which would avenge it. Indeed, he can be "heathen," neither Jew nor Christian, and in the youthful innocence of "summersaults and chestnut battles" he can love his beautiful losers, the saint eaten by insects, the insects in turn crushed under "the reason of the heel."

The final stanza confirms this choice. "Raging and weeping" — the alternatives of stanzas two and one respectively — "are left on the early road." There remains the neutral stance of the comparative mythographer, who can see the story of the crucifixion as an "elaborate lie," reminiscent of the image of a generalized vegetation god dying in the fall of the year. The conclusion proclaims a break away from any single or narrow religious view; Cohen believes in mythologies, but not in any one system, except that which he can assemble himself by comparison and assembly of fragments.

The dialectic of this poem is continued in the next two poems of the book. "The Song of the Hellenist" (16) adopts the persona of a Jew who attempts to abandon his own tradition and become part of another. This attempt is immediately balanced by the formal "Prayer for Messiah" (18); then the two poems, thesis and antithesis, are followed by the attempted synthesis of "Rites" (19). Here the poet acknowledges fully the force and importance of his inheritance; nevertheless, it is only when the father is dead that the eldest son can begin to shout in his own voice, drowning the prophecies of the uncles.

Another effect of the religious metaphor is to give a sense of timelessness to the poetry. As remarked in the introduction, Cohen does not see the present as discontinuous from the past: the old gods are still alive, Orpheus and Christ in their modern settings. In the final poem of the book, the Apocalypse arrives on the most ordinary of mornings:

> Well finally it has happened,
> Imagines someone in another house,
> Staring one more minute out his window
> Before waking up his wife.
>
> (70)

In "Exodus" (66), Cohen retells the story of the plagues of Egypt, but, in a remarkable extension of sympathy to "My distant enemy" (1956 was the year of the Suez war), he tells it from the Egyptian side. "Saviours" (64) sees an almost continuous replay of the great religious myths:

> And all the saints and prophets
> are nailed to stakes and desert trees
> All the Kings and men of ages
> with deathless words and singing harps
> are exhumed to die again in the wilderness.

In "City Christ" (25), Christ himself "has returned from count-
less wars," and now "counts ages in a Peel Street room," like the
old men "with rotting noses and tweed caps" who sit in Phillips
Square, "letters of reference crumbling in their wallets" (62).

There is, however, one poem in the book which takes a
different approach, and that is "Saint Catherine Street" (44).
Here the protagonists long to "be saints and live in golden coffins," but find instead that in this present age "There are no
ordeals . . . Our eyes are worthless to an inquisitor's heel / No
prince will waste hot lead / or build a spiked casket for us."
What is still typically Cohen about this poem is that the protagonists are failures, losers who have lost even the possibility of
a glorious death. What is not typical is the idea that the age of
ordeals is over; most of Cohen's writing insists that the tortures
and the golden coffins are still here.

Let Us Compare Mythologies remains a quite extraordinary first book. It deals almost exclusively with subjects which
can only be phrased in the most absolute terms, and it treats
them with the assurance of a position already formed and con-
solidated. The language is vivid, exotic, and above all confident:
confident enough to accommodate some deliberate excursions
into excess.

There are reminiscences of Eliot in "Rededication" (20),
in which "Spring disturbs us" like the cruelest month, and in
"Just the Worst Time" (69), whose title is acknowledged as a
quotation (from "Journey of the Magi"[6]). Donne is invoked in
"The Fly" (60), a rather poor imitation of "The Flea," and in
many of the startling openings, such as "How you murdered
your family / means nothing to me" (36).

These are the gestures any young poet might make, but
Cohen is also deliberately courting the absurdities of excess, as
in "Prayer for Sunset" (41), which drowns its ostensible subject-
matter in extraordinarily overstated images. More successful is the "Fragment of Baroque" (52), where the lushness of
the language is only keeping pace with the lushness of the
subject-matter; most successful of all is the delightful "When
This American Woman" (27), with its two extremes of vulgarity
and delicacy. Its success is due to the faintly humorous tone set
up by the word "thundering." *Let Us Compare Mythologies* is
not, overall, a very funny book (Cohen is always more inclined

towards humour in his novels than he is in his poetry), but here one can detect the poet smiling at the extremeness of the image he has created: a smile which extends from the "Mongol tribe" of the American woman to the "embroidered Chinese girls." Of course Cohen takes their fragile beauty seriously as well, but he is creating a deliberate contrast of extremes, on both sides of which there is a playful element.

These few poems seem to exist mainly, if not solely, as explorations of the limits of a style, but the style remains constant throughout the book. In some ways it can act as a hindrance: too often, readers of Cohen have been content with the general impression of something exotic, sensuous, and romantic, without pushing through to the actual meanings, often very "black" meanings, which this use of language carries. This is a tendency which *The Spice-Box of Earth* continued strongly and against which *Flowers for Hitler* was in some measure an attempted revolt.

(ii) *The Spice-Box of Earth* (1961)

The Spice-Box of Earth[7] is the most popular single volume of Cohen's poetry. The reasons for this popularity are fairly obvious: it contains much of the most beautiful and uncomplicated of his love poetry, and it is the volume in which the darker sides of his imagination are least obtrusive. It is a book in which the imperceptive reader can easily lose himself in the richness and sensuousness of the language without worrying too much about the meaning. Like the poem from which it draws its title, "Out of the Land of Heaven" (71), it appears to be nothing more than a joyous celebration, richly seasoned.

On the surface, *The Spice-Box of Earth* may appear to be a more limited book than *Let Us Compare Mythologies* or *Flowers for Hitler*. It concentrates on three main themes — the role of the poet; love; the inheritance of Jewish tradition — and it treats them, at least part of the time, from a Romantic rather than from a Black Romantic standpoint. But in reality, much of the sunniness of the book's atmosphere lies only on the surface. Each of the three themes, but especially the central theme of love, has a dark underside to it, and it is partly because of the contrast provided by their apparently sunny context that

Michael Ondaatje is able to describe the book as "far nastier and far more frightening"[8] than *Flowers for Hitler*.

The book takes the form of a continuing dialectic argument between different ways of approaching the same subjects. Structurally, it opens with a group of poems about poetry and Cohen's role as a poet; balancing this is a closing group of poems on the Jewish tradition and Cohen's position as inheritor of it. The major part of the book consists of love poems, which fall into two groups: those which may be seen as "conventional" Romantic love poems, and those which explore the darker, more "perverted" Black Romantic directions. The conflict between these two attitudes is similar to that present in *The Favourite Game*. Like Breavman, Cohen occasionally pauses to try on the mask of the conventional love poet. But the beauty of the poems attests more to Cohen's skill as a writer than to any conviction that ideal love is possible.

The opening poem of the book, "A Kite Is A Victim" (1), sets the tone and initiates the themes even more firmly than "Elegy" did for *Let Us Compare Mythologies*. The language has a strong sensuous appeal, but it is also direct and precise. The image of the kite is developed through a rising series of comparisons — falcon, fish, poem, moon — and at each stage a balance is maintained between its independence and the poet's control over it, until finally the moon breaks totally free, "cordless," leaving the poet in a humble state of religious veneration, praying that he may become "worthy." This balance relates to that paradox mentioned in the introduction: the theme of the loss of personality being expressed by a very strong ego. Although the first stanzas present a balance, one has the sense that the poet is always in control. The falcon is "desperate" but also "trained"; the fish is "already caught"; the poem is "given to the wind" only "until someone finds you / something else to do." (Not even something better, just something "else.") There is even a hint of the darker side of Cohen's imagination in the sadistic implications of the language. Somehow the beauty of the poem tends to gloss over the unpleasantness of "a victim you are sure of." The fish, "already caught," is to be played "carefully and long," its suffering and death extended in the name of sport, or art. At any time the kite can be pulled down out of "the high, sweet air" and tamed in a drawer. These suggestions of slightly sadistic personal power serve also to underline the about-face in the final stanza, where master becomes slave, submits himself to the elements, and prays for worthiness. The cordless moon exercises over the poet the same domination which he has previously exercised over the kite; as so often happens in Cohen, the roles are reversed, the personalities are interchangeable.

The kite itself is one of Cohen's most successful and most richly complex images. Like all good images, it exists first of all at the literal level, as itself: this is an excellent poem about kite-flying. But precisely because Cohen has been true to the emotional integrity of this level, the image is able to expand onto other levels as well, at least one of which — kite as poem — is explicitly mentioned. The tension between independence and control, the degree to which a poem seems to take on a life of its own, is well known to any writer. The kite could also, obviously, stand for a lover; a similar tension exists in all personal relationships, which Cohen tends to view as power games. At a still more general level, Ondaatje sees the kite as "symbolic of our ego and ambitions, of all that is original and free in us."[9]

Synthesizing these views, it is possible to see the kite as the "other": anything which the ego feels to be separate enough from itself to demand that some kind of relationship be set up. These "other" things — kite, lover, poem, "all that is original and free" — are presented initially as things to be dominated. The self will play games with them, give them the illusion of freedom, but in reality always retain power over them, the ability to pull them down to the closed drawer. They are victims the ego is sure of. But this game — the game of being in control, of winning — is not finally a satisfactory one. As the "other" increases in intensity and purity it finally breaks free, the cordless moon; the roles are reversed; the commanding self is now the victim praying to be worthy, is now the beautiful loser. The ego finds its ultimate gratification in self-dissolution. But the paradox remains, for this conclusion does not give the "other" any more real life and individuality than it had before. It is still the poet's creation, still subordinate to the demands he makes upon it. The game of losing may only be a refinement of the game of winning. Even the masters of a beautiful loser are still, in a sense, victims he is sure of.

The other poems about the role of the poet continue to revolve around this shifting balance of power and powerlessness. Sometimes the poet is in control, exercising power to transform the outer world into the images of his beauty. Other poems are directed, somewhat equivocally, against this Romantic conception of the poet, and discount the dignity of his role.

"If It Were Spring" (6) begins with a startling image (reminiscent of Donne's opening lines): "If it were Spring / and I killed a man." The poem is about the poet's power over his material. We commonly speak of writers "bringing things to life," but Cohen's formulation is, typically, a reversal: he creates beauty by bringing something to death. The dead man would be changed to leaves on a shelter-giving tree; "Wind would make him / part of song"; he would become a dance, a map, a flag. His death would produce a "language" to explain anguish and relieve sorrow; his death becomes in the end a "mercy." The poem asserts the poet's complete power and control over this process: the final stanza rings out with the assertions of his supremacy. "*I* will kill . . . *I* will hang . . . *I* will see" (my emphasis). And, of course, the man to be killed has no say in the matter. He does not exist in the poem at all, has no more personality than a kite; he is only a victim the poet is sure of.

The reversal of the role of poet as life-bringer is also hinted at in the brief poem "The Sleeping Beauty" (33). Here the narrator refuses to play the role of "Kissing Prince," but the Beauty (who has obviously seen Cocteau's film) intimates that she prefers him as Beast. The poet, however, is reluctant to be confined to this definition either, and (comparing mythologies) hints a switch to the role of Swan, with all the implications of Leda and the twin eggs. The poem is too short and whimsical to be more than a clever little game, but again it indicates the poet's impulse to dominate and change external reality. This impulse is given its quietest and most dignified expression in the poem "There Are Some Men" (8)—though even here the emphasis seems to be more on the poet's ability to name the mountain than on the virtues which make the (unnamed) friend worthy of such commemoration.

"The Flowers That I Left in the Ground" (4) repeats the familiar idea of beauty growing out of death and decay, "rotted" flowers and "wrecked" ships. Indeed, the first three stanzas are so regular and formulaic that they suggest a kind of disenchantment with the idea. The second half of the poem switches to "renunciation, betrayal," a movement away from the loved one (accompanied by the most explicit of all Cohen's allusions to Donne: "I go for weariness of thee"). Whereas the formulas of the first half involve the poet's control ("*I* bring them back"), the withdrawal of the second half is connected with the counter-movement: the poet beginning to disparage himself, to see himself as a loser. "Who owns anything he has not made?" the poet asks, an assertion of the poet's supremacy used here as a reason for backing off from the physical beauty of the lover, which he has not "made," with which he is "uninvolved." All he can do is marshal the same old tired words to describe it: "Gold, ivory, flesh, love, God, blood, moon— / I have become the expert of the catalogue." This is, in fact, perceptive self-criticism; but, though he claims "This is my last catalogue," it isn't.

Just as the loser may be only a more subtle form of the winner, so too the pose of the anti-poet is only another of the poet's masks. In "When I Uncovered Your Body" (31), Cohen claims that "the real and violent proportions of your body / made obsolete old treaties of excellence, / measures and poems." But this disclaimer of poetry is itself contained in a poem (not one of Cohen's best poems, but by no means his worst, either). The role of anti-poet can never be anything other than a para-doxical one; a poem attacking poetry is always less successful in its aim the more successful it is in its execution.

Similarly, "The Cuckold's Song" (42) begins with a dis-claimer: "If this looks like a poem / I might as well warn you at the beginning / that it's not meant to be one." But it is a poem, and, in its fine control of the modulations of the bitterly ironic tone, a very good one. In "Gift" (3) Cohen seems to ac-knowledge this inevitability in an ironic way: whatever he says will be accepted as a poem; even silence may be. A bitter aware-ness of the supposed futility of the poet's role is also projected in "I Wonder How Many People in This City" (11), which features the poet in his favoured role as loser, gazing in his lone-liness out of the window at all the other losers whose only con-solation is to turn away, go back to their desks, and write the same poem, about all the other lonely losers whose only con-solation . . . etc., in a circle of futility.

"After the Sabbath Prayers" (2) deliberately balances the

two views, presenting in the first stanza the poet's flight of creation, his vision of the "miracle" of the Baal Shem's butterfly, and in the second the dejection of the poet in his "loser" role, forced to "spend this night in darkness, / Hands pocketed against the flies and cold." There is no resolution to this contrast: it is simply presented, perhaps as a cause for wonder (the second role is as great a "miracle" as the first), but not as something which could or should be changed. A more subtle balance is sought in "I Have Not Lingered in European Monasteries" (22). The bulk of this poem consists of a rejection of the old roles and attributes of the Romantic poet, but in the rejection itself there is another kind of "lingering," and the very flat, objective closing statement is obviously inadequate to account for the poetic imagination which has produced the first part of the poem. Here the anti-poetic tone becomes so ironic that the poem contrives to mean the opposite of what it says.

The central part of the book is taken up with love poems, among them some of Cohen's best-known pieces, such as the exquisite lyric "As the Mist Leaves No Scar" (56). These poems, however, vary in tone and attitude. Some of them are expressions of entirely conventional and normal love relationships, without any hints of Cohen's individual twists and obsessions; some (including those associated with *The Favourite Game*) seem to reflect an uncertainty, or a debate, as to whether these attitudes are possible or desirable; but the majority, in one form or another, involve Black Romantic conceptions which all their luxuriance of language cannot entirely conceal.

Even the conventional love lyrics only succeed, Michael Ondaatje claims, when Cohen "is able to inject just the smallest touch of irony and self-consciousness of himself as a romantic, aware of his pose." [10] Ondaatje claims that this balance is achieved in "For Anne":

> With Annie gone,
> whose eyes to compare
> With the morning sun?
>
> Not that I did compare,
> But I do compare
> Now that she's gone.
>
> (64)

The degree of irony present in this poem is debatable (I feel that it is so slight as to be almost imperceptible); the poem succeeds more because of its absolute simplicity and lucidity. For once Cohen is not "loading every rift with ore," perhaps because there are no rifts in the complete purity of this poem and its emotion.[11]

The other poem for Annie, "Now of Sleeping" (60), is more elaborate and less successful. The primary emotion is a watchful, protective tenderness (with the implication that Annie is a small child). But compared to the simple beauty of the shorter poem, there is something gratuitous and tediously image-spinning about such lines as the comparison of her eyelids to "ages of weightless snow / on tiny oceans filled with light." Nor can the extended form exclude an image as bizarre and violent as that of the third stanza:

> The small banner of blood
> kept and flown by Brother Wind
> long after the pierced bird fell down
> is like her red mouth
> among the squalls of pillow

Cohen erects around the sleeping girl the protective powers of "mighty Mother Goose / and Farmer Brown and all good stories"—an interesting example of Cohen's totally serious use of "pop" mythologies—but one wonders who the "Bearers of evil fancy" are against whom these worthies are being invoked. There is the uneasy awareness that Annie's "one true lover" is also the poet who has created the "evil fancy" of the "pierced bird."

On some occasions, Cohen's tone seems inapposite to the emotion, as in "Celebration" (55), where the uneasiness is caused by the equivocation of the language. The poem is about an act of fellatio, but Cohen has not yet found the diction to say so. Later, in *Beautiful Losers,* he is able to use direct and colloquial obscenity, but here the equivocation moves towards a grandiosity of language. The penis becomes "my manhood," then "a sceptre," then "the amber jewel"; the act becomes a religious ceremony like ancient phallic dances; the climax is likened to the collapse of the "roof / that Samson pulled down." The self-aggrandizement in this poem may raise a smile. More seriously, it is a failure of tone: there is too large a gap between the portentousness of the imagery and the reality of the blow-job.

One of the central aspects of Breavman's character in *The Favourite Game* is the attraction he feels, especially with Shell, towards some kind of secure, reciprocal, loving relationship. Breavman wants also to be alone, self-sufficient, independent, working towards a conception of himself as an artist, and prepared to sacrifice anything for that goal. A small group of poems in *The Spice-Box of Earth* share this conflict.

"Owning Everything" (34) starts as an elaborate compliment to the loved one: "Because you are close, / everything that men make, observe / or plant is close, is mine." This premise affords the basis for the conclusion:

> You worry that I will leave you.
> I will not leave you.
> Only strangers travel.
> Owning everything,
> I have nowhere to go.

This is in some ways a beautiful formulation of a secure and continuing relationship—even if there is the slightly uneasy suggestion that he is staying only because there is nowhere else to go. But both Cohen and Breavman are always attracted to the role of travelling stranger, and the penultimate stanza raises their questions:

> With your body and your speaking
> you have spoken for everything,
> robbed me of my strangerhood,
> made me one
> with the root and gull and stone,
> and because I sleep so near to you
> I cannot embrace
> or have my private love with them.

Breavman, and Cohen, are not at all sure that they *want* to be robbed of their strangerhood: they see it as a necessary condition for their art, the "embrace" and "private love" from which this secure relationship is cutting them off. This particular poem seems to accept the loss of strangerhood, albeit with regret; others present a different view.

In "Travel" (52), the division (and thus the choice) is clear between "the way I had to take" and the woman in whose hair the poet may become "lost." But while the division is clear, the resolution is not. The poem opens with a retrospect: when, in the past, he loved her "flesh to flesh" ("flesh" is Cohen's favourite word), then he thought of travelling to meet a "master," who would teach him how "to love alone," in his strangerhood, isolated and intact. The second stanza states the conflict and describes its initial resolution:

> Lost in the fields of your hair I was never lost
> Enough to lose a way I had to take;
> Breathless beside your body I could not exhaust
> The will that forbid me contract, vow,
> Or promise, and often while you slept
> I looked in awe beyond your beauty.

What is described here is essentially Breavman's solution, when he decides that he must leave Shell. The third stanza, however, introduced by the rhythmically isolated "Now," looks back with regret and nostalgia, and introduces the element of doubt, the question of whether "travel leads . . . anywhere." The nostalgia is then reinforced, in the final lines of the poem, by two of Cohen's most gorgeous images: "Horizons keep the soft line of your cheek, / The windy sky's a locket for your hair." The beauty of these lines tends to overpower the lonely resolution of the earlier part of the poem.

Similarly, in "Song" (62) a choice is set up between the saint with his "disdain" for "each body rare" and the poet's continuing attraction to "The naked girls with silver combs . . . combing out their hair." Less ambiguously than "Travel," this poem ends with a firm commitment to "the mortal ring / Of flesh on flesh in dark." Later, Cohen shows this conflict to be illusory; in *Beautiful Losers,* all the saints live within that mortal ring, and sexuality is not an alternative to but the centre of the saint's experience.

The two poems most closely associated with *The Favourite Game* are "Beneath My Hands" (57), the writing of which is described in the novel, and "As the Mist Leaves No Scar" (56), which serves as an epigraph to the book.[12] "Beneath My Hands," like "Owning Everything," is a straightforward, rather lush love poem which, within the novel, relates in subtle ways to Shell's

specific character. "As the Mist Leaves No Scar" also has implications within *The Favourite Game,* especially in relation to
the imagery of scars, but it also stands up as a beautiful and
quite complex poem in its own right.

It opens with the lovely image of the mist and the hill, reminiscent of Bliss Carman's "Softer than the hill-fog to the forest."
But whereas Carman's line expresses only softness and tenderness, Cohen's also includes the element of detachment, of non-
involvement. The abrupt "nor ever will" signals the end of a
relationship, not its non-hurting continuation. In the second
stanza, the soft images of mist and hill are replaced by the harsh
heroics of "Wind and hawk"; and no continuing love-relationship
can be read into the almost military "encounter" or the scorn
of "keep." The third stanza modifies the tone back to a softer
level; the verb "endure" is more ambiguous, at least allowing
for the possibility of the couple enduring together (emotionally
if not physically) rather than enduring apart, as solitary beings.
Nevertheless, the strength of the second stanza leaves the reader
with little doubt as to which of the two will soon be "gone and
far."

The element of strangerhood always pulls Cohen away
from the simple expression of love for another. Most of the love
poems in *The Spice-Box of Earth* are imbued with darker tones:
images of pain, cruelty, and victims; images of the third party
and of the dissolution of the self; images of the master and
slave, saint and disciple, and the ways they have to take.

Under the innocent title "Morning Song" (44), we find,
not a joyful aubade, but a nightmare image of disfigurement;
"I Have Two Bars of Soap" (53) takes the love-poem convention
of the lover offering various exotic gifts and twists it into a tale
of cruelty and murder. "I Long to Hold Some Lady" (59) opens
with a courtly compliment — "There is no flesh so perfect / As
on my lady's bone" — but the singular "bone" already suggests
the tone of the conclusion — "Cold skeletons go marching / Each
night beside my feet." In "The Cuckold Song" (42), the first
necessary step on the way to turning to gold is to turn to clay.

The title of "The Girl Toy" (48) may be taken to indicate
the kind of relationship implicit in many of these poems: Cohen
controlling, the women being manipulated as depersonalized
toys. But in this particular poem, the sex-machine, precisely

because it is depersonalized, is more perfect than a woman, and therefore takes the dominant role. In some ways, "The Girl Toy" is a dry run for *Beautiful Losers'* Danish Vibrator and other "ordinary eternal machinery." As the opening allusion to Yeats's "Sailing to Byzantium" suggests, the girl toy may also be taken as an image of art: the impersonal, perfect, eternal machine to which the king, like Breavman, devotes himself. "Deep in the palace" the lovers isolate themselves from the world, to the ruinous neglect of the kingdom. Perfection brings with it cruelty, but the king "didn't care if sometimes he tasted gold in her mouth / or cut his aging lips on a jewelled eye." The toy retains the mechanical beauty of "a pendulum" or "perfect machines," but the king, involved in his self-destructive quest, grows "obese and old" until "he fell and wept and spit up blood." At that point, when his self-destruction is as complete as it can be, short of death, she offers him a perfect mechanical consolation, and would "hum or sing a ballad of their wedding feast." The jewelled perfection of the toy offers the timeless consolation of art: the wedding song is as present and as changeless as the girl, in the face of the obese old man's mortality. Cohen's images of the king's physical decay are merciless, yet the poem appears to endorse the value of his quest, and of its reward.

Yet some sort of debate, or dialectic movement, continues. The commitment to suffering and death is not always absolute. "Credo" (25) opens along characteristic lines: the image of the lovers juxtaposed to images of destruction. The poet's mind seems drawn towards ever more bizarre scenes of destruction, from a farm devoured to a slave people freed to "pyramids overturned" to Pharaoh, like Mussolini, "hanging by the feet, / his body smeared —." And at this point, as the imagination seems to start revelling in the images of violence, "my love drew me down / to conclude what I had begun." The act of love can then be seen either as a distraction from the sequence of violent images, or, equally, as its culmination. After the lovers have finished, the grasshoppers return, "fat and flying slow," and "The smell that burning cities give / was in the air." The implication is that the grasshoppers' orgy of destruction has been parallel to the poet's lovemaking.

The exiles follow, "batallions of the wretched," and the poet "had two thoughts," both highly characteristic Cohen responses. One is "to leave my love / and join their wandering," casting himself in the role of holy exiled prophet; the other is to "take my love / to the city they had fled," to the heart of destruction, which would be a proper environment for their love. This particular poem, however, rejects both alternatives. "Our ordinary morning lust / claimed my body first / and made me sane." Just as "Song" (62) rejects the asceticism of the saints in favour of "the mortal ring / Of flesh on flesh in dark," "Credo" embraces the sanity of "ordinary morning lust" and elects to preserve "the small oasis where we lie." A knowledge of the world of cruelty and violence surrounds them, but that nightmare world is, for once, kept at a distance. "Credo" preserves a balance between the ruined city of the imagination of cruelty and the oasis of the sanity of lust, but such a balance is precarious in Cohen, and his imagination always pulls him towards that "diseased sensuousness that one cannot eradicate because it is also beautiful." [13]

The central poem of the book, then, and the poem which expresses most fully the themes which are to reach culmination in *Beautiful Losers,* is "You Have the Lovers" (29). In this poem we find the central Cohen themes: the lovers as saints who have transcended ordinary human values, such as individuality, and have entered a new, religious dimension, into which the protagonist, or disciple, is initiated. Here indeed the disciple is robbed of strangerhood, but not by any "ordinary morning lust"; the oasis of the room is not the oasis of normality of "Credo" but rather the secret room, "deep in the palace," where the king cuts his lips on a jewelled eye.

The poem opens almost clinically, as if setting up the terms of a scientific experiment: "you have," given to you as the basic ingredients, the raw materials, "the lovers" themselves, and the equipment, "the room, the bed and the windows." Whatever is not absolutely necessary is discarded: "blacken the windows." It is not important, then, that the lovers are individual people: they have no names, and their histories are only for each other. Here they are completely and adequately defined by their function: they are lovers, those who love. "Pretend it is a ritual." A ritual is a formalized ceremony in which the personalities of those taking part are made transparent to the will of the impersonal process. The lovers' "histories" are not important, any more than are the idiosyncracies of any parish priest celebrating a Mass. The bed is then "unfurled," like a ceremonial flag, and the lovers are "buried." The experience they will go through is in fact very close to death, and death-related imagery recurs later in the poem. It is a "death" to all normal human life and ordinary relations; it also recalls the intimate connection between sex and death that underlay the Elizabethan pun.

After setting the tone of a scientific experiment in the opening phrase, the generalizing "you" becomes slightly more specific. "You" is the disciple, the one who watches over the lovers and who must eventually join them. The gender of this third person is, as usual, unknown and irrelevant.

The first stage of the ritual is to "let them live in that house for a generation or two." (The familiar pun on "generation" is ironically cancelled by the fact that sex, in Cohen's writing, never seems to have a procreative function.) The purpose of this is to allow time for the lovers to go beyond humanity, like the period spent in the treehouse in *Beautiful Losers*. When "you" finally enters the room, the lovers will no longer be, strictly speaking, human. No sign of their activity penetrates to the outside world, but "You know they are not dead, / you can feel the presence of their intense love." Compared to this intensity, the details of normal life are mundane and transitory. In a few curt, almost brutal lines, Cohen dismisses the lives of his protagonist's children and "mate." The word "mate" is particularly contemptuous, almost animalistic, but it also serves to preserve the ambiguity of the protagonist's sex. "Who knows you?" Cohen seems to be jeering. "Who remembers you?" The only importance, the only value that the protagonist can ever find in his or her life is in the fulfillment of the role of disciple.

"But in your house a ritual is in progress: / it is not finished: it needs more people." This is a central line for Cohen's extension of relationships beyond the couple: two are never enough; his rituals keep on demanding more people. With two, the ego and the individual personality are still too clearly involved: with greater numbers, these things can be lost.

"One day the door is opened to the lover's chamber." Both *The Spice-Box of Earth* and the *Selected Poems* print the line that way, with "lover's" in the singular; some anthologies print it as the plural, "lovers'."[14] The plural is logical, but the singular is thematically right: the two lovers have, to all intents and purposes, become one. The room has been transformed into a "dense garden, / full of colours, smells, sounds you have never known." It has passed beyond reality to become a new Garden of Eden, serpentless, in which Adam and Eve explore the innocence of their sexuality. The bed, standing like an altar alone "in the midst of the garden," has become "smooth as a wafer of sunlight." (It is tempting here to read the unusual word "wafer" in its theological sense as the sacramental bread of the Mass, the body of Christ.)

The lovers have now been reduced (or extended) to their sole function: "slowly and deliberately and silently, / [they] perform the act of love." This function has taken them through death and beyond: heavy coins lie on their eyes, the traditional coins placed on the eyes of corpses, but, in Cohen's cosmology, made out of flesh. The intensity of their passion has bruised their lips, and continues to do so. Their physical bodies are merging with each other: it is not just that "her hair and his beard are hopelessly tangled," but that all their physical sensations have become interchangeable. "All her flesh is like a mouth": a preview of F.'s more direct statement in *Beautiful Losers*, "All flesh can come!" "He carries his fingers along her waist / and feels his own waist caressed." They have broken down all the barriers between them, not just the psychological barriers of individuality but also the physical barriers of the senses, of pleasure and pain. They have no histories now, not even for each other: they are each other.

This vision of the complete mingling of two beings into each other is Cohen's ultimate statement of the sainthood achieved through love. The presence of the third party will, briefly, give us the human context within which this sainthood is only a surreal image; but it is the central image towards which Cohen's imagination works. Talking through characters distanced in the second and third persons, Cohen is able to achieve a more convincing image of the dissolution of personality than in any of the poems containing the dominating "I." "You Have the Lovers" is essentially fiction, rather than a lyric poem, and therefore prepares the way for Cohen as novelist. The true gloss on this poem is *Beautiful Losers*.

The disciple, all mortal ties stripped away, is now ready for initiation. The ritual demands more people, and the disciple must now be absorbed into the lovers' condition, merging his or her personality with theirs, as they have merged one into the other. "As you undress you sing out, and your voice is magnificent / because now you believe it is the first human voice / heard in that room." Also the last: the lovers have gone beyond humanity, and the disciple is about to join them. The voice is "magnificent" only by the old, human standards. "You climb into bed and recover the flesh": the flesh, momentarily uncovered when the disciple peeled away the sheet, is now re-covered; but it is also recovered, as the disciple moves to a deeper, more elemental state of being, as if recovering something long lost: the womb, Eden, or whatever. The disciple begins to lose individual perceptions: previously his or her eyes had been "filled with tears" so that "you barely make out the lovers": now, more ruthlessly, "You close your eyes and allow them to be sewn shut." This startling and cruel image comes from falconry, where the eyes of young hawks used to be sewn shut in training; used here, it evokes the "wind and hawk" of "As the Mist Leaves No Scar" and the "desperate trained falcon" of "A Kite Is a Victim."

"You create an embrace and fall into it": the disciple creates a form (a poem, a ritual), and submerges all individual personality into it. There remains only one fleeting "moment of pain or doubt," as the old values surface in the question, "how many multitudes are lying beside your body," but then the ritual is completed. "A mouth kisses and a hand soothes the moment away." In this poem, the disciple's transition into union with the saints is easy and smooth; but Cohen was to come to realize that so radical a departure from normal human values could not always be achieved so easily. In *Beautiful Losers,* that "one moment of pain or doubt" is extended throughout the whole novel: it is *I*'s complete course in F.'s "classroom of hysteria."

"You Have the Lovers" is a stunning poem: in gorgeously exact and sensuous language, it defines the central themes and scenes of Cohen's imagination. Much of his later work can do little more than elaborate on what is implied here. The pattern it uses is that of disciple and saint, which, as suggested in the introduction, modulates to the patterns of teacher and pupil, master and slave. Ideally, "the master and the slave embrace"

(19), and become interchangeable. At the end of "You Have The Lovers," the disciple is fully embodied in the saints' pattern, and would himself in turn be a saint to anyone coming after. What is missing from the poem is, principally, the sense of pain, destruction, and terrible loss which the saints must go through: the sense in which master and slave not only embrace but also "punish one another" (19).

Two other poems, "To a Teacher" (21) and "A Poem to Detain Me" (39), suggest this aspect of the saints' experience. "To a Teacher" opens with a stark image of the saint/poet who has gone through an ultimate dissolution: "Hurt once and for all into silence. / A long pain ending without a song to prove it." This teacher (whose sex is again unidentified, though the lines about "the Messiah" suggest a male) has gone so far from ordinary humanity that the disciple (the speaker of the poem) asks him with awe: "Who could stand beside you so close to Eden, / when you glinted in every eye the held-high razor, / shivering every ram and son?" (This image is to be picked up in "Prayer for My Wild Grandfather" (74), and later in the song "Story of Isaac.")

"A Poem to Detain Me" (39) presents Cohen himself in the role of saint and wanderer: "I'm heading for another border, my scrapbook stuffed with murder." The stanza on Cain reflects Cohen's continuing obsession with that character (cf. "Last Year's Man") and contains a hint of the themes of *Flowers for Hitler*: "the voice accuses so many names / I do not know which name is mine." Cohen feels strongly in this poem the gap between the saint and even the most sympathetic of his followers:

> O you will be listening for music
> while I turn on a spit of song;
> you will increase your love
> while I experiment with pain.

In these lines, the poet seems proud of his suffering, but there is still a longing to return to the more secure world of "you." The poem opens with an admission, "I am probably wrong," and closes with a desperate plea:

> Believe nothing of me
> except that I felt your beauty
> more closely than my own.

> I did not see any cities burn.
> I heard no promises of endless night.
> I felt your beauty
> more closely than my own.
> Promise me that I will return.

A brief series of poems addressed to other poets and artists leads Cohen into the final stage of *The Spice-Box of Earth*. These poems contain only faint overtones of the saint poems. The poem on Van Gogh (68) concentrates not on his madness but on the exuberant sunniness of his imagination, and the poem on Klein (67) views him as a singer who can still heal himself, if not the world around him. Frank and Marian Scott are given, in "Summer Haiku" (69), a moment of delicate and silent beauty, while "Last Dance at the Four Penny" (65) finds Cohen and "Layton, my friend Lazarovitch" dancing together in joyous and boisterous celebration. Celebration is also the keynote of the poem addressed to Marc Chagall, "Out of the Land of Heaven" (71).

These poems call on all the richness and sensuousness of Cohen's language, and they are by and large successful in their evocation of mood. Yet there is still something slightly uneasy about them. In the poem on Van Gogh, Cohen feels the need to "overwhelm" those who "tell tales of tragic art," but the reader is still aware of Van Gogh's tragedy, as he is of Klein's. Cohen and Layton's dance is modified by the final line: "we know that freilachs end." "Out of the Land of Heaven" reflects an almost aggressive self-consciousness about the separate Jewish identity: the Queen who "makes every Jew her lover" could just as easily order their deaths. The darker side of the Jewish inheritance is clear in "The Genius" (78), where Cohen cynically, and in a tone of self-disgust, rehearses all the stereotyped Jewish roles he can play, culminating in the image which is never far from his mind:

> For you
> I will be a Dachau Jew
> and lie down in lime
> with twisted limbs
> and bloated pain
> no mind can understand.

Like Layton,[15] Cohen compares his role as poet with that

of the old prophets, the supreme interpreters of their age; and within the Jewish tradition, the image of the saint gives way to the image of the prophet. In "Isaiah" (75), Cohen begins by drawing the familiar contrast between the complacency of a society secure in its own prosperity and luxury, and the prophet, the voice of the wilderness, who rages and cries "Jerusalem is ruined, / your cities are burned with fire." Isaiah is the outcast, "smelling vaguely of the wilderness," who proclaims a desolation. Yet he also proclaims love: his central speech in the poem is a sensual "song of my beloved touching her hair." Isaiah is a prophet/saint, "plunged in unutterable love," who brings both destruction and renewal to those around him. "Heavy trees he sleeps under / mature into cinder and crumble," but he also "gently hums a sound" (like the girl toy), through which "all men, truthfully desolate and lonely, / as though witnessing a miracle, / behold in beauty the faces of one another."

The other prophet celebrated in the final poems of the book is Cohen's own grandfather. In "Priests 1957" (70), one of the frequent allusions to the name "Cohen" meaning "priest," he presents an ironic portrait of how this man's wild, strange character makes all the rest of the family feel that their work is "prosaic" in comparison; in "Prayer of My Wild Grandfather" (74), Cohen sees him as a mad prophet or saint whose madness is the product and proof of God's love.

The major use of the grandfather is in the book's closing piece — an extended meditation, or prose poem, "Lines from My Grandfather's Journal" (80). As a poem, this piece is more impressive in its parts than in its whole: individual ideas and images are very striking and moving, but the overall form and development is uncertain, and Cohen never defines precisely enough the relationship between author and persona. The use of the figure of the grandfather is another move in the direction of fiction, the distancing of Cohen's ideas away from the dominating first person in the lyric; but in this poem the distinctions between Cohen as poet and his grandfather as character are not kept clear enough.

The central subject of the meditation is tradition: the strength and the attractiveness of the Jewish tradition which Cohen inherits, his need to understand it, and also his need to resist it, to live outside it. The poem opens with a vivid image of the grandfather's knowledge of the holy books: "I am one of those who could tell every word the pin went through. Page after page I could imagine the scar in a thousand crowned letters. . . ." The image attests to the thoroughness of his knowledge of the tradition, yet it is also an image of that tradition being attacked: it is not the words themselves in which he rejoices as much as in their scars. To stay within this tradition, even if it is a "tyranny," is still the easiest course: "Why make trouble? It is better to stutter than sing. . . . Become like a weak Rachel: be comforted, not comfortless."

But the persona has to "sing," and later in the poem this easy way is explicitly rejected: "Let me refuse solutions, refuse to be comforted. . . ." Instead, like Isaiah, he seeks a desolation, and finds that "The real deserts are outside of tradition. . . ." The tradition is "composed of the exuviae of visions. I must resist it." Exuviae are the cast-off skins of larvae and insects, stages of growth which must be left behind. The tradition must be grown out of: "Let judges secretly despair of justice: their verdicts will be more acute. . . . Let priests secretly despair of faith: their compassion will be true. It is the tension. . . ."

This "tension," however, remains. Even the wildest prophet needs a tradition outside of which to live, needs the words through which a pin can pierce. The poem closes with a formal gesture: "Inscription for the family spice-box." The grandfather is forced to comment that "It is strange that even now prayer is my natural language" — prayer which "makes speech a ceremony." The force of this tension comes, again, from the awareness of the Jews' immediate past. Although he admits that "I do not thrill to the sight of Jewish batallions," the grandfather sees "only one choice": "Who dares disdain an answer to the ovens? Any answer." This knowledge is with him all the time, each morning as he wakes: "It is painful to recall a past intensity, to estimate your distance from the Belsen heap, to make your peace with numbers. Just to get up each morning is to make a kind of peace."

"Lines from My Grandfather's Journal" is Cohen's most complex attempt to balance and evaluate the various aspects of his relationship to the Jewish tradition. It is still couched in the sensuous language of *The Spice-Box of Earth;* for all its doubts and reservations, it is still, like "Out of the Land of Heaven," a celebration. But the painful intensity of estimating his "distance from the Belsen heap" was demanding of Cohen a new language, a new kind of poetic pose. It is with a surrealistic harshness that his next book, *Flowers for Hitler,* undertakes that act of measurement.

(iii) *Flowers for Hitler* (1964)

Like all of Cohen's gestures and stances, the announcement of *Flowers for Hitler*[16] was extreme and flamboyant. The blurb contained an extravagant statement by Cohen about the book's importance and Cohen is reported to have asked later that this blurb be suppressed, but allowing for its inflated style, it is an important guide to the stance of the book:

> This book moves me from the world of the golden-boy poet into the dung pile of the front-line writer. I didn't plan it this way. I loved the tender notices *Spice-Box* got but they embarrassed me a little. *Hitler* won't get the same hospitality from the papers. My sounds are too new, therefore people will say: this is derivative, this is slight, his power has failed. Well, I say that there has never been a book like this, prose or poetry, written in Canada. All I ask is that you put it in the hands of my generation and it will be recognized.[17]

It is significant that Cohen is here directing attention not so much towards the individual poems as towards the stance of the book as a whole. The poems of *Flowers for Hitler* are an all-out assault on the "pretty" image of the "golden-boy poet": they are deliberately ugly, disjointed, clumsy, surrealistic, evoking nightmare images of things broken and without connections.

There also seems to be little in the way of discrimination. Whereas Cohen's two previous books had been carefully edited, and contain relatively few poems which are completely bad or without interest, *Flowers for Hitler* seems thrown together in a much more slapdash manner, and contains a good deal of inferior material. Michael Ondaatje comments:

> There are nearly a hundred poems in *Flowers for Hitler*: about forty good ones. Cohen himself chose fifty-five for his *Selected Poems*. Most of the bad qualities . . . could have been avoided by careful or less egotistical editing. Layton has made it fashion-

able to print all, saying time will pick the good poems anyway, but it seems pointless to waste everyone's time with poems that are obviously poor or obviously just private jokes.[18]

The reference to Layton is interesting, because Cohen has always had close affinities with him, and also because the phrase "the dung pile of the front-line writer" sounds very Laytonic. Layton's Preface to *Balls for a One-Armed Juggler* (published just one year before *Flowers for Hitler*)[19] stridently calls for the poet to encounter head-on the realities of twentieth-century evil. "Where is the poet who can make clear for us Belsen?" Layton demands; Cohen obviously decided to take up the challenge.

Yet, like Layton, Cohen does not tackle his subject head-on, but rather by the indirect routes of symbolism and surrealism. (Layton's best poems, after all, are not direct social satire, but "The Birth of Tragedy" and "A Tall Man Executes a Jig.") Too often, in *Flowers for Hitler*, this method goes astray and Cohen simply gets lost in a cloud of surrealist images, impenetrable to the reader.

I am not sure that it is as easy as Michael Ondaatje suggests to separate the "good" poems from the "bad" ones: both the faults and the virtues of the book are widespread. Some of the best lines occur in some of the worst poems, and vice versa. What matters is that the whole stance of the book is directed *against* writing formally "good" poems: "I will forget my style," Cohen insists; "I will have no style" (27). The economy and precision of a poem like "As the Mist Leaves No Scar" are frequently abandoned: the majority of the poems go on too long and seem as if they could go on longer. Those written in rhyming quatrains often stumble clumsily across the metrical patterns. A whole group of poems (81–85) written on one day, July 4th 1963, flaunt the date as if to say: "Look, I didn't revise them, I didn't write them carefully and slowly, they just all came rushing out and I left them that way."

But of course it is impossible for a poet to have no style; the pose of having no style is itself a style. *Flowers for Hitler* does possess a unity of tone, atmosphere, and emotional effect (sometimes an irritating one) which quite clearly sets it off from Cohen's other books. And Cohen is too good a writer to be lost in surrealism all the time: under the pressure of his imagination, the familiar thematic concerns break through, time and again, into vivid and energetic expression. *Flowers for Hitler* is in places the most absurd book that Cohen has written, but it is certainly not negligible.

Much of the surrealistic detail, then, is intended more to create a general tone or atmosphere for the book than to convey any very precise meaning. There seems little point in attempting to follow an argument through the myriad images of a poem like "The Glass Dog" (70). One of the tricks to which Cohen descends is that of the list of incongruous details. There is almost a formula to it, as John Glassco indicates in his description of surrealist writing: "I . . . was struck . . . by a certain sameness and monotony of treatment and even of syntax . . . where an endless number of out-of-the-way objects were placed in apposition to adjectives and verbs to which they had no relation but that of surprise."[20] This trick can be seen throughout *Flowers for Hitler,* in such poems as "The Drawer's Condition on November 28, 1961" (16) and "The Suit" (17).

Ondaatje, in discussing the style of the book, points out that its publication was linked with a reading tour, "and the tour was to be his new poetry's best medium, for he was now following a public rather than a private rhetoric." Some of the satirical poems especially contain "the sort of rhetorical wit that cannot fail at a public reading."[21] The list-making piling on of details is certainly of this sort: it sounds good, but it soon becomes tiresome. It substitutes a general impression of fevered imagistic activity for the precisions of the individual image placed and directed at exactly the right spot.

Yet few of these poems can be entirely dismissed. "The Drawer's Condition" is a feeble joke, but in another context the image of the searching hand "like a rat / in an experiment of mazes" could be very powerful. "Three Good Nights" (48) contains one very typical formulation of the master/pupil power game — "In the end you offered me the dogma you taught / me to disdain and I good pupil disdained it" — but its first two stanzas remain entangled in obscurity. The third stanza, however, breaks through to a lucid and beautiful expression of such central Cohen themes as the holiness of matter and the perfection of machines:

> Long live the unknown machine
> or heart
> which by will or accident
> pours with victor's grace
> endlessly perfect weather
> on the perfect creatures
> the world grows.

Flowers for Hitler contains various stylistic experiments directed towards the destruction of "style." The very prolixity of the book, its scorn of discrimination, can be seen as a gesture in this direction. In "Indictment of the Blue Hole" (19), Cohen offers us another list — "3 loaves of suicide / 2 razorblade pies," etc. — and deletes two of the lines, leaving the deletion marks in, followed by "(sic)," with the words underneath still legible. This seems to be intended as a parody of the kind of discrimination involved in revising poems: "Look," Cohen might be saying, "I'll do some revision, I'll show it to you, and really what difference does it make?" The lines deleted are as arbitrarily bizarre as the lines left in. Similarly, "The Pure List and the Commentary" (89) offers us a series of condensed imagistic phrases, followed by a commentary intended to show how much has been left out, how much experience the poet must always exclude in his selections and revisions. Both of these poems, however, completely misfire. It really does not matter what lines are left in or out of "Indictment of the Blue Hole": it is a bad poem anyway, and no amount of revision could save it. The "Commentary" is really no commentary: it explains nothing about the list, merely expands it arbitrarily.

In several poems, Cohen consciously turns against conventional "poetic" gestures. In "Montreal 1964" (35) he offers us a "literary allusion"; indeed he parades it before us: "Canada is a dying animal / I will not be fastened to a dying animal." Then he immediately pours on the obvious, unsubtle scorn: "That's the sort of thing to say, that's good, / that will change my life." The most outrageous of these reversals comes when Cohen takes the title "The Music Crept by Us" (113) from *The Tempest* and degrades it with one of his most excessive pictures of ugliness and corruption.

The most direct attack on "style" comes in the poem actually called "Style" (27): but here the paradoxes of Cohen's position overwhelm him. He insists that he "will have no style" in a poem which very clearly does have style. In the last few lines he envisages a terrible silence, the end of all style, but to do this he uses a couple of striking images (the silence is "Beyond the numbered band" of the radio, and is "like the space / between insects in a swarm") and concludes with a carefully arranged and notated rhythmic climax (the parenthesis of the penultimate line, the lack of punctuation at the end). A poem like "Indictment of the Blue Hole" may succeed in being anti-style, though only at the cost of being nothing at all, but a poem like "Style" (as the title perhaps acknowledges?) cannot; it is far too well written.

A more interesting modification of the "golden-boy" stance is found in "The Hearth" (14), which begins with a series of comic admissions that the poet is not, after all, unique, and that his lust is "not so rare a masterpiece." The routine images of "stars and hurricanes" are at first rejected, then finally offered back to him as a kind of consolation prize from an indulgent lover. The humorous tone of this poem makes it more effective than the overwrought protestations of other "anti-style" poems, but none of the mock-humility can cancel out the impression that there is still an entirely non-humble intelligence behind the poem, deliberately shaping this pose.

As Ondaatje comments, the "public rhetoric" works best in the satirical poems, where the satiric intent gives point and direction to the catalogues of absurdist imagery. It is easy to imagine the impact at a public reading of, especially, "The Only Tourist in Havana Turns His Thoughts Homeward" (38). This is the best of Cohen's satirical poems in *Flowers for Hitler*: its images strike an acute balance between what is totally absurd and what is just barely possible, its tone is sustained throughout, and it stops before the joke is worn out. There is also a genuine sense of fun to it: too much of Cohen's humour in *Flowers for Hitler* seems doggedly determined, but here one can see the delight with which one idea sparks another: "let us have another official language, / let us determine what it will be, / let us give a Canada Council Fellowship / to the most original suggestion." Slightly less successful, because less subtle in the points it is making, is "Business As Usual" (18), a standard attack on Canadian politicians.

"The Bus" (74) opens in a similar satirical vein, though more muted; from an interestingly absurd premise it moves through one standard joke (Cohen and the black driver changing places in "the racial cities") to a curiously haunting final image of the bus on the Florida sands "pointing out, / metallic, painted, solitary, / with New York plates." There is a sense of forlornness in this image of the displaced bus which gives emotion to the surrealist image, lodging it more firmly in the reader's imagination than the purely intellectual surrealism of many other poems can do.

One other very interesting satirical poem is the one called "Destiny" (87): what is interesting about it is that, for once, the object of the satire is Cohen himself, and the grandiose conception of his own role as poet. "Destiny!" he cries, "why do you find me in this bathtub, / idle, alone, unwashed?" As Cohen lists the more "heroic" places in which Destiny might have found him, the sense of self-parody is open and joyous: "Why don't you find me explaining machines / to underprivileged pupils, negroid Spaniards, / happy it is not a course in creative writing?"

The final satirical poem which I wish to discuss is "A Migrating Dialogue" (72), which also serves as an introduction to the group of poems which directly use the Nazi imagery of the title. It is a diffuse and scattered poem in which the parts do not fit very closely together, but many of these parts are interesting. The satirical rhetoric is used mainly as an attempt to comprehend the horrors of the Nazi atrocities through the medium of black farce. Sandra Djwa sees such witty but sick asides as "I say let sleeping ashes lie" as an "attempt to exorcise evil by filtering it through the comic mode."[22] Throughout the book, the satire also implicates the whole of Western culture in the collective guilt. Cohen insists, with his references to western pop figures, that Hitler was not an exclusively German phenomenon.

> Captain Marvel signed the whip contract.
> Joe Palooka manufactured whips.
> Li'l Abner packed the whips in cases.
> The Katzenjammer Kids thought up experiments.

This black farce portrait of the evil of an absurd world is the major line of argument in the poem, but there are two curious asides which call for some comment. Despite the fact that this poem, like all the Nazi poems, insists on the importance of remembering what was done in the camps, it also contains one of Cohen's gestures against history: "I believe with a perfect faith in all the history / I remember, but it's getting harder and harder / to remember much history." This statement links up with the stanza in "On Hearing a Name Long Unspoken" (25):

> History is a needle
> for putting men asleep
> anointed with the poison
> of all they want to keep.

This stanza in turn is reworked by F. in *Beautiful Losers*, where it is the centre of that novel's attack on history.[23]

The other unusual section is the ending. Cohen prepares for it in the most elaborate style of his satirical public rhetoric: "I apologize in advance to all the folks / in this fine wide audience for my tasteless closing remarks." But it is surely debatable just how "tasteless" (apart from the supercilious parenthesis) the closing lines are:

> Braun, Raubal and him
> (I have some experience in these matters),
> these three humans,
> I can't get their nude and loving bodies out of my mind.[24]

Here we are given a startlingly human and even emotionally moving picture of Hitler and the two women he loved (Eva Braun; and Geli Raubal, who died, possibly by suicide, in 1931, and for whom Hitler retained to the last a sentimental affection.)[25] As the image sticks in Cohen's mind, so it sticks in the reader's. The association of Hitler with something as sensuous, vulnerable, beautiful, or just plain human as "nude and loving bodies" is deeply disturbing, and inexplicable in its power.

The image of Hitler is, obviously, a very highly charged one. Gail Fox, the Kingston poet, has talked of the power that certain words or sounds can have:

Sophocles, Aeschylus and Euripides recognized the power of words, the vibratory force of speech and the danger of bad or inharmonious combinations of language for unformed and undisciplined minds. It is not so difficult to remember the fear that merely the *name* of the German dictator—its vibratory sound—struck in people and still continues to strike today. When we use a single word like that infamous name, one word that carries so rich and terrifying a range of associations that most people cannot even begin to articulate what these associations are, *think* then of the power of such a carefully forged structure and group of highly subtle and vivid words that is the poem.[26]

In some ways, Cohen's book is not adequate to the associations of mass horror, in that it seldom deals with them directly, but this may be because he assumes that all these associations are there, and that we have no need of further poems detailing the atrocities of the camps or proclaiming the evils of anti-Semitism. The image of Hitler is absorbed into the overall surrealist tone of the book, and the major stress of the poems which deal by name with the leading Nazi figures is on their ordinariness, on the fact that they are not monstrous paragons of evil but simply people not unlike ourselves.

This appears to be the point of these closing lines of "A Migrating Dialogue," though the erotic context of the image gives it a lasting and disturbing power. A similar portrait of Hitler is attempted in "Police Gazette" (21): "Hitler is alive. / He is fourteen years old. / He does not shave. / He wants to be an architect." Here, however, the mood is ominous; destruction, behind this innocent exterior, is only waiting to be unleashed: "I have one hour of peace / before the documented planets / burn me down."

The most celebrated of these poems is "All There Is To Know About Adolph Eichmann" (66), in which the flat, factual, anti-poetic arrangement of the poem reflects the prosaic nature of the real Eichmann as against the "poetic" extravagances of talons, oversized incisors, green saliva, and madness. It is partly for this very reason that Cohen is less successful in "Goebbels Abandons His Novel and Joins the Party" (28). A medium Eichmann is a much more terrifying figure than a surrealistic Goebbels.

The force of evil may often be felt more strongly in an apparently sunny, innocent setting. In "Folk" (81), we are given a picture of sunny innocence which is, deliberately, ever so slightly overdrawn, like a child's painting book:

> here is a little village
> they are painting it for a holiday
> here is a little church
> here is a school
> here are some doggies making love
> the flags are bright as laundry

The childish "doggies" strikes a slightly false note, suggesting something fundamentally unreal about the scene. And on either side of this idyllic picture, framing it as the first and last lines of the poem, we read: "flowers for hitler the summer yawned." There are several possible associations and interpretations for this line, which of course carries special weight because of the book's title. "Flowers for Hitler," as a title, obviously evokes Baudelaire's *Fleurs du Mal* and thus the complete tradition of decadence and Black Romanticism. But in the context of this poem, the "flowers all over my new grass" are part of a lazy, yawning summer: indifferent Nature. Evil is a human phenomenon, and it is up to humans to perceive it, even within the most innocent of contexts. Meanwhile, "yawning" at our feet (in another sense of the word) is a terrifying abyss.

Evil works by a drugging of human consciousness and perceptivity. If one is to perceive the Hitlers in the little painted village, or in the "medium" Eichmanns, or in oneself, then one needs an acute awareness. Evil works to drug that awareness: "Several faiths / bid him leap— / opium and Hitler / let him sleep" (78). At the end of "Opium and Hitler" Cohen portrays this acquiescence, using again the image of history itself as a drug; sex also can act this way, blurring out distinctions, acting as a retreat from consciousness rather than as (in poems like "You Have The Lovers") an advance beyond it:

> No! He fumbled
> for his history dose.
> The sun came loose,
> his woman close.
>
> Lost in a darkness
> their bodies would reach,
> the Leader started
> a racial speech.

This acquiescence is all the easier because we each carry within us the possibility of being Hitler. He digs in our brains like a mole:

Hitler the brain-mole looks out of my eyes
Goering boils ingots of gold in my bowels
My Adam's Apple bulges with the whole head of Goebbels
(43)

This immanence of evil becomes even clearer in the book's final poem about the Nazi leaders, which is simply called "Hitler" (125). It starts as a kind of farewell: the book is ending, our thoughts have gone through this particular hell, now

let him go to sleep with history,
the real skeleton stinking of gasoline,
the mutt and jeff henchmen beside him;
let them sleep among our precious poppies.

But the opium-bearing poppies, among which the comic-book Nazi leaders may be left to the drugged sleep of history, are *ours*. The second stanza proceeds to show that it is in *our* minds and fantasies that such images begin as well as end:

Cadres of SS waken in our minds
where they began before we ransomed them
to that actual empty realm we people
with the shadows that disturb our inward peace.

The true site of terror is not in the camps, but, as Primo Levi warns in the epigraph to the book, in our own homes. Here begin the "shadows" which we project into that "actual empty realm" which is always waiting for them. No wonder, then, that "The leader's vast design, the tilt of his chin / seem excessively familiar to minds at peace."

One of the reasons, then, that the book does not rely to as great an extent as might have been expected on direct imagery of the Nazi atrocities is that the horror has been thoroughly internalized. It does not belong *out there*: it is inside, domesticated, and the external images are only projections. This process is most obvious in "The Invisible Trouble" (39), in which a man pretends that he carries on his wrist "numbers of the war," whereas in fact "His arm is unburned / his flesh whole: / the numbers he learned / from a movie reel." The "projection" image is here almost literal: the man lives in a horror movie he is projecting from his own mind onto the screen of reality. The reason is that he is "Too fevered to insist: / 'My world is terror.'"

But his world, which is also our world, *is* terror: that is what we have inherited. In a few poems, Cohen touches on the sources of this terror; the statement is clearest in "Congratulations" (15). The first stanza points to the same source as Jeff Nuttall does: the omnipresent awareness of the bomb. Cohen uses a familiar pun on "mushrooms" as he presents a portrait of the contemporary mystic contemplating death in its new forms:

> Here we are eating the sacred mushrooms
> out of the Japanese heaven
> eating the flower
> in the sands of Nevada.

This is one of Cohen's very few direct references to the bomb. (In the poem for Alexander Trocchi he describes it as something he is "distracted by" (45), and in "What I'm Doing Here" (13) he refuses its "universal alibi.") In the rest of "Congratulations" he returns to the central image of "the jewelled house of Dachau / Belsen's drunk fraternity." He calls upon Marco Polo and Arthur Rimbaud to examine these atrocities, and concludes "Don't your boats seem / like floating violins / playing Jack Benny tunes?" Rimbaud's boat is of course the "bâteau ivre" of his poems, drunk like the fraternity of Belsen, evoking the whole tradition of the nineteenth-century French poets in the same way as the title *Flowers for Hitler* evokes Baudelaire. The sources of the mental, internalized terror are to be seen, then, in the awareness of impending nuclear catastrophe, in the memory of Dachau and Belsen, and also in the literary tradition within which Cohen himself is working. These things have shattered the old world-views of progress and optimism; messages of hope and comfort now seem merely sinister.

> *All things can be done*
> whisper museum ovens of
> a war that Freedom won.
> (31)

The sources strike close to home: the terror is domestic.

In "A Migrating Dialogue," Cohen insists that "Captain Marvel signed the whip contract": in "The New Leader" (67) the protagonist is motivated by his realization that "his father had the oven contract." As Sandra Djwa has pointed out,[27] this discovery wipes "the sky clean" of all moral imperatives and categories, leaving him "free to shiver, free to hate, free to begin." In "Why Commands Are Obeyed" (30), another father insists to a son that the real terror, the real ordeal, is to be found in "this familiar room where I say the bench is dangerous" and where terror invades the simplest images of innocence: "the Mother Goose wallpaper goes black."

The domestic setting of terror is clear in the way in which "Heirloom" (56) views a "torture scene developed under a glass bell" like an elaborate clock, or like toys or a music box. At the end of the poem, a bored girl is advised: "Look through your grandmother's house again. / There is an heirloom somewhere." The skeletons in Cohen's cupboards come from the Gestapo cellars.

Yet the domestic scene contains possibilities for the infliction of pain far greater than that suggested by these melodramatic images. In "The Failure of a Secular Life" (53), the "pain-monger" coming home is bested at his own trade when "His wife hit him with an open nerve / and a cry the trade never heard." Cohen miscalculates in turning this poem into a flip, cynical joke (the torturer's career is ruined because "A man's got to be able / to bring his wife something"), but the force of the idea remains. Terror is inside us; we do suffer in our own homes what was inflicted in the camps. So of course "the drinks are watered / and the hat-check girl / has syphilis" (113) — what else did we expect? — and the best thing to do is just to "place my / paper hat on my / concussion and dance."

This, then, is the view of the world which *Flowers for Hitler* presents: a world still dominated by the Nazi image, now made so completely, domestically our own that terror is the very condition of our lives. And this is the setting for the second main theme of *Flowers for Hitler:* the actions of a series of exceptional individuals who have embraced the terror and thus transcended it: the saints of destruction, the beautiful losers. The connection between the two themes is shown in the chilling final couplet of "For Anyone Dressed in Marble" (80): "Bred

close to the ovens, he's burnt inside. / Light, wind, cold, dark
—they use him like a bride."

Michael Ondaatje has commented that "The best moments
in *Flowers for Hitler* . . . would not seem out of place in a novel,"[28]
suggesting that some of the rhetorical "rant" in the poems needs
a character like F. to give it a context. The group of poems I
wish to examine now may certainly be seen as preparation for
Beautiful Losers, as explorations of the themes and techniques
of that novel. In my introductory chapter, I outlined briefly
a concept of "saints": these exceptional characters, living self-
destructive lives outside the bounds of normal society, may also
be described as "beautiful losers." It is an exact phrase. Their
beauty, for Cohen, lies precisely in their loss, in their destruction.
"I'd rather sleep with ashes," he asserts, "than priestly wisdom.
/ Of all the lonely places in the world / this is best / where
debris is human" (21).

Cohen's exaltation of the losers finds interesting expression
in the movie poem "Order" (86). Cohen sides not only with the
stereotype "losers" of African-safari-adventure movies but also,
more radically, with the very nature of bad movies. He likes
them because they *are* bad movies, with no pretentions to "art"
or to permanence.

Pop art is to become an increasingly important image for
Cohen; he embraces it because it is itself a loser, despised by
the critical elite, essentially ephemeral, and energized only by
the immediate emotional charge it provides: cheap thrills. The
bad movies of "Order" do provide a kind of "order," but it is
the order of beautiful loss, in defiance of all ideals of permanence and solidity. "Come my darlings," he writes, "the movies
are true"—and proceeds to a prophetic image of himself as a
pop-romantic "lost sweet singer" (120).

"Disguises" (116) seems at first to be satirical, with Cohen
rather heavily playing up his ironic affection for the disappear-
ing aristocracy and their complementary workers. But within
the pop-art framework of Cohen's exaltation of the loser, the
"dope fiends of North Eastern Lunch" and the "sex fiends of
Beaver pond" are objects of satire only insofar as they have
abandoned these roles and opted for the dead respectabilities
of patriotism and of writing for the learned journals. They
have, paradoxically, betrayed their own nature as "incorrigible

betrayers of the self"; and in the final stage of the poem, Cohen
turns his own "butchered mind" to a celebration of the true
betrayers who have not betrayed their betrayal of themselves.
"Disguises" is a poem in which the style of *Flowers for Hitler* is
working rather impressively: the images are striking and well
controlled, even if they are rhetorical. The poem is entertaining, in its perverse sort of way (especially the stanza on the sex
fiends), but the humour, and the bizarreness of the imagery,
are far from arbitrary: they are directed towards a conclusion
which is central to the book's themes.

Who, then, are the beautiful losers, the "incorrigible betrayers of the self"? In "The Project" (63), one such character
is presented through an interior monologue; indeed, the piece
is not so much a poem as a condensed short story. Most of these
characters are in fact presented in semi-fictional modes, or
dramatized in the third person: Cohen does not use the first-
person lyric for this purpose. The protagonist of "The Project"
is in hospital, being drained of his blood, remembering past
acts of destruction and lovingly anticipating more. There is an
order of society ("white bottles standing in front of a million
doors"; factory and hospital as images for each other) against
which the protagonist sets an ideal of pure destructiveness and
sadistic delight: "I'll be comforting. Oh dear, pyjama flannel
seared right on to the flesh. Let me pull it off." The form of
the story invites the reader to a measure of identification with
this character; the final paragraph even suggests that he is a
kind of artist, and that his "imagination," however perversely
directed, is preferable to the sterility of a society in which even
the power of sex is reduced to the feeble gesture of self-exposure.

The monologue of "The Project" is replaced by the objec-
tification of a stage presentation in "The New Step" (91), which,
although presented in printed form, was intended for the stage
and can only be fully realized there.[29] Here Cohen goes out of
his way to emphasize the bizarre nature of his central image, in
a set of stage directions which would pose a formidable challenge to any actress. The Collector's dance is "grotesque but
military, excruciating but triumphant. It is a woman-creature
proclaiming a disease of the flesh." As one of the Obese, she is
one of the losers of society, yet she has learned to see herself as
beautiful; her project of revenge is more advanced than that of

the protagonist of "The Project." Her vision is one of "uncompromising domination," and she is confident that soon "We'll be teaching everybody."

The objective form of the stage play forces us to see this character from the outside, rather than from the subjective viewpoint of the poems. The perspective is that of "normal" society, as represented by the girls, Mary and Diane. Their opening dialogue is wholly naturalistic, often very funny (Mary's bitter interpretation of Diane's praise of her hands as "Sexiest knuckles on the block"), and completely sympathetic. So the true force of the Collector's image is seen most clearly in her effect on Mary, a character already established and accepted on a naturalistic level.

The ending of the play presents each of the characters in a paradoxical situation, the paradoxes playing with the ideas of beauty and power implicit in the notion of a "beautiful loser." The Collector, by accepting and exulting in her own ugliness and lack of power, has become both beautiful and powerful. Diane, for all her conventional beauty, has lost her lover and also her power over her room-mate. Mary is beginning to follow the same course as the Collector, but her immediate goal and inspiration is still the conventional beauty of Harry. As a final situation, this is all considerably more complex (and therefore, I feel, more satisfying) than the single exposure result of many of the poems; it is also, through the characters of Mary and Diane, more accessible to the reader's experience. This success confirms that the themes with which Cohen was working at that time were more suitable for dramatic than for lyrical presentation: i.e., that *Beautiful Losers* was the only satisfactory resolution of *Flowers for Hitler*.

But the most interesting group of these poems in *Flowers for Hitler* centres on characters who are not completely fictional but rather versions of historical figures: Kerensky, Queen Victoria, Irving Layton, and Alexander Trocchi. It is in these poems that Cohen comes closest to defining the kind of experience involved in responding adequately to the terrors of Hitler's world.

The historical figure of Kerensky is used (127) as an image for the character of a nameless "friend." It is a sympathetic and generous portrayal recognizing the nobility as well as the futility of the man's attitude. Cohen himself is more detached, or even hostile, towards history and the political process than is "Kerensky," who sees, with a weary resignation, that "It will all come round again"; his "vision of Revolution" is that it is "Possible and brief." But at least possible.

He is akin to the other beautiful losers in that he accepts the impermanence, the broken nature of what he is doing. Not for him the absolute systems of the professionals, "they of the pure smiling eyes / trained only for Form... who need our daily lives perfect." "Kerensky" accepts imperfection, knows that the "moment when / everything is possible" must of necessity be "tiny," and that "There is nothing for him to do but preside / over the last official meeting." His rewards are small, but the moments do come when, in a phrase so typical of Cohen that it is almost a cliché, "poems grew like butterflies on the garbage of his life." Even this reward is undercut in one flat, laconic line: "How many times? The sad answer is: they can be counted."

In the final, prose paragraph, the falling snow confers ironic epaulets upon him as he sees the night itself around him being consumed by the greed of "The carved gargoyles of the City Hall... the bankers — of History." History has no place for Kerensky: neither Tsar nor Lenin, he creates no significant act. He too will be consumed.

Kerensky is one of the losers of history, and the compassion which Cohen extends to him is also extended to perhaps the most unfashionable figure of all: Queen Victoria (88). "The most artistically ostracized woman in history," Ondaatje calls her,[30] and thus she is a perfect candidate for Cohen's roll-call of saints, though the poem is at times a little too conscious of its own outrageousness: "Queen Victoria / The 20th century belongs to you and me." There is an astute, controlled use of detail: the "huge pink maps" of the British Empire; the "glass roof in a train station" and "cast-iron exhibition" of Victorian architecture; the notoriously English vice of flagellation combined with a fascination for clockwork toys in "will you spank her with a mechanical corset"; the passing allusion to Meredith's *Modern Love* (1862). All these establish a full, almost sensuous impression of the period, but what really unites "Queen Victoria and me" is "our incomparable sense of loss." As losers, outsiders, they "turn up unwelcome at every World's Fair" (one Victorian idea enthusiastically endorsed by the 1960s), disrupting order and complacency, confusing the "star-dazed tourists." Ondaatje describes the poem as "witty and moving." To a greater extent even than in "Kerensky," the harshness of Cohen's vision is mitigated by his real sympathy for the much-maligned character he is writing about.

The poem "For My Old Layton" (36) is less directly connected with its "real life" protagonist. Rather, the image which Layton projects of himself in some of his poems (such as "The Cold Green Element") is here used as a starting-point for the portrayal of a character pursuing the career of a typical Cohen saint. He starts by rejecting his own personality, leaving his "pain" behind, "unowned." Now he is "clean" (as the sky in "The New Leader" is "clean"); now he is "arrogant" and "swift." He enters a town and accepts the "garbage" showered upon him as "praise . . . like ticker-tape." He disrupts "the peace of gentle folk" by "throwing his shadow" into their private lives. He is beyond envy: rather, he feels a vast, impersonal love, which can just as easily turn into the misanthropy of Timon. He retires to the seashore to live like a hermit and sleep "on stone cribs," and here "the salt-bright atmosphere" provides him with an image of beauty transcending its context, "building crystals in his hair."

This pattern of conduct contains several adumbrations of *Beautiful Losers*: the swift arrogance of F., the hermit withdrawal of *I*, the final transcendence and metamorphosis of *IF*. But, to return to Layton, there are also echoes of "A Tall Man Executes a Jig," especially in the parallel between the atmosphere building crystals in the one man's hair and the snake coiling a green halo above the other's head. As with all the best poems in *Flowers for Hitler*, the poem is tightly ordered and concise in its imagery; nothing is wasted; it makes nonsense of the "I will abandon my style" posturings.

The image of the saint/disciple relationship is most fully laid out in "Alexander Trocchi, Public Junkie, Priez pour Nous" (45). Trocchi himself is well in line with the book's other self-destructive heroes, with his insistence that "healthy skin is grey" and his dedication to the project of "changing the Law," but above all, Cohen sees in him the qualities of "purity" and simplicity. Ondaatje comments that the poem is "very close in form to *Beautiful Losers*" in its structural use of the disciple figure, "awkward, uncertain, and more conservative than the saint he admires."[31] The alternation of stanzas between the two points of view begs for the more fully dramatic structure a novel allows. The religious imagery of *Beautiful Losers* is also present in the title of the poem, which explicitly casts Trocchi in the role of a saint. The text then becomes like a prayer with responses, as the disciple confesses his own unworthiness and asks for guidance.

If this poem has a shortcoming, it is that it is rather too systematic in its rejection of systems. (This paradox persists in the novel.) The contrast between saint and disciple is too fixed, too unvarying; the lessons to be learned are rather too clearly set out. Cohen's views of teachers and the teaching process are rather more paradoxically (and therefore accurately) set out in poems such as "My Mentors" (54) and especially "Old Dialogue" (107):

> — Has this new life deepened your perceptions?
> — I suppose so.
> — Then you are being trained correctly.
> — For what?
> — If you knew we could not train you.

This state of uncertainty is a necessary part of F.'s "classroom of hysteria" in *Beautiful Losers;* Trocchi's disciple knows too clearly what it is he is being trained for.

Neither saint nor disciple should be confused with the figure of the poet himself. Cohen as poet continues to stand slightly apart from all the configurations of the world in which the flowers yawn for Hitler, and in which the incorrigible betrayers of the self pursue their course to destruction. He partakes in it all, of course, but as a poet he is still able to transcend it by giving expression to it.

Although many of the poems in which he discusses his own role are taken up by the superficial "anti-poet" stance, not all of them are. For instance, the opening poem of the book, "What I'm Doing Here" (13), is a much more serious poem than, say, "Style," or the more whimsical "The Hearth," which immediately follows it. "The Hearth" makes a mock-humble joke out of the poet's discovery that he is not unique; the opening confessions of "What I'm Doing Here" are altogether more serious: "I do not know if the world has lied / I have lied / I do not know if the world has conspired against love / I have conspired against love." Cohen declares, "I refuse the universal alibi" of "the mushroom cloud": evil is not external but internal, the poet is part of it and must admit that he is. Moreover, he must make us admit it also: his function as poet is to "wait / for each one of you to confess." But if this is his central aim in the book (no longer the "golden-boy poet" telling us his loves, but the "front-line writer" waiting for our confessions), the bizarre images of the second stanza (telephone booth, mirrors, nymphomaniac) are already starting to attract attention towards themselves, towards the insistent *style* of the book rather than the simplicity of that initially announced commitment.

The paradoxes of *Flowers for Hitler* are never, in fact, fully resolved. Despite "The Hearth," Cohen's lusts still assert themselves as unique masterpieces; despite the cover blurb, Cohen cannot wholly shake the image of the "sweet lost singer." A final group of poems in *Flowers for Hitler* reassert the beauty of poetry itself as an absolute. "Nothing I Can Lose" (20) presents a familiar image of the poet as a tightrope-walker, balanced over Niagara, undisturbed even by the news of his father's death. Final trust is placed in the elements with which he works, and this trust will be repaid by some new gift of grace:

> Tomorrow I'll invent a trick
> I do not know tonight,
> the wind, the pole will tell me what
> and the friendly blinding light.

The light is friendly, but also blinding; the light is blinding, but also friendly.

"For E. J. P." (69) starts off as if it were going to be a confession poem: "I once believed a single line / in a Chinese poem could change / forever how blossoms fell." The implication is, obviously, that he no longer holds this belief, and that the poem will expose its foolishness. But in fact this exposé never happens. The re-creation of the atmosphere of Pound's Chinese translations (the "E. J. P." looks as if it should refer to Pratt, but the text of the poem is much more apposite to Ezra without the J.) is so complete and so beautiful that finally it takes over the whole poem, and the expected reversal never occurs. The poet's sense of the absolute beauty of words destroys whatever satiric intent he may have started with. So we are left with a sense of remote beauty. In "Sky" (58), "The great ones pass" in a sense of isolation and grandeur quite distinct from the general tone of the book, and it is to this sense that Cohen returns for his view of the poet in the closing poem of the book, "Another Night with Telescope" (128). The poet himself is as usual "broken"; he disdains all roles; the patterns he spins "on an eternal unimportant loom . . . do not last the night." But the great ones remain, and the poet, ultimately, is subject to them:

> I know the stars
> are wild as dust
> and wait for no man's discipline
> but as they wheel
> from sky to sky they rake
> our lives with pins of light.

(iv) *Parasites of Heaven* (1966)

Even Cohen's greatest admirers will readily admit that *Parasites of Heaven* [32] is a pretty bad book. Perhaps the kindest adjective that can be applied to it is "uneven." For Michael Ondaatje, it has the same kind of interest as a bad movie: "the director's struggle with his material . . . holds our concentration." [33] More unkindly, it could be argued, as the title suggests, that the publication of the book was "parasitical" on the notoriety of *Beautiful Losers* (published earlier the same year) and on Cohen's dawning fame as a pop-singer. Moreover, because the book contains a number of poems dated as early as 1957 and 1958, we can suspect that we are being given the rejects from earlier collections. The cynical conclusion is that the book was a slap-dash attempt to cash in on Cohen's popularity.

This conclusion is unfair, but the fact remains that *Parasites of Heaven* does not have the coherence of purpose of any of Cohen's other volumes. Whereas such collections as *Flowers for Hitler* and *The Energy of Slaves*, however uneven they may be in overall quality, still possess a purposeful thematic unity, *Parasites of Heaven* seems to wander, held together only loosely by its vague lack of concern for anything outside the surreal workings of the poet's mind. The book contains a higher proportion of totally negligible poems than does any other volume, and of the few poems in it which may be thought totally successful, a significant number have shown their best qualities in another medium, as songs. In their musical form, they have a firmness and clarity that is missing from the other poems in *Parasites of Heaven*.

It may be only because we are so familiar with these poems as songs — "Suzanne" (70), "The Master Song" (76), "Teachers" (56), and to a lesser extent "Avalanche" (78) — that they should stand out as we read through the book. In any case, I intend to exclude them from consideration in this section and return to them in the later chapter on Cohen as songwriter.

There are a number of formal experiments in *Parasites of Heaven*, of which the songs are the most notable. Apart from those which were finally recorded, there are a number of poems which appear to be failed or rejected songs, such as "I was standing on the stairs" (52) and "I've seen some lonely history" (59). Other poems look like sketches or rehearsals for later songs. "Suzanne wears a leather coat" (31) and "Nancy lies in London grass" (33) attempt portraits which later songs were to achieve in a much more satisfying and complex manner.

Besides the songs, there are a number of conventionally rhymed poems, of which the most interesting is "Give me back my fingerprints" (72). Here Cohen uses the rhymes, and a kind of deadpan manner, to produce a humorous, even a whimsical effect. The poem may be seen as a restatement, in comic terms, of the scar motif from *The Favourite Game*, but the whimsy and the serious theme remain separate from each other rather than being identified, as they so often are in the novels.

The other major formal aspect of the book is the number of short prose-poems. (The two forms are oddly crossed in "I guess it's time to say goodbye" (50), which is set out as prose but actually consists of long, rambling and irregular rhymed quatrains.) Many of the prose pieces are similar in style to *Beautiful Losers*, but, deprived of the dramatic context of the novel, they stand rather shakily and pretentiously on their own. The prose is best when it can achieve an informal, colloquial tone, when it moves in the rhythms of speech rather than in the rhythms of pseudo-poetry. Thus, a piece like "It's not so hard to say goodbye" (12), with its nicely turned ending — "look! that's a smile on the skull. Last year we thought only hypocrites did that to their mouths" — is far more successful than the impossible conglomeration of "Found once again shamelessly ignoring the swans" (39).

The book also contains a few gestures towards the "anti-poem" stance, of which the most interesting are those which use flat, factual statement. The love poem "Snow is falling" (53) is the most successful here: each line is a factual, "unpoetic" statement, but the selection, economy, and juxtaposition give them poetic form. "A cross didn't fall on me" (14) attempts to use the same technique, but in a looser, more random manner. Here Cohen is exploiting his own poem's pointlessness and lack of connections, appealing to the reader: "Love me because nothing happens." It doesn't seem a particularly good reason.

The main thematic preoccupation is, once again, the subjective self. The outward-turning social concerns of *Flowers for Hitler* have dropped out of sight. Stylistically, the result is a total immersion in the kind of surrealist language which was one of the weakest aspects of the earlier book. In many poems in *Parasites of Heaven*, the subject-matter never becomes clear; the images are trapped entirely within Cohen's private and arbitrary associations. They illuminate nothing: they make no aspect of experience, even Cohen's, clearer to the reader; they merely play obfuscating games with words.

A good example is the poem "The nightmares do not suddenly" (13). The first stanza presents a moderately interesting image, though the comparison is still more showmanship than illumination:

> The nightmares do not suddenly
> develop happy endings
>   I merely step out of them
> as a five year old scientist
> leaves the room
> where he has dissected an alarm clock

This stanza is followed by an image of startling clarity and bril-

liance, in four lines in which all Cohen's genius suddenly shines
clear:

> Love wears out
> like overused mirrors unsilvering
> and parts of your faces
> make room for the wall behind

Here everything works: the image of the mirrors "unsilvering"
makes a nice play between the literal decay of a mirror and the
figurative loss of glamour and value in a love affair; there is
the implication that the affair ends because it has become too
narcissistic; and the pain of the moment, even its terror, is
caught in the idea of "parts of your faces" physically falling
away to leave only a blank wall behind. But this moment of
illumination is immediately lost in an arbitrarily bizarre and
meaningless gesture:

> If terror needs my round green eyes
> for a masterpiece
> let it lure them with nude key-holes
> mounted on an egg

The final stanza dissipates whatever is left of the mood, as it
indulges in further irrelevances:

> And should Love decide
> I am not the one
> to stand scratching his head
> wondering what wall to lean on
> send King Farouk to argue
> or come to me dressed as a fast

This one poem, with its single moment of insight surrounded
by inconsequential nonsense, could well serve as a diagram of
the whole book.

In a few poems the familiar Cohen themes emerge with
startling economy and clarity. One of the best prose pieces is
"You are the Model" (58), which amounts to a brief character
sketch of a girl longing to break into the world of "real power
movies." In some ways it is an accomplished piece of fiction,
the creation—all too rare in Cohen—of a credible character
separate from himself. The girl is confused, unsure of herself,
worrying "can any girl be discovered after Bardot?" But ob-

viously Cohen's empathy with the character derives from their shared obsession with the mythology of the movies—the trivia-quiz details of Bardot, Vadim, and Jean Shrimpton—and with the overriding sense of power in the popular medium, a power which amounts almost to sainthood: the girl dreams that she is "Walking home without autograph disciples for the last time."

Also characteristically of Cohen, the girl is a failure, and will probably stay on her "poor, unfashionable Greek island," never getting the chance to "threaten Paris." A similar sense of lost possibilities exists in the book's other successful pop-culture poem, "I met Doc Dog The Poker Hound" (38). Here, in the setting and atmosphere of comic books, Cohen sets up an idea of grace and beauty which derives its force not only from the incongruity of the setting but also from the fact that it is bound to be destroyed:

> One of these days
> I'm going to open up a cafeteria
> that serves coffee in thin cups
> bone thin China cups
> What we lose in cups we make up
> in gratitude

Other "loser" poems in the book are more serious in tone. "Give me dog, dogs" (19) is an intense and savage hymn to destruction, using a long line split up into short, gasping phrases: "bring me in their wild midst, in the spiked ring / of white teeth, sharp fangs, wet mouths, cast me hard / and down." The poet has been "sent to love" but in order to achieve this he must be "clawed first, cleansed first, taught to fight, to lose." The poem is dated 1961, and one wonders why it was not included in an earlier book; perhaps it was too harsh in tone for *The Spice-Box of Earth* and too self-centred for *Flowers for Hitler*. At any rate, it is one of Cohen's strongest statements of the necessity of embracing destruction.

The brief reference to "the calf, the ewe" prepares for the slaughterhouse image which dominates the strongest piece of prose writing in the book, "Here was the Market" (54). This is a sustained tour-de-force of descriptive writing in which the realistic details of the scene gradually amass a terrifyingly surreal power of suggestion that culminates in the brilliantly ominous final phrase: "watching out for the black puddles under-foot, for who knows how deep they went."

But whereas Cohen is outraged by the images of the cruelty suffered by animal victims, he continues to regard his human losers as beautiful, and the experience of loss as leading to a higher vision. In another earlier poem, from 1959, "O love intrude into this strangerhood" (25), the following lines express as concisely as possible the situation of the would-be saint: "Silence be my wilderness / Where I can learn to master / As my heroes did / The visionary discipline." At the end of the poem he seeks to "lose with grace / The pine trees to the early mist." Grace for Cohen is always in the losing, the dissolution of identity.

As usual, the book contains several poems on Cohen's own conception of himself as a poet. In the prose piece "I wonder if my brother will ever read this" (29), Cohen places himself, with his compulsion to write, in the position of the disciple not yet possessing the "balance" (a key word in *Beautiful Losers'* definition of the saint) of the "Heroes and near-heroes, anointed children" who can "disdain to implore the horizontal world with words and organizing metaphors." This humility, however marginal it may be in a book as obsessively self-centred as *Parasites of Heaven,* is in fact the keynote of all the poems on Cohen's role as poet. He is even able to take a humorous swipe at his own messianic status: "If you are the Light / give me a light / buddy" (46).

A similar humility, and a more serious religious tone, are to be found in "Created fires I cannot love" (62): "Make me poor so I may be / servant in the world I see." In this, and several other poems, Cohen is talking about a religious sense of a higher order which serves as the inspiration of his poetry. A key image for this is the sky, continuing the imagery of the poem "Sky" in *Flowers for Hitler.* In "Here was the Harbour" (45), Cohen asks, "Who doesn't give his heart to things that soar, kites or jet planes or a sharp distant sail?" The sense of the sky as wide, open, clean, and demanding permeates the poem. "It demands stories; of men the sky demands all manner of stories, entertainments, embroideries, just as it does of its stars and constellations."

This use of imagery is even more striking when the following paragraph emerges from the weary parade of surreal images in "Somewhere in my trophy room" (49):

> There ahead of me extended an impossible trophy: the bright, great sky, where no men lived. Beautiful and empty, now luminous with a splendour emanating from my own flesh, the tuneless sky washed and washed my lineless face and bathed in waves my heart like a red translucent stone. Until my eyes gave out I lived there as my home.

Even though a trace of egoism lingers in the idea that the splendour here emanates from Cohen's own flesh, it is clear that the sky in these poems is an image of a higher order before which the poet feels humble but which is also capable of extending its blessing, as in the beautiful short poem "This morning I was dressed by the wind" (75).

The pose of humility is, of course, only another pose, only another mask tried on by the restless ego, but it was a direction in which Cohen was to move, increasingly, through the "New Poems" and some of the songs, to the full self-abasement pose of *The Energy of Slaves*. Most of *Parasites of Heaven* does not project humility. Rather, there is the almost arrogant assumption that the most obscure, arbitrary and bizarre concoctions of Leonard Cohen's subconscious will be of interest to the reader. If "heaven" is still present in the book, it is present in the occasional glimpses of Cohen's true poetic power, but in too many of the poems Cohen is the parasite of his own ability.

(v) *New Poems* (1968)

When Cohen's *Selected Poems* appeared in 1968, there was at the end of it a twenty-page section called "New Poems."[34] These poems — the smallest "collection" Cohen has ever published — are in fact very interesting, and quite distinctive in style.

Although they continue the personal, non-socially-oriented tone of *Parasites of Heaven,* they are written in much simpler language. The greatest excesses of surrealist imagery have gone; Michael Ondaatje describes it as "a reaction to the high-swinging language" of the previous books. For Ondaatje, "It is a catching simplicity," and the poems are "very moving . . . simply because of the gracious low-key tone."[35] Most of the poems are written in a looser, more conversational verse form—there is only one poem in quatrains—and there is a tendency towards a greater length than is usual for Cohen.

This move towards a simpler, or, to use Ondaatje's word, more gracious style is matched, in the best of these poems, by a slight shift in Cohen's attitude. The poetry is still self-centred—at one point Cohen confesses "I can't connect you with / anything but myself" (224)—but at least Cohen is now able to say that as a confession, rather than as a boast. There is a softening in the harshness of Cohen's isolation, and of his insistence on the destruction of the self: a retreat, in some measure, from the apocalyptic absoluteness of the vision in *Beautiful Losers*. Such a softening is also visible in the songs, and in this respect it is interesting that the image of Joan of Arc is first used in "I Met You" (227). This softening raises at least the possibility of a relationship in which the other may be viewed as an equal, and in which personality, rather than being destroyed, may be allowed to flourish.

"This is for you," the first poem begins (221), and it seems to be the first time that Cohen has seriously shown himself to be writing *for* someone else. (Cynically, this might be seen as just another pose: the outward-turning self as another disguise of the same consuming ego. And maybe we *want* to believe it, because it is more humane. But it does seem to me that the tone achieved in these poems and in the songs is a genuine one.)

The poems reach for an end to Cohen's "strangerhood," his compulsive isolation. "I long for the boundaries / of my wandering," he writes, ". . . and I move toward a love / you have dreamed for me" (222). A value is placed on being part of a community, being with other people: "you welcomed me into the circle / more than a guest" (221). The title of the collection's longest poem sums this up: "It's good to sit with people" (236). In the poem "Edmonton, Alberta, December 1966, 4 a.m." (225) (which, despite the particularity of its title, manages to rename Jasper Avenue) the idea of a community is extended to the whole natural scene. Interestingly enough, considering the use of the image in *Parasites of Heaven,* this embrace includes the sky:

> Grass and honey, the singing radiator,
> the shadow of bridges on the ice

of the North Saskatchewan River,
the cold blue hospital of the sky —
it all keeps us such sweet company.

The central fact about these poems, though, is that they are love poems, and that in them Cohen is attempting to extend a love which is tender, sympathetic, and helpful, rather than demanding or destructive. "It's good to sit with people" (236) builds up a convincing and sympathetic portrait of its central character, Frédérique, who shares some of the saintlike qualities of Suzanne. Of her, Cohen is able to say, "Only with you / I did not imitate myself / only with you / I asked for nothing." The poem's closing lines are, in their total simplicity and understatement, as moving as any Cohen has ever written: "Come to me if you grow old / come to me if you need coffee."

This gentler conception of love is also linked with the (inevitable) poems about his own role as a poet. Cohen shows the contrast between his growing public role as a singer and his private identity as a lover: "I've sung to a thousand people / and I've written a small new song" (225). In another poem he states, "The reason I write / is to make something / as beautiful as you are" (231).

But this poem continues with a flash of the older Cohen, as, echoing the "soldier and the whore" imagery of *The Favourite Game,* he goes on to say that "When I'm with you" he wants to fulfill his childhood dream of being "a perfect man / who kills." In the final poem of the book, it is possible that Cohen is describing himself and the paradoxes of his own position:

He studies to describe
the lover he cannot become
failing the widest dreams of the mind
& settling for visions of God

The tatters of his discipline
have no beauty
that he can hold so easily
    as your beauty

He does not know how
to trade himself for your love
Do not trust him
unless you love him   (239)

Placed at the very end of the *Selected Poems,* these lines may be seen as a summary and judgement of all of Cohen's poetry up to that point. (Certainly, the second stanza seems to repeat exactly the debate of *The Spice-Box of Earth.*) Having gone through the fire of *Flowers for Hitler* and *Beautiful Losers,* Cohen is now seeking to become a lover. But he does not yet know how.

CHAPTER THREE

The Novels

Your teacher shows you how it happens.
(*Leonard Cohen,* Beautiful Losers)

Leonard Cohen's novels examine and develop the themes apparent in his poetry, and to a certain extent they may be seen as "a poet's novels." Whereas the centre of attention in a novel is normally on such narrative elements as plot, character, and dramatic situation, in Cohen's novels these elements are subservient to theme, imagery, and linguistic texture. Neither *The Favourite Game* nor *Beautiful Losers* adheres to a clearly developed plot line, and the latter novel is as much concerned with the destruction of character as with its creation. The linguistic texture of both novels is thrust to the forefront of the reader's attention: the concise, cinematic imagery of *The Favourite Game,* the grotesque elaborations of imagery in *Beautiful Losers.* Cohen is clearly not interested in writing "conventional" novels. Though *The Favourite Game* displays certain similarities to the *Kunstlerroman* pattern (and most critics have talked of the parallel to Joyce's *Portrait of the Artist as a Young Man*), this basic pattern is less important than the highly individual variations which Cohen plays on it. And part of the fun of *Beautiful Losers* is the outrageousness with which it breaks every possible convention and taboo.

But however much he may modify it, the novel form still inevitably produces certain changes in Cohen's writing: it affords some possibilities, imposes some limitations. The most important effect of the novel form, an effect which makes itself felt both in Cohen's writing and in the reader's response, is the distancing produced by the (actual or implied) third person narration. The novel deprives Cohen of the urgency and the authority of the lyric "I": writer and reader are forced to look objectively not only at the central characters but also at those with whom they come into contact. In *The Favourite Game*, Cohen's irony is continually holding Breavman at arm's length, and, whereas Breavman longs for the lyric isolation of his own beautiful pain, the novel must also present Shell. In *Beautiful Losers* the effect is more complex, with a subtle interaction of different characters and different narrative voices in, progressively, first, second and third persons. The result is that in the novels the outlines of Cohen's vision appear in their clearest, harshest terms. Beyond *Beautiful Losers* there can be no advance, only the retreat into the muted gentleness of the songs.

The objectivity of the form also allows Cohen opportunities to do some things more easily than in the poems. Some of the excesses of style gain significance by being the speech-habits of specific characters in a dramatic context.[1] Even more important, the novel allows Cohen to indulge the fantasies of his humour, which the "dignity" of the lyric "I" had held in check except in the occasional poem such as "Destiny." Cohen the novelist is not afraid to laugh at his protagonists, and this humour is an effective instrument of his vision.

Part of the fascination of the novels, then, is to see the ways in which the workings of the form give shape and direction to Cohen's writing, and, conversely, how the force of Cohen's vision alters and moulds the novel form to his own needs.

(i) *The Favourite Game* (1963)

"The Favourite Game, then, is love," wrote George Robertson[2] in one of the early reviews of Cohen's first novel;[3] this interpretation has been taken as gospel by the commercial blurb writers. It is repeated, more or less verbatim, on the back of the New Canadian Library edition, whereas the somewhat more lurid Avon paperback offers as a come-on to its buyers: "love, with a very modern set of rules."[4] Patricia Morley offers a different view: "The pursuit of truth by means of fun is Cohen's favourite game." [5] This comment is accurate in pointing to an interdependence of farce and seriousness in the novel, but it rather ignores the point that *The Favourite Game* does not seem particularly concerned with "the pursuit of truth." In fact, the title's reference is very precisely to the novel's final paragraph, and it is there that we should primarily look for our interpretation. For whatever else may be the central meaning of the favourite game and *The Favourite Game,* it is not love.

> Jesus! I just remembered what Lisa's favourite game was. After a heavy snow we would go into a back yard with a few of our friends. The expanse of snow would be white and unbroken. Bertha was the spinner. You held her hands while she turned on her heels, you circled her until your feet left the ground. Then she let go and you flew over the snow. You remained still in whatever position you landed. When everyone had been flung in this fashion into the fresh snow, the beautiful part of the game began. You stood up carefully, taking great pains not to disturb the impression you had made. Now the comparisons. Of course you would have done your best to land in some crazy position, arms and legs sticking out. Then we walked away, leaving a lovely white field of blossom-like shapes with footprint stems.
>
> (223)

The essence of the game may be stated thus: you start with a field of snow; something white, blank, unmarked. The possible analogies are obvious enough in the book: the artist confronting the white sheet of paper, or two people meeting for the first time, their relationship still open to all potentialities. Then, acting *on* this blankness, violently imposing your will upon it, you create an image. The more distorted, grotesque and "crazy" the image is, the more beautiful it is. Then you walk away and leave it; you break the connection, leaving nothing real or permanent of yourself behind. The image created is as beautiful as a flower, but only because you have abandoned it, breaking off the "footprint stems." (It is important to note that "stems" is the last word of *The Favourite Game,* since one of the central images of *Beautiful Losers* is to be the "stem" broken from the "system.")

This total image of the favourite game serves as a paradigm of what Breavman seeks for himself as an artist and in his personal relationships. He seeks to create beautiful and grotesque images, which he can leave. The pun on his name has often been noted, but Cohen maintains a careful balance between acts by which Breavman bereaves others and acts by which he is himself bereaved. The whole book can be read as a judgement on how far the ideals of the favourite game can in fact be achieved in the areas in which Breavman wishes to apply them.

The complexity of the image lies in what is left behind. It is necessary for the game that marks should remain: that the snow (page, person) be no longer untouched. But there must be nothing vital of the artist himself, no commitment, left behind. He must make his mark and then go, "As the mist leaves no scar / On the dark green hill." Hence the importance of this poem, which is reprinted as an epigraph to the book in the original English edition (but not in the American edition.⁶) This poem, which I have already discussed in the context of *The Spice-Box of Earth,* is one of Cohen's most beautiful lyrics, but in the context of *The Favourite Game* it becomes the expression of Breavman's longing for easy escape routes, ways of getting out of relationships which leave behind only the lovely grotesque marks of his own art, not the real scars of real pain. But the book's obsession with the imagery of scars shows Cohen's awareness of the impossibility of Breavman's project.

The first page of the novel (8) is taken up with a discussion of scars. They are viewed romantically as "the proud scars of combat," and as secrets for lovers to reveal: or, ironically, as the result of arguments on aesthetic principle. But even here Cohen cannot keep out the uglier implications: "His mother regarded her whole body as a scar grown over some earlier perfection which she sought in mirrors and windows and hub-caps." A scar is also, most interestingly of all, "what happens when the word is made flesh." Although the immediate allusion is biblical, the phrase clearly applies to Breavman's own writing. When Breavman attempts to realize the image of himself as artist in the flesh of his human relationships, the results are always scars. Mist may leave no scars, but Breavman cannot.

Detachment is possible for Breavman only in the innocence, or naivety, of childhood, to which he obsessively returns. "I'm the keeper," he tells Krantz. "I'm the sentimental dirty old man in front of a classroom of children" (69). And later, to Lisa:

"I don't want to forget anyone I was ever connected with" (111). His courtship of Shell consists of a long, lovingly detailed re-creation of the romantic dreams of his childhood, seen in a romantic glow. Breavman and Lisa, playing their game, "had no knowledge of the sordid aspect of brothels, and who knows if there is one?" (28) The discovery of true sexuality comes in a rush which leaves young Breavman wondering, "Why was any-body working?" (30)

This passage (29–30) is worth a closer look, for it is entirely typical of Cohen's method. Its message is central to the book: sexuality liberates Breavman in some ways and yet limits him in others. The presentation of the message, however, is all-out farce. Even Cohen's love of the pop media is present, since knowledge arrives in the form of "a two-foot strip of film" in which "you saw everything." Cohen breaks from the narrative to announce, in portentous tones, "Let us praise this film, which has disappeared with the maid into the Canadian wilderness." His tongue now firmly in his cheek, and the absolute seriousness of the passage thus assured, Cohen proceeds to "praise" this "wilderness" film, "titled in English, with beguiling simplicity, 'Thirty Ways to Screw,'" which could have such a liberating effect on the uptight "garrisons" of Canadian morality. At one moment he is announcing, with all the understated solemnity of a sociological treatise, "This tiny strip of celluloid shown widely in Canadian theatres might revitalize the tedious mar-riages which are reported to abound in our country"; the next moment he launches into a quasi-biblical encomium, "Where are you, working girl with supreme device? The National Film Board hath need of you."

The control of tone is exact, and the passage is outrageously funny, but its very humour directs the alert reader to its intense seriousness in the novel's thematic structure. Breavman and Lisa, looking at this instructive strip of celluloid, "knew it would be like this"; in its idealism, its impersonal perfection, its detach-ment, its lack of scars, it becomes the Romantic, childhood image which Breavman never quite gives up hope of finding again in his own real life. Lisa, however, is immediately cut off from it by "the Curse" (31), which marks the end of childhood. At the time, Breavman "hadn't the remotest idea" what this means; in a sense, he never does. As "the keeper," he is reverting to an age, and an ideal, from which Lisa is permanently separated.

Breavman attempts various ways of realizing this detachment. Each involves the invention of some kind of impersonal form, or ritual, in which he can take part as an actor rather than as an individual. He creates roles for himself and stands back to watch himself playing them (while Cohen stands farther back, to watch him watching). The most fully developed of these roles is that of the artist.

This type of role-playing is first seen, and most clearly seen, in the childhood games he plays with Lisa. A game is a way of coming to terms with aspects of reality by reducing them to manageable proportions, by making them "small scale models." In this respect, there is a great deal of similarity between games and art — the major difference being that games often introduce concepts of winning and losing which are (or should be) alien to the artist. In *The Savage Mind,* Claude Lévi-Strauss talks about the process of art as a "small-scale model," and one of the illustrations he uses is that of the children's game.

> A child's doll is no longer an enemy, a rival or even an interlocutor. . . . In the case of miniatures, in contrast to what happens when we try to understand an object or living creature of real dimensions, knowledge of the whole precedes knowledge of the parts. And even if this is an illusion, the point of the procedure is to create or sustain the illusion, which gratifies the intelligence and gives rise to a sense of pleasure which can already be called aesthetic on these grounds alone.[7]

It may be argued that Breavman never fully learns to cope with the "contrast" between games and the "living creature of real dimensions."

Thus the "games of flesh, love, curiosity" (26) which Breavman and Lisa play serve as controlled initiations into reality. Lisa understands perfectly the distinction between game and reality; within the game she is willing to be naked, but "Now outside of the game, she made them turn while she put on her dress" (18). Breavman's trouble is that he wants the games to go on forever. Within the games, everything is perfect: "Whores were ideal women just as soldiers were ideal men" (28). Most important of all, no scars are left behind: the red welts that "dance all over Lisa's imaginary body" (17) are inherent only in the string, which is later "lost" (18).

Ideally, all the actors in the game remain separate from it, lost in their parts. Their real identities are as forbidden as "talking dirty or roughhouse" are in "their great game, The Soldier and The Whore" (27–28). Note the generalizing, de-individualizing capital letters. One occasion on which this impersonality is disturbed is the whipping game, when Breavman is so spellbound by the perfection of Lisa's naked body that he "didn't take his turn whipping." Instead, his reaction is the possessive, and illegitimately personal, "Oh my, my, my." His distraction breaks the spell and forces Lisa out of the game: "What's the matter with him? I'm getting dressed" (18).

In fact, Breavman's control of the game situation, in whatever mode, is always precarious. He is frequently in danger of becoming narcissistically absorbed in the beauty of his own creations, and he always ignores (or tries to ignore) the existence that his human material continues to lead outside the games. Preoccupied, for instance, by his own Kleenex creation, he assumes that Muffin also participates in it (39); Cohen has time for one line of sympathy (her "nightmare had just begun"), but Breavman has none.

The ideal form of Breavman's experience comes to him in his hypnotism of the maid Heather (52–56). Breavman, playing the role of hypnotist, is in perfect control, and the material with which he is working, while necessarily human, is in the ideal depersonalized state of being unconscious and without memory, without the possibility of scars. Within these limits, the experience becomes transcendent: "The tungsten light was the same as the moon." The precariousness of Breavman's control is demonstrated by Heather's double awakening and by the moment of panic when he believes he has driven her insane; then Cohen dissolves the scene in characteristic humour with Heather's response of "genuine admiration." This experience becomes another paradigm for Breavman's relationships with women: with all of them, he seeks the same control and the same detachment. He wishes that all the scars of memory could be hypnotically cancelled.

These early roles (Soldier, torturer, hypnotist) all lead towards Breavman's ultimate role as artist. All his responses to the world are compulsively verbal. When he has his first sexual experience, with Norma, "His mind broke into postcards" (74). For most of the book, this verbal response is shown mainly (apart from his writing, of course) in the running "dialogue" with Krantz through which the two friends are "interpreting the world for one another" (109). These dialogues are the training ground for Breavman's epigrammatic wit and, more seriously, for the literary vision which he attempts to impose on his world.

Breavman is perfectly capable of regarding this role, cynically, as a means to an end. In his short and savage satire of the fashionable "literary life" of Montreal, Cohen shows Breavman playing the role for sexual gratification: "Canadians are desperate for a Keats. Literary meetings are the manner in which Anglophiles express passion.... He slept with as many pretty chairwomen as he could.... He could maintain an oppressive silence at a dinner-table to make the lovely daughter of the house believe he was brooding over her soul" (101–102). Although Breavman becomes increasingly serious in his view of himself as an artist, he is always capable of using his art in this way. The poems he writes to Shell are propaganda, at least in origin, because "It made it easier for him if she liked her body" (162). He uses a short story to help break his relationship with Tamara, and his diary for the same purpose with Shell.

Tamara complains of the short story that "I don't talk that way" (92), but Breavman refuses to acknowledge any responsibility for what the story may do to their relationship. Although from different bases, both responses point to the separation between what Breavman writes and what Breavman is. As an artist, he creates a version of his own world which is separate from the reality, so that he can be in control of it. Tamara further complains that both characters talk like Breavman; in other words, she has become, in the story, as much his mouthpiece as he himself is. She is reduced to the status of ventriloquist's dummy — or hypnotist's victim. As artist, Breavman can narcissistically recreate the world in his own image — without scars.

Within the work of art, Breavman is in control, in control even of time. He seeks the ideal stasis of art: Canadian literati may be looking for a Keats, but Breavman is after the Grecian Urn. Patricia Morley connects this stasis with another possible pun on Breavman's name: "*brief-man* suggests man's participation in time and decay . . . a brevity which the novel contrasts with the stasis of art."[8] Book Two begins with the explicit statement, "Breavman loves the pictures of Henri Rousseau, the way he stops time" (58).[9] This stasis is most fully presented in the scene (95–98) where Breavman, riding in Krantz's car at night, puts to himself the "proposition" of choosing between the fifty years or so of varied experience still awaiting him in life, and the prolongation of the present moment in all its component parts. "And Breavman never hesitated in his choice." Cohen treats the moment rhapsodically; the writing takes off into a three-page *tour-de-force* expanding on the details of this particular, eternal moment. They include all of Breavman's memories and dreams of women (here quite savagely depersonalized), but the central experience is the car on the road with the pop song on the radio. These are images of speed and transience and isolation. The car rushes through the night, always in motion and never at rest; its microcosm isolates Breavman and Krantz from the rest of the world, locked inside their dialogue; the pop song, itself a transient cultural artefact, gives its usual message of loneliness and pain. And it is precisely these images of transience which Breavman proposes to extend indefinitely into the stasis of art, the lovers of Pat Boone's song frozen, "forever young,"[10] on Keats's Urn. It is a glorious piece of writing, the sheer force of which convinces the reader, if only for a moment, of the validity of Breavman's desires.

But if stasis is possible at all, it is possible in art, not in life. Later, Breavman speaks of the bodies of those he comes in contact with, preserved "in the condition of their highest beauty" (176). (Michael Ondaatje sees the whole novel as a "lyric" in which all the scenes are viewed this way.[11]) But this condition is only possible if the bodies have also been "lost . . . in fire where they persist whole and perfect," and Cohen is forced to admit that "This kind of permanence is no comfort to anyone." For Breavman as artist, "comfort" can only be seen as a betrayal of his role.

Cohen's use of film imagery in the novel has been widely commented on.[12] Film is a medium which offers a very complete control of time, and Cohen introduces it several times to show Breavman attempting a similar control over his perceptions of himself. He objectifies himself in longshot, meditates upon him-

self in slow motion. But when he attempts to stop time altogether, he fails. In showing the family movies, Breavman stops
the film to study certain frames, and the image "is eaten by a
spreading orange-rimmed stain as the film melts. . . . Breavman
is mutilating the film in his efforts at history" (10). The film
finally goes out of control—not only Breavman's control as projectionist but also his father's, as cameraman, as he "staggers
under another attack." This image may be seen as another of
Cohen's attacks on history—the flow of life is mutilated—but
the burning film is also beautiful. Breavman's attempt to stop
time may fail, but it produces lovely scars.

I would like to propose an interpretation of the book as a
judgement on Breavman's attempts and failures as an artist and
as a human being. Although much of the book is told from
Breavman's viewpoint, it is far from being indulgent of that
viewpoint. As I mentioned earlier, the very form of the novel
forces a certain objectivity on Cohen. Breavman has no refuge
in the self-sufficient lyric; we must also see the people around
him and the actual scars that his passing leaves. This is not to
say that Cohen's judgement on Breavman is as harsh as that of
some of his readers is likely to be. Rather, Cohen creates both
sympathy and distance: in much of its language, the book extends itself into Breavman's point of view, but through the
minor characters who provide a judgement upon him, it maintains distance. What holds these responses in balance is an irony
similar to that with which Joyce treats Stephen Daedalus in *Portrait of the Artist as a Young Man*. This ambivalence is finally
what is most intriguing about the book.

One can never be fully sure how much of what the contemporary reader would see as a judgement on Breavman was in
fact intended as such by Cohen. For instance, in dealing with
the car ride sequence, I mentioned that Breavman's memories
and dreams of the women in his life are "savagely depersonalized." Certainly this is one of the major points in the book: That
Breavman never takes his women seriously as individuals, and
that this is one reason for his failure as a human being himself.
But would Cohen, writing in the early sixties, and holding in
any case many fundamental premises which would now be described as "sexist," have intended a reaction as adverse as he
would now get to this passage? "There will be many lovely cunts

to lie in, different colours of skin to kiss, various orgasms to encounter, and many nights you will walk out your lust, bitter
and alone" (95). The effect of this passage, with its reduction
of all women to cunts, orgasms, and colours of skin, is to show
a drastic limitation on the range of Breavman's human sensibilities. The question is, how far does Cohen share that limitation?

Certainly the novel offers ample evidence for condemning
Breavman. He is totally and obsessively self-centred, and ruth-
less in his treatment of all around him. To some extent, this
may be seen as the necessary self-centredness of the artist, but
Rowland J. Smith comments that

> The pathological nature of Breavman's horror of becoming en-
> trammelled with his women is not made explicit, and Cohen is
> too consistently ironic in his treatment of "normal" relation-
> ships to suggest that Breavman's attitude is to be judged as merely
> neurotic. Nevertheless, his alienation is so constant a feature of
> the second half of the book that there is a continual sense of this
> detachment being something more deep-seated than simply a
> desire for artistic isolation.[13]

The only redeeming qualities that Breavman can offer are his
wit, his energy, his honesty (such as it is) with himself and others,
and his art. Very little judgement is passed, in the novel, on the
quality of Breavman's work. The book of Montreal sketches is
a success, but only with critics, who are themselves the subject
of Cohen's satire; the short story based on Tamara is laboriously
overwritten; the poems for Shell are not, in a sense, those of
Breavman but of Cohen, having been reprinted from *The Spice-
Box of Earth*. In any case, the question remains of whether or
not any form of artistic genius either needs or justifies Breavman's type of isolationism.

"Bertha was the spinner" (223), and the first grotesque
shape in the snow of *The Favourite Game* is that of Bertha,
whose twisted leg as she falls is described by the extraordinarily
callous phrase, "A position she could never achieve in the gym."
(14). Breavman attributes her fall to the power of his words,
but he feels no special guilt. Later, he romanticizes her into
"Bertha, who had fallen out of a tree for his sake!" (69) She

becomes a central part of his private mythology, the hub of the favourite game, but for her real pain he shows no feeling.

Bertha is associated, through her limp, with Norma, the first of Breavman's patient women who service him and are then abandoned. Breavman suppresses much of Norma's story in his long confessional to Shell (which itself has an air of self-justification throughout). It emerges only as a result of a rigorous internal dialogue (70–75) in which one part of Breavman's mind appears to be forcing the truth out of his memory like a police interrogator. The "guilty" Breavman responds with his most elaborate technique of cinematic distancing ("The camera takes them from faraway. . . . Sudden close-up of her body. . . .") attempting to isolate "that important second" of sexual union. That isolation achieved, Norma is forgotten. She goes off to phone her boyfriend (an important image of detachment) and Breavman promptly abandons her. Like Bertha, however, she limps; she bears a scar.

Although, most of the time, Breavman wants to leave no scars behind him, except those beautified by his art, there are times when he is unable to leave well enough alone. Even Heather, the hypnotized maid, is not permitted a full escape from his fantasies. After she runs off with her soldier,

> Sometimes Breavman likes to think that she is somewhere in the world, not fully awake, sleeping under his power. And a man in a tattered uniform asks:
> "Where are you, Heather?"
>
> (56)

Again, a scar remains; and the romantic sidestep of "a man in a tattered uniform" evades the human considerations involved.

Breavman's encounter with the adult, married Lisa is also instructive. In their first meeting, he approaches her with all the naive romanticism of their childhood faith. "If you remembered what I remember you'd be in bed with me right now" (111). But Lisa wisely and gently repulses him. This incident is surely sufficient to show the difference between them, and Lisa's greater maturity, at least in personal affairs. But Cohen goes on to a second meeting, which seems designed mainly to bolster Breavman's (or Cohen's?) masculine pride at the expense of Lisa's dignity. None of the women can be allowed to find

Breavman resistible. Now he is given the chance to play wise marriage counsellor, and, when that fails, to approach their sexual encounter with a superior air of "weary inevitability." At the end, he agrees to "let her go free" (as if he had ownership rights) for the significant reason that "*he* had all *he* needed of *her*" (my emphasis) (117). This episode, in which Lisa's feelings are callously manipulated and trivialized, is at least one instance in which insensitivity can definitely be attributed as much to Cohen as to his character.

The most spectacular casualty in Breavman's world is his mother, yet of all his personal relationships this is the one in which Breavman is least to blame. Cohen sketches in only briefly the background of Breavman's attitudes towards his parents, but it is clear that Breavman prefers his weak, wounded father, whom he associates romantically with a war that the veteran would no longer be capable of fighting. Cohen wisely refrains from stressing the Freudian implications of Breavman's identification with his father rather than with his mother, but nevertheless the conflict is present, and comes to a head with the quarrel over the closed coffin (23–25).

Breavman's dissociation of himself from his parents' world view is a natural part of the maturing of any adult, and especially of an artist with a highly individual world view to forge. But in Breavman's case, it is emphasized by his almost pathological fear of being smothered by other people. Indeed, a simplistic psychological explanation would trace this fear directly to Breavman's experience with his mother and her constant concern for his well-being that is expressed by a hilariously monomaniac obsession with food. Breavman's reaction is to break away, as decisively though gently as possible. What anguish he does feel is carefully concealed from her (65).

Breavman's mother's fate is largely self-destruction, and Cohen's presentation of her character emphasizes those elements which lead her to martyrdom; it is even possible to conclude that she enjoys her condition. But it is destruction, and Cohen's most daring touch is to present that destruction as an increasingly horrific parody of the stock figure of the Jewish mother. The early insistence on Breavman's eating is very funny, and within a conventional comic tradition, but Cohen increasingly plays on a note of hysteria which finally tips over the edge into something that is not funny at all. Whether or not Breav-man's mother ever possessed an "earlier perfection," it is cer-tainly true that by the end of the novel "her whole body" is a scar (8).

Such scars are the inevitable results, on those around him, of Breavman's isolation. Yet he clings to that isolation, seeing it to be necessary for his integrity as an artist. This conflict between his need for isolation and his need for human contact is first shown in the relationship with Tamara, then is stated in its most uncompromising form in the relationship with Shell, and finally is restated, in a more bizarre form and from a slightly different angle, in the relationship with Martin Stark.

Breavman sees his relationship with Tamara as a "ritual of love and deceit" (79): what love there is is on her part, the de-ceit is his. Right from the start he tries to force himself: "Tell her you love her, Breavman...Say I love you. Say it. One-two-three, now" (78). But he cannot. Later, with Shell, Breavman is able to create a version of himself who can; here he can only struggle in a silence which becomes at times "catatonic" (93).

Tamara sees the reserve, and interprets it as a conventional fear of marriage and commitment. She herself apologizes in advance for saying "I love you," knowing that "it hurts you in some way" (85). Breavman first expresses his fears, typically, in comic terms: "I can't make things happen so easily these days, alas. Things happen to *me*. I couldn't even hypnotize you last night" (80). Underneath this comment is Breavman's quite seri-ous fear that, once he lets himself become committed to the full demands of a personal relationship, he will lose the control and detachment of the artist/hypnotist. Tamara's reply, equally comic, is also equally serious: "You're a failure, Larry, but I'm still crazy about your balls. Yummy."

For a while, Breavman is content to be a "failure" in exactly the terms that Tamara's sexuality defines: "How could he run from that body?" (85). He makes one attempt to "put distance between himself and the hot room where he couldn't make things happen" (85), but it fails. For Breavman at this stage, "Commitment was oppressive but the thought of flesh-loneliness was worse" (85), so he returns to Tamara, knowing that "He should have kept running that bright morning" (88).

Their relationship degenerates into a bitter deadlock out

of which Breavman writes the short story in which "Tamara" is cruelly and unjustly satirized for an ineptly romantic use of language which is in fact much closer to Breavman than it is to her. The story only intensifies the deadlock between them and moves Breavman farther into silence and into visions of "Miles he would never cover because he could never abandon this bed" (94).

Cohen does not directly present the final collapse of the affair; all he says is "They were lucky the parting was not bitter" (100). This may be seen as a narrative failure, but perhaps it is necessary to allow for Tamara's later reappearance in the book. When she comes back, she is more prepared to play by Breavman's rules and to accept his kind of detachment.[14] She is even prepared to help him seek a substitute for the lost dialogue with Krantz. This is a different Tamara, one who has learned, like Breavman, to hide the scars. She no longer makes the kind of demand, implicit in their first relationship, which seems to threaten his commitment to loneliness.

What the affair with Tamara demonstrates, then, is that for Breavman there seems to be an absolute choice between the roles of artist and lover; they cannot be combined. That is the central assertion of the book concerning Breavman's character and concerning the nature of the artist. The impatience, even the anger, which many readers may feel towards Breavman may all be directed to this point. Showing Breavman's inability to bring the two roles together, does Cohen intend us to see it as a pathological failure in Breavman's character, for which he is to be pitied or condemned? Or does Cohen intend us to see this inability as a general truth about the position of the Romantic artist?

The problem is restated, in even more uncompromising terms, with Shell. It is important for the reader to have some concept of Shell as a human being separate from Breavman, so Cohen attempts a more detailed and conventional account of her background and previous life than he does of any other character. These passages are in some ways the least convincing of the book; as a writer, Cohen has always been too self-centred to operate outside his own milieu, or to write in depth about any character who is not, in some aspect, himself. We are given an elaborate but terribly artificial history of lesbian encounters and an impotent husband, linked to the clichéd concept of "the extinct American male" (141). There is something self-consciously stilted and awkward in Cohen's handling of these scenes: "'Ha ha,' cried Miss McTavish, flinging herself backwards in the snow. 'I'm brave. I'm very brave'" (133).

But in a deeper sense, Shell never does emerge as a real character. She is "the most beautiful person" (120), and her name suggests something beautiful and delicate, like the shell on which Botticelli's Venus rides ashore. But a "shell" is also an outer surface, protective or sometimes hollow; it has no depth, nothing to offer beyond its immediate and superficial beauty. It is also fragile and easy to break; in fact, what Breavman eventually does is exactly that. As the unusual full form of her name — "Marshell" — suggests, the effect of Breavman's encounter with her is to mar Shell, to leave her more scarred than before.

Shell is closely connected with scars. In the first paragraph of the book, we are told how her pierced ears "festered" (8); later, examining herself in a mirror, she thinks that her "appendix scar was an appalling gash ruining her body" (141). Another time, she makes herself believe that "her breasts were stuffed with cancer" (136). But these supposed scars are all minor in comparison to the true scars which Breavman can inflict.

Cohen wants us to believe that Shell "knows everything" about Breavman (130–131), but he gives us very little warrant in her previous experience for this kind of subtlety and maturity. At one stage Shell thinks that "People who walk into desolation, beggars, saints, call to those they leave behind, and these cries are nobler than the victory shouts of generals" (133). It is an entirely typical, almost *too* typical, Cohen statement; for Shell it is knowledge which is not fully her own: "She knew this from books and her house." Its validity is also undercut by the unconvincing nature of the dramatic situation in which it occurs. She needs Breavman, "her Compleat Physician" (136), to make her whole, but the very fact that he accomplishes this integration only makes his final desertion of her all the more shattering.

Breavman's attitude towards Shell is, right from the start, a divided one; indeed, it becomes so split that Cohen can only describe it as a kind of conscious schizophrenia. He starts by seeing her as "the most beautiful person" and deciding to "pur-

sue" her (120); at the same time he abandons all of his pretentious self-images: "He didn't want to smash his fist across
the city, lead the Jews, have visions, love multitudes, bear a
mark on his forehead, look in every mirror, lake, hub-cap, for
reflection of the mark. Please no. He wanted comfort. He wanted
to be comforted" (146–147). On the one hand, he sets her up as
an idol to be pursued and worshipped through his art; on the
other, he seeks a human being to comfort him. The two desires
finally become irreconcilable.

In the remarkable sequence which documents the con-
struction of one of Breavman's poems for Shell, we are told that
"Breavman always envied the old artists who had great and accepted ideas to serve. Then the colour of gold could be laid on
and glory written down" (161). Shell provides such a subject for
him: "Once, for a while, he seemed to serve something other
than himself. Those were the only poems he ever wrote. They
were for Shell" (162). This passage is interesting for several
reasons. It provides a kind of rationale for Cohen's own Romanticism, colours of gold and glory. It identifies the particular
kind of Romantic artist that Breavman aspires to be. It indicates
that for Breavman as artist, Shell is not so much a person as
an ideal to be served. But there are also a couple of uneasy
questions raised by it. The poem, we know, is Cohen's as well
as Breavman's — it appeared in *The Spice-Box of Earth* — so it
really does not serve *Shell*; and what authority does Cohen have
to tell us that it is so good? More seriously, is this really a case
where Breavman is being unselfish? Cohen himself immediately
qualifies the claim by pointing out how the poem also works as
erotic propaganda, but this is not the whole point. Breavman
as artist is never unselfish; everything relates back to his image
of himself, and the poem's lyric form ultimately tells us more
about Breavman the worshipper than it can about Shell the
worshipped. This kind of "devotion," as Cohen himself points
out (166), is not love. Breavman the self-centred artist is even
able to foresee "the guilt that would nourish him if he left her"
(171). Both the beauty and the fragility of the shell can be
made to nourish Breavman's art.

But for a while, Breavman is content to "retire into comfort" (161). In order to do this, he builds what is in effect a
separate character of himself, his "deputy," the "lover." "He

was a skilful product, riveted with care, whom Breavman wouldn't have minded being himself. . . . The lover, being planned so well, had a life of his own and often left Breavman behind" (163). This schizophrenic split in his character deepens steadily.

> He was very comfortable. He had begun to accept his deputy's joy. This lover was the most successful thing he had ever made, and the temptation was to supply him with wallet and identification and drown the master Breavman in a particularly garbage-strewn stretch of the Hudson River. . . . More and more the lover had Shell to himself. These are the times Breavman does not remember too well because he was so happy.
>
> (168)

Yet one part of his mind still sees this "comfort" as a "temptation." A revealing incident (169) shows Breavman writing, believing so completely that he is alone that Shell's sudden presence startles him: "He wheeled in surprise, pencil in hand, and scraped skin from her cheek." Another scar. He begins to consider the possibilities of leaving her, knowing that "Otherwise he'd stay beside her always" (170). The conflict is the same as that with Tamara, but here made more intense by Shell's perfection and by Breavman's schizophrenia. When he goes, he tells her — and half believes himself — that "he didn't want to leave for good. He needed to be by himself, so he could miss her, to get perspective" (171). Their last exchange reveals the growing separation between them: " 'I wish you'd be more miserable.' / She smiled." (173)

At this stage the possibilities remain open; Breavman is balanced between his roles, and could still, theoretically, go either way. The letters he writes to Shell are beautiful, in his usual affected style. What determines his final decision is his disturbing and paradoxical encounter with Martin Stark. When the decison does come, it is direct and brutal:

> I don't want to see or hear from you. I'd like to counterpoint this with tenderness but I'm not going to. I want no attachments. I want to begin again. I think I love you, but I love the idea of a clean slate more.
>
> (215)

Although Breavman tries to set up a context for it, this statement remains almost intolerably cruel, and to emphasize this cruelty Cohen adds the despicable indulgence of Breavman's telephone call in which he tortures and betrays Shell all over again. The end of it shows Breavman's total self-centredness in its least attractive light: "For himself, he had exhausted the emotion that impelled the call. He didn't need to go to New York" (220). This is reminiscent of his dismissal of Lisa ("he had all he needed of her"); whether or not Shell needs him to go to New York is never even considered. Even after this, he longs, in his usual infantile retentive way, to keep some connection with her:

> He must always be connected with her. That must never be severed.... One day what he did to her...would enter his understanding with such a smash of guilt that he would sit motionless for days...But that was not today.
>
> (222)

This awareness is kept at arm's length, dismissed into a future that the novel will never show. But it is at precisely the moment when he is thinking this that Breavman is driven to the memory of the favourite game, the scars in the snow.

As for Shell herself, the novel shows us just enough for us to sense her pain. "Lawrence, you can't treat people like this" (219). It is all compressed into that sentence, an understated scream of agony, a final judgement on Lawrence Breavman.

What produces this decision is, as I have said, Martin Stark. Again, the name is significant, for Martin presents the issues in an even starker form than Shell does. In his relationship with Shell, Breavman was balanced between his two characters: the lover, who can operate within the normal forms of society, and the artist, who cannot. Martin cannot conform to the routine of the camp (a microcosm of society), and Breavman refuses to join the forces which try to force him into conformity. Rather, Breavman encourages him in his isolation, an isolation which leads directly to his death.

Breavman sees Martin as the "divine idiot" (190), a figure (as Patricia Morley points out)[15] with a long tradition in romantic literature. Martin is "that rarest creature, a blissful mad-child" (185), who "enjoys his madness. He's the only free person I've ever met. Nothing that anybody else does is as im-

portant as what he does" (203). In recognizing these qualities
in Martin, Breavman sees an image of what he himself would
like to be, and so he establishes with Martin a private anti-
social relationship complete with complicities and rituals.

Martin's genius and Martin's madness are inseparable.
There is no mitigating factor such as the social "respectability"
of art. The conception of the artist, and the Romantic dignity
of that "calling," could be used as shields or excuses for Breavman's behaviour; Martin has no such disguise. He exults in systems, especially arithmetical systems, and by pushing them to
their extremes he destroys them. Counting is sane and rational,
but counting grass is insane and anti-rational. This disruption
of systems is one of the ways in which Martin foreshadows *Beautiful Losers*; the other way is of course the image of him as he
"stuck his index fingers in his ears for no apparent reason,
squinting as if he were expecting some drum-splitting explosion"
(191). This action reappears in *Beautiful Losers* as the Telephone Dance, which represents insight into the workings of
"ordinary eternal machinery."

Martin's genius, then, can only be approached or explained
in terms of ritual. Breavman feels that the camp's "institutions
should be constructed around him, the traditionally incoherent
oracle"; he cannot explain this to Krantz except in terms of
their own ritual: "tempered by the dialogue, it wouldn't sound
so mad" (190). But since the dialogue with Krantz is no longer
possible, Breavman can only set it up with Martin himself.

At the centre of Martin's experience is the letter (197) in
which he spews out all his hate on his brother, who appears to
be a figure from Martin's imagination (185). This is another aspect of Martin's calculation. He knows, logically, that he must
vent his emotions somehow, so he creates a "safe" outlet, an
imaginary figure. For Breavman, the relevance is obvious:
imaginary people bear no scars; they cannot suffer like Shell. In
Martin's punctuation, the letter ends "love your brother": love,
that is, the imaginary creation upon which all your scars are
left. Breavman is never fully capable of the love which Martin
commands.

In the end, Martin's obsession with numbers and machinery
kills him, and Cohen ironically records the fact with the only
precise date in the book: "the first week of August 1958" (211).

Martin's death is the logical conclusion to his isolation: the society which excludes him must inevitably, even if inadvertently, kill him. In Breavman, Martin's death causes an ambivalent reaction. It drives him irrevocably out of the camp, out of society; it causes his final break with Krantz. On the other hand, he writes to Shell, "When you read my journal you'll see how close I am to murder" (214). While rejecting the social world, he cannot entirely rid himself of the practice of moral judgement — accusing himself of "murder," for example — which the social world entails. Breavman is balanced again between his two selves.

But in the course of writing to Shell, he comes to a decision. The "comfortable world," i.e. the world of "comfort" which he shared with Shell, "has been destroyed irrevocably," and "something important," i.e. the vision which he shared with Martin, has been "guaranteed" (214). The letter then proceeds to the brutal break with Shell. Breavman has accepted his own isolation, knowing, from Martin's death, all that it may imply.

Martin's death is also the cause of the final break with Krantz. Krantz is the embodiment, in a way, of Breavman's alternative persona, "the lover." The progression of Krantz's character throughout the book is one of gradual but decisive divergence from Breavman. Krantz remains solid and normal, a kind of touchstone by which Breavman's aberrance from the social norm may be measured. In the early chapters, Krantz appears to be as non-conformist as Breavman. He shares in Breavman's games and rituals, and he "had a reputation for being wild" (40). But in fact, Krantz is always at heart a conformist; even his "reputation" is based on nothing more than his "having been spotted from time to time smoking two cigarettes at once on obscure Westmount streets." Krantz's rebellion is the conventional rebellion of youth, a socially acceptable stage to be passed through. His essential conformity is shown by the fact that he "had worked many summers at a children's camp" (98): Breavman had always thought of this as an extension of the game, and it comes as a surprise to him to find Krantz "in the role of disciplinarian" (98).

Nevertheless, for the first half of the book at any rate, Krantz is essentially at one with Breavman. Their "dialogue" has already been mentioned as the training ground of Breavman's wit. But there is more to it than that. Krantz, and the dialogue, are essential to Breavman. They provide what he always needs: an audience. It is with Krantz that he is best able to articulate his response to life and also his response to art (the moment of timeless stasis in Krantz's car). The irony and the wit of their dialogue hold the world at arm's length: this detachment is what makes it so entertaining for the reader. No real issues enter, no demands are made.

Krantz's development, then, can be seen as an alternative to Breavman's. He is what Breavman might have become, and his attitude to Anne (significantly named, remembering *The Spice-Box of Earth*) is close to Breavman-the-lover's attitude to Shell. However, there is one brief incident between Breavman and Anne (200–202) which shows the extent of the divergence. Breavman's poem for Anne is "I don't know you"; standing close to her "he received no trace of the radar signal to embrace"; when he sets up a game (with overtones of the old whipping game with Lisa), Anne laughs, but she also "ran to the lights of the camp."

The camp is Krantz's territory: it defines what he has become. He sums up his own attitude to the past in terms similar to Lisa's: "I remember everything, Breavman. But I can't live in it" (203). For Breavman, who is always trying to live in it, the break is complete. He rejects Krantz's attempts to restart the dialogue, correctly perceiving them as false, "Some sort of charitable therapy" (196). What Krantz in reality substitutes for the old dialogue is the cynical "pool" on Wanda, the tired cliché of a middle-aged lecher. Breavman asks himself, with bitter irony, "What did you expect, Breavman, reunion on a windy hill, a knife ceremony and the exchange of blood?" (182). So when the confrontation between them reaches its climax at Martin's death, it is this betrayal which Breavman flings back into Krantz's face as the insult which starts their fight (212).

Krantz's withdrawal from the dialogue leaves Breavman terrifyingly alone, and throughout the book he attempts to start it up with other people. He comes closest to success in his renewed acquaintance with Tamara, who creates with him the Compassionate Philistines (179), an organization from which Krantz is specifically excluded (198). But even this attempt breaks down, in what Michael Ondaatje calls "the most powerful scene in the novel":[16] "He leaped up, ran to the window, smashed his fist through the glass. / *'Get the car, Krantz,'* he screamed. *'Get the car, get the car!...'"* (216).

The note of desperation here confirms the paradox of Breavman's character: he has committed himself to an aesthetic ideal which calls for his total isolation and self-sufficiency, and yet he continually needs a dialogue, needs an audience.[17] In his agony, Breavman turns and turns desperately about, seeking an audience: to Tamara, in his attempt to re-create Krantz; to Shell, in his brutal phone call; even to the paper-thin image of Patricia, the most negligible of all the women in the book; finally, predictably and retrogressively, to his memories of Lisa and the favourite game.

By the end of the novel, Breavman has made his choice. His compulsive need for other people suggests that it may not be a very secure conclusion, but for the moment at least he has accepted his isolation, accepted his guilt, accepted that the lovely grotesque shapes he makes demand that he breaks off the stems. Like the river with his name, Saint Lawrence is moving on alone.

The foregoing analysis of *The Favourite Game* may suggest a harsher, more disenchanted view of the character of Lawrence Breavman than Cohen perhaps intended. Certainly the tone of the novel does not always imply this kind of distancing. It is necessary in any novel that the reader maintain a certain degree of identification with the central character if he is to go on reading, and the force of the images, the brilliant wit and sensuous surface of Cohen's writing carry the reader along. It would be possible to argue that the whole novel is in fact intended as a justification of Breavman's choice, and that his status as an artist excuses his failure as a human being. But if this is the intention, then the degree to which it is carried out has to be seen as modified by the form of the novel, the objectivity of which I spoke earlier. For all the weakness of her characterization, Shell does exist, and her pain is real, as is the pain of all those who (for reasons which are not perhaps totally understandable) attempt to love Lawrence Breavman. Cohen's tone is ironical, in a defensive manner, but the whole dramatic structure of events, and the insistence on the imagery of scars, imply a much more drastic judgement.

This judgement must, however, be balanced against the energy, complexity and empathy of Cohen's creation of Breavman. To whatever degree, great or small, the novel passes judgement on Breavman, there is also a degree to which Breavman is a self-portrait. If the analogy is to be made to Joyce's *Portrait of the Artist As a Young Man,* then the analogy must be carried through to *Ulysses.* By the end of *The Favourite Game,* Cohen no less than his protagonist is ready to move on alone, into the stark self-destruction of *Beautiful Losers.*

(ii) *Beautiful Losers* (1966)

One of the best descriptions of *Beautiful Losers* is still that given on the dust jacket of the first edition: [18]

> *Beautiful Losers* is a love story, a psalm, a Black Mass, a monument, a satire, a prayer, a shriek, a road map through the wilderness, a joke, a tasteless affront, an hallucination, a bore, an irrelevant display of diseased virtuosity, a Jesuitical tract, an Orange sneer, a scatological Lutheran extravagance—in short a disagreeable religious epic of incomparable beauty.

This description suggests a disorganized jumble, Cohen trying to be all things to all readers. But in fact the book is highly organized, held tightly together by a network of images and connections. Douglas Barbour has pointed [19] to the paradox of a book which proclaims "Connect nothing" (16) and then insistently offers connections which must be made; a book which "prepares to abandon all systems" (39) in a systematic manner. This paradox may itself be seen as part of Cohen's attack on rational order: why be consistent? The reader, no less than the protagonist, is being put through a classroom of hysteria. A critical account which attempts to elucidate this order may then be running directly contrary to the spirit of the book, but if *Beautiful Losers* is "a road map through the wilderness," then perhaps it will not be amiss to attempt a legend.

At the centre, then, there is a narrative situation. I say "situation" rather than "story," because there is no conventional linear development. For most of the book, the situation is static, and even when a change of some sort occurs, the time sequence is deliberately distorted, indeed abandoned. The movement in the book is movement within a fixed pattern, and this containment contributes to its sense of energy and tension, even when there is no narrative progression or suspense. The situation is defined by the four main characters: Edith, Catherine Tekakwitha, F., and the nameless protagonist. I shall refer to this character as *I*, although strictly speaking he is only in the first person for the first section of the book. I use this denotation to help clarify the notion that the composite character in Book Three is *IF*, "a remote human possibility" (95).

The relationships of these four characters are set out in terms of images of saints and disciples, masters and pupils. But, as is usual in Cohen, the roles are interchangeable, so none of the four is ever entirely fixed within one definition. The most obvious saint, in the conventional religious sense, is Catherine Tekakwitha, but her life shifts in the novel between recorded historical fact, Québecois popular mythology, imaginative reconstructions by the novel's other characters, and the decidedly unconventional uses which are reserved for her as a character. Edith also partakes of sainthood, and even, in her incarnation as Isis, of divinity, but she and her body are the creations of F. and are entirely subservient to him. F. has all the characteristics of the master, but as such he is more teacher than saint, and finally must recognize the limitations imposed by his power. These three characters could all be seen as saints, with *I* as their disciple, but in the end these positions are reversed and it is only the disciple who can, through metamorphosis, attain his own full sainthood and make theirs possible. At the end of the book, Catherine Tekakwitha has still to be beatified.

The central definition of a "saint" is given in a passage which is among Cohen's most gorgeous pieces of writing:

> What is a saint? A saint is someone who has achieved a remote human possibility. It is impossible to say what that possibility is. I think it has something to do with the energy of love. Contact with this energy results in the exercise of a kind of balance in the chaos of existence. A saint does not dissolve the chaos; if he did the world would have changed long ago. I do not think that a saint dissolves the chaos even for himself, for there is something arrogant and warlike in the notion of a man setting the universe in order. It is a kind of balance that is his glory. He rides the drifts like an escaped ski. His course is a caress of the hill. His

track is a drawing of the snow in a moment of its particular arrangement with wind and rock. Something in him so loves the world that he gives himself to the laws of gravity and chance. Far from flying with the angels, he traces with the fidelity of a seismograph needle the state of the solid bloody landscape. His house is dangerous and finite, but he is at home in the world. He can love the shapes of human beings, the fine and twisted shapes of the heart. It is good to have among us such men, such balancing monsters of love.

(95–96)

The first thing to notice about this passage is its commentary on various kinds of systems. The definition emphasizes qualities which are not susceptible to being systematized. The saint achieves only a "possibility," which is "remote" and impossible to define but is connected with "energy" and "balance." Energy and balance are dynamic rather than static qualities which cannot be reduced to any system for "setting the universe in order." They are anarchic and disruptive like an "escaped ski"; they depend not on generalizations but on "a moment of . . . particular arrangement"; they submit to, rather than attempt to control, "the laws of gravity and chance."

This passage's context is also essential to its meaning. It follows immediately on from the night drive to Parliament, one of the most brilliantly outrageous and serio-comic scenes in the novel. Further, the passage continues without a break from this gorgeously poetic definition into "But why fuck one? I remember once slobbering over Edith's thigh . . ." and so into one of Cohen's most direct and "obscene" images of the attainment of sainthood through sexuality.

The phrase "fuck a saint" is the one which compresses most exactly the central project to which *I* is committed, even if he himself does not fully understand it. "I merely wanted to fuck a saint, as F. advised. I don't know why it seemed like such a good idea" (34). The project is, of course, literally impossible. (There are several accounts of saints' bodies being preserved incorruptible in the grave, but there is never any suggestion that *I* will try to dig up Catherine's remains.) But as F. prays, "lead me from the Desert of the Possible" (178). Fucking a saint can only happen outside time, outside the limits of event; it is an act which breaks down the barriers of possibility, the barriers between flesh and spirit, between past and future. It is the ultimate union of the sexual and religious modes; it is the metaphor of the *Song of Solomon* restated in its most direct terms.

In the novel, as it turns out, *I* never does get to "fuck" a saint; the phrase itself is not used again after the definition passage quoted above, but is replaced by "go down on" a saint — which is what *I* does achieve, in the car in Book Three.[20] Most of the major sexual scenes in the novel are oral rather than genital; sexuality is throughout divorced from reproduction. The novel presents a closed system, a circle which cannot renew itself.

The whole pattern of the novel, then, is centred on this project for which fucking a saint is the major metaphor. It may be summarized in several ways: to escape the bounds of time; to destroy history; to move beyond individual personality; to become Magic; to enter what Dave Godfrey calls the "overworld"; to transcend the limitations of reason, of humanity, of mortality itself. This is the goal towards which *I* is driven by his teachers, and the main method of teaching is the breaking down of systems.

"I am a born teacher," says F. (148), and teaching is his function throughout the book. F. urges his pupil on towards sainthood, using Edith (alive) and Catherine (dead) as his examples. Even when he is feeling his way up under Mary Voolnd's skirt, F. turns aside to comment, "Do you see how I cannot stop teaching?" (151) The reasons for this obsession are suggested in a long speech addressed to Edith (174–175): as usual, its seriousness is both undercut and underlined by the fact that F. is also using it to distract Edith's attention from the Danish Vibrator so that he can grab it for himself. "Was it selfish of me," he asks, "to try to end your pain, yours and his (you, dear old comrade)? I saw pain everywhere." The speech proceeds in F.'s typical style, picturing his world as a vast auto wreck, in the middle of which, "Dr. Frankenstein with a deadline" (a possible reference for the initial), F. is frantically trying to piece something together: an ideal which, like the definition of a saint, is never fixed or static. "I had an idea of what a man should look like, but it kept changing."

F.'s teaching is not done in an ordered, intellectual manner, though he is in fact capable of such teaching, as is shown by his entirely lucid account of "The last four years of Tekakwitha's life and the ensuing miracles" (190). F.'s account very completely achieves what *I*'s floundering narration has failed to do. But mostly, F. scorns conventional teaching methods, parodying them in his little games with the ruler and the answers to be filled in. "Did you fill in the lines? You didn't have to, you know. Did I trick you again?" (147) In keeping with the book's attack on rational systems, F.'s main teaching method is hysteria. "Hysteria is my classroom," he says, and *I* recalls that "he was ready to use any damn method to keep me hysterical" (56). These methods include such elaborately prepared incidents as the silk wall on the night drive to Ottawa (91–95), and such on-the-spot improvisations as the didactic removal of the wart (101–104). F. also uses and exploits *I*'s feelings towards himself and Edith: "Jealousy is the education you have chosen" (33). Several times, F.'s tactics are referred to as "tricks": the note at the bottom of the fireworks box is one of "many compassionate tricks" (78) by which *I* is led out of the basement of his misery into the treehouse of his transformation.

On one occasion, *I* refers to F.'s tactics as "your cheap koans" (116). F. M. Macri has elucidated the pun: "In Zen, a koan is a nonsensical question posed to students because the stress of meditation on it may prove beneficial."[21] This describes F.'s teaching exactly—especially the word "stress." Poor *I* does not always appreciate the experience. At one point he tells F., "I'm not going to take your cowardly guru shit" (25)—"cowardly" is an unusual adjective here—and later he complains, "it's been too hard, too much crazy education, and God knows for what. Every second day I've had to learn something, some lesson, some lousy parable, and what am I this morning, a Doctor of Shit" (32). But *I* also acknowledges his debt: "Thank you, F. Thank you, my lover. When will I be able to see the world without you, my dear?" (84).

Finally, of course, the roles are reversed. F. writes in his letter to *I*, "We lay in each other's arms, each of us the other's teacher" (154), and appeals to him, "I pray you, dear friend, interpret me, go beyond me.... Go forth, teach the world what I meant to be" (158).

The major focus of instruction in the novel is the concept of Systems. One of the many historical details with which Cohen ironically surrounds the events of Catherine Tekakwitha's life is that of the Marquis de Laplace beginning to develop his *"Exposition du Système du Monde"* (83). Cohen sees world-systems everywhere, and he sees them as dangerous. (Cf., in "Story of Isaac," "a scheme is not a vision.") F., for all his hysteria, is obsessed and limited by systems; as such he envies the totally unsystematic *I*: "Times I felt depleted: you with all that torment, me with nothing but a System" (152). His ideal for his pupil is something "greater than my Systems conceived" (160). In a fascinating speculation on the nature of systems, F. posits that "Jesus probably designed his system so that it would fail in the hands of other men." This is the way in which "the greatest creators . . . guarantee the desperate power of their own originality" (55). *I*'s instruction is to "abandon all systems" (39) — or rather, to concentrate on systems that fail.

The central image of Systems is the System Theatre, Montreal's flophouse cinema. This is the site of the most important events in the book: the rediscovery of the Telephone Dance (27–34), F.'s vision of the newsreel invading the feature (221–224), and the beginnings of *IF*'s metamorphosis (235–236). Even the politically symbolic statue of Queen Victoria, site of F.'s attempted martyrdom, is something "passed . . . on our way to the darkness of the System Theatre" (135). Linda Hutcheon claims that the name should make "the wary reader . . . suspicious,"[22] but she overlooks the fact that the System Theatre is not the place where systems triumph but where systems are broken.

The cinema is at the heart of the banal pop culture which Cohen celebrates, but much more importantly, it "displays the only neon failure in miles of light: dropping two letters which will never be repaired, it signals itself as stem Theatre, stem Theatre, stem Theatre" (221). I take this to be the central "signal" of the novel. Systems in themselves are useless unless they are broken, but once they are broken the "stem" appears. "Stems," it will be remembered, was the final word of *The Favourite Game,* and it reappears, very beautifully, in the song "Sisters of Mercy." The stem is always present inside the system, once it has failed. The book reviews various systems, and as each one breaks, something is eclectically picked up from it: some possibility for growth. (Of course, to the extent that this

is done systematically, the book is heading into the same paradox as is implied in "Connect nothing.")

The major systems which are reviewed are those of religion,
sexuality, politics, history, and that general area which Dave
Godfrey has called the banal, of which the main sub-systems
are pop songs, movies, and machinery.

Beautiful Losers is obviously, in the most general sense, a
religious book. Its main premise is a religious dimension to
human experience, and it speaks of human beings having access
to the mystical. But, like *Let Us Compare Mythologies,* it does
not confine itself to any one religious system or dogma. When
I, in one of his three capitalized prayers, says "O God, Your
Morning Is Perfect. People Are Alive In Your World" (53), he
expresses very beautifully a sense of divine immanence in all
things, but he is clearly using "God" in the very generalized
sense indicated by Cohen in the interview quoted in the introduction.[23]

A religious system exists only to be broken. Even Catherine
Tekakwitha, who follows a rigidly constructed system of religious
discipline, realizes this. She is consistently more tolerant to-
wards other people's beliefs than are either the Jesuits or her
Indian aunts, and her dying prayer, one of the most beautiful
and moving things in the book, is the perfect expression of
Cohen's religious ideal: "O God, show me that the Ceremony
belongs to Thee. Reveal to your servant a fissure in the Ritual.
Change Thy World with the jawbone of a broken Idea. O my
Lord, play with me" (207). Here ritual becomes perfect when it
is fissured, and the idea which changes the world is "broken."
The final sentence, besides its startling sexual connotation,
evokes F.'s observation that "the truly Messianic vision of the
brotherhood of creatures must be based on the idea of the game"
(29).

Accordingly the Jesuit order is praised for accepting the
possibility that miracles can break up the rational structure of
the world. "I love the Jesuits," *I* writes, "because they saw miracles. Homage to the Jesuit who has done so much to conquer
the frontier between the natural and the supernatural" (99).
At Catherine's death, the Jesuits are forced to choose "History
or Miracle, or to put it more heroically, History or Possible
Miracle" (207). The choice of "Possible Miracle" confirms the

Jesuits' heroic stature, and it is on this basis, I believe, that Cohen is prepared to "rent" the final page to the Jesuits to demand "the official beatification of Catherine Tekakwitha" (242). It is also worth noting that it is the Jesuit priests, even those who are "Terribly happy" to be priests, not saints, whose voices sound in Catherine's ears as "Ordinary eternal machinery" (204).

But apart from this, the book's attitude towards institutionalized Christianity is negative. In one peroration, *I* accuses the Church of a variety of personal and social crimes, culminating in "female circumcision in French Canada" (47); the Church's inability to come to terms with sexuality is one of the central points in Cohen's accusation. Whereas Catherine Tekakwitha finds the Fuck Cure "acceptable," the priest Sagard can only comment, "Dieu veuille abolir une si damnable et malheureuse cérémonie" (132). This puritanism in fact traps the Church into a kind of salaciousness. Even Le P. Edouard Lecompte, S.J., who loved Catherine (67), is described as "whetting our sexual appetite in his expert Company manner" (21). And *I* accuses the Church of being one of the social forces implicitly approving of Edith's rape (58).

The most serious accusation on *I*'s list, however, is that of "killing Indians" (47), in the sense that the rigidity of the Christian system is used to destroy the Indian religion. Of all the religious systems in the book, it is the Indian system that Cohen is most sympathetic to, perhaps because it has been destroyed, but more because of its openness to the stems of the irrational and the unknown.

The Jesuit tactics are portrayed at their crudest in the form of a hellfire sermon, with visual aids, aimed at destroying the Telephone Dance. The success of this tactic is recorded by Cohen in deeply elegiac terms:

> As those waxy digits were withdrawn a wall of silence was thrown up between the forest and the hearth, and the old people gathered at the priest's hem shivered with a new kind of loneliness. They could not hear the raspberries breaking into domes, they could not smell the numberless pine needles combing out the wind, they could not remember the last moment of a trout as it lived between a flat white pebble on the streaked bed of a stream and the fast shadow of a bear claw. Like children who listen in vain

to the sea in plastic sea shells they sat bewildered. Like children at the end of a long bedtime story they were suddenly thirsty.

(82)

This passage is typical in its strong identification of the Indian religion with natural life. Catherine's uncle, for example, sees a religious immanence in all things: the "First and Perfect Deer" in the deer he has killed, the courage of the wolf in its wood carving (88). Singing the Corn-Planting Song, "He could feel the powers of the seeds, their longing to be covered with earth and explode" (85). This is a religious system which is open to miracles at all points, which incorporates the essence of Magic. In this sense, it is scarcely a "system" at all: it is almost pure "stem."

This is clearest in the passage describing the Andacwandet, the "Fuck Cure" (128–132); again, it should be stressed that Catherine Tekakwitha, Iroquois virgin, describes the ceremony as "acceptable." The core of its meaning lies in the prayer which the old man sings, "the first prayer in which Manitou had manifest himself, the greatest and truest sacred formula." Prayer is important throughout the book — *I*'s capitalized passages are all prayers, F. gives him a "prayerbook" (of sorts) as a gift — but this is the profoundest prayer of all. "I change / I am the same." Singing this, Catherine's uncle "saw it change and every change was a return and every return was a change." The power of this chant cannot easily be analyzed: the best way to experience it is to try it yourself, for an extended period. The chant asserts both permanence and impermanence, eternity and mortality, at once: in its very form it enacts itself. By repetition within time, it transcends time. Sequentially, it destroys sequence. It admits time and change into the closed circle of eternity. Even more than F.'s "God is alive, Magic is afoot," it provides the definitive image of the religious dimension which the whole book is directed towards capturing.

The other important image from Indian religion is that of Oscotarach,[24] an emblem of the rejection of rationality, the preference for emotion over intellect. It is also one of the links between the characters, or one of the disruptions of time sequence, since F.'s description (184) is based word for word on *I*'s (132), which, "realistically," F. cannot have seen. Catherine's uncle states the image first: "Beside the path there is a bark hut. In the hut lives Oscotarach, the Head-Piercer. I will stand beneath him and he will remove the brain from my skull. . . . It is the necessary preparation for the Eternal Hunt" (114). *I* and F. both make the identification of the treehouse with the hut, and of F. with Oscotarach; both describe the operation as "long and clumsy," using "a blunt tomahawk." F. in turn has to "apply to public wards" for his operation: one of his limitations is that he cannot perform it on himself.

The removal of the brain "as a necessary preparation for immortality" (184) is a theme repeated throughout the book. *I* states that he has always had "little respect" for his brain (19), which he later describes as "ruined" (96); he says, "I want to be consumed by unreason. I want to be swept along" (46). F. says that he "feared the rational mind, therefore I tried to make you a little mad" (151). *I*'s interpretation of the very name Iroquois, Hiro-Koué, sees the "koué" as an attempt "to subvert the beguiling intellect with the noise of true emotion" (8). The Indian image, then, provides the stem for breaking the system of rationalism.

The stem of all religious systems—that which, within the system, is not classifiable or reducible to dogma—is Magic. F. says of his anti-rational teaching that "I wanted your confusion to be a butterfly net for magic" (160). The "New Jew" is described as "the founder of Magic Canada, Magic French Québec, and Magic America" (161). F. sees his great peroration to Magic as "the sweet burden of my argument" (156), his ultimate proclamation. The passage itself—"God is alive. Magic is afoot" (157–158)—is one of Cohen's great *tours-de-force* of writing. The qualities it stresses are similar to those stressed in the definition of a saint: those which are unclassifiable and dynamic rather than static. The key words are "alive" and "afoot," and Magic is always on the move: "Police arrested Magic and Magic went with them for Magic loves the hungry. But Magic would not tarry. It moves from arm to arm. It would not stay with them." At the climax of the definition, Magic is moving, coursing, dancing through the material world of mind and flesh, transforming time itself into "the Magic Length of God."

The passage is so magnificent that it is only natural that it should have been isolated and taken out of context, but as usual, the context is important. While F. is writing it with one hand,

his other hand is moving up Mary Voolnd's cunt: another outrageous example of Cohen's unlikely unions of the sacred and
the profane. But further, this other hand goes "limp" during
the writing, and F. is forced to ask, "If my instruction were gospel, would it wither up my hand?" (158). In fact, F. sees himself at this point as "a hopeless case"; the great peroration is
really a failure, and it is this failure which leads F. to make his
distinction between being (as he is) only a magician, and being
(as *IF* is to become) Magic itself.

The final group of religious images is that centering on
the idea of apocalypse and the figure of Isis. The word "apocalyptic" is first used by *I* after his account of the feast at which
Catherine Tekakwitha spills the wine (97–98).[25] Linda Hutcheon
links this image with Revelations 6:12 and makes other parallels.[26]
The story of the feast, since it comes not from history but from
Edith, is in a sense our "truest" picture of Catherine, and Cohen
tops it off with that magnificent anticlimax—"I guess I owe
you all an apology"—which by its very ludicrousness confirms
the deep seriousness of the image. *I* then says, in mock-tentative
tones, "It is my impression that the above is apocalyptic," and
proceeds into a mock-scholarly account of the derivations of
the word.

> It comes from the Greek *apokalupsis,* which means revelation.
> This derives from the Greek *apokaluptein,* meaning uncover or
> disclose. *Apo* is a Greek prefix meaning from, derived from.
> *Kaluptein* means to cover. This is cognate with *kalube* which is
> cabin, and *kalumma* which means woman's veil. Therefore
> apocalyptic describes that which is revealed when the woman's
> veil is lifted. What have I done, what have I not done, to get
> under your blanket, Kateri Tekakwitha?
>
> (98–99)

There are two strands here. The first is the idea of the lifting of
the veil, which connects with *I*'s longing to "know what goes on
under that rosy blanket" (3). These references to veils and blan-
kets are connected with the inscription spoken by Isis (183),
which uses the word ἀπεκαλυψεν when it says that "no mortal
has lifted my robe." In fact, the robe, veil, or blanket is lifted
twice in the novel: first by Catherine Tekakwitha when she re-
moves her uncle's blanket to see his "old Mohawk body" and

hear the story of Oscotarach (113); secondly by *IF* in the second encounter with Isis (235), by which time the veil has been removed entirely.

The second strand, planted by Cohen and then mischievously ignored, is the derivation from καλυβη, cabin. What is "apocalyptic" is also that which comes *apo kalube,* down from the cabin, Oscotarach's hut or *I*'s treehouse. This derivation also is connected with Isis, who recovered the dismembered body of her brother Osiris from a "treehouse" (he was concealed inside a tamarisk tree) and brought him back to life.

The figure of Isis in the novel has been well described by Douglas Barbour, who shows that Isis "had the happy ability of being able to incorporate into her worship all goddesses and all manners of living."[27] Thus she is "both virgin and sexual goddess," and is also associated with healing the sick, so Catherine, Edith, and Mary Voolnd can all be assimilated into her image. Barbour also mentions strong links between Isis and Mariolatry. The figure of Isis suggests connections throughout the novel. The great inscription—"I am Isis, I am all things which have been, and are, and shall be, and no mortal has lifted my robe"— is ostensibly spoken by Edith, at the climax of the novel's most extreme sexual scene, but Edith immediately follows it up with "Wiggle," which links directly to Catherine Tekakwitha and the Jesuit priest (87). All these references are drawn together into the appearance of Isis (in moccasins) in Book Three (234– 235). Finally, given the repeated attack on history's past tense, there is a possible pun in the fact that the name Isis is a repeated insistence on the present tense.

The next major system through which F. attempts to drive *I* towards Magic is sexuality. This is of course the most sensationalistic aspect of the book, and Cohen's belief in excess is nowhere shown more clearly than in his wholehearted adoption of the methods and language of pornography. Yet after a while the shock value wears off and the book's sexual systems can be viewed as calmly as any other. For even in sexuality, systems are imposed, and have to be broken into stems.

One may start with the creation of Edith, an almost wholly sexual creature. *I* gives an ecstatic description of her body (26– 27), especially the texture of her skin and her "wondrous nipples." F. reveals that this perfection was not natural but created according to a system. Her skin was originally acned, then cured by F.'s "famous soap collection" (134, 159); as for the rest: "Her buttocks were my masterpiece. Call her nipples an eccentric extravagance, but the bum was perfect. It's true that from year to year it required electronic massage and applications of hormone mold, but the conception was perfect" (164–165).

F.'s project here is to create, systematically, a sexually perfect object, a body in which "All flesh can come" (32). But the system of sexual perfectionism is continually being broken, and it is at the breaking points that the stems grow. The project of creating a "pan-orgasmic body" breaks down when Edith confesses that "I can't make myself come any more" (167), but it is at this point that the Danish Vibrator is introduced. *I* complains to F. about Edith's "unspecific" kisses, which keep him from climax, but it is *I*'s very failure to reach climax, even when facing the rushing silk wall, which marks him as a beautiful loser. Finally, F.'s system escapes his control, as did Pygmalion's (183): Edith transcends her creator to become Isis. The central breaking of this system is, of course, the crushing of Edith's perfect body in the elevator shaft. This may be seen as the ultimate purpose, conscious or unconscious, of F.'s creation; in Phyllis Webb's words, "What are we whole or beautiful or good for / but to be absolutely broken?"[28]

Edith herself achieves, at times, a level of experience comparable to that of Catherine's uncle's chant, but she does this only at the cost of her personality. What is broken is not only Edith's body but also her existence as an individual. *I* remembers one ideal time when "it wasn't Thigh or Cunt . . . it was just a shape of Edith: then it was just a humanoid shape: then it was just a shape — and for a blessed second truly I was not alone, I was part of a family" (96). Similarly, F. describes her as reaching, in the Argentine orgy, "that blind realm, so like sleep, so like death, that journey of pleasure beyond pleasure, where each man travels as an orphan toward an atomic ancestry, more anonymous, more nourishing than the arms of blood or foster family" (173). Edith herself states it more directly when, coated with red grease, she appeals, "let's be other people" (14). Finally, the Danish Vibrator reduces her to "nothing but a buffet of juice, flesh, excrement, muscle to serve its appetite" (179):

another "shape of Edith," not too far removed from the shape left at the bottom of the elevator shaft.

F. also creates a perfect body for himself, using the Charles Axis system. Like any other system, it can be dangerous and repressive, as is suggested by the political overtones of the name. But as a system for sexual perfection, it is always breaking down. Axis himself turns out to be not the perfect man but "the worst nuisance on the beach" (73). Whereas F. hopes to create a pan-orgasmic body, Axis's own "immaculate white bathing suit" is "unshadowed by topography of genitalia" (166). It is Axis who observes the Danish Vibrator disappear into the ocean, and his presence frames the whole orgy sequence (166, 180), but he takes no direct part in it.

F. tries to impose the Axis system on *I*, instructing him where his buttocks should be when he is squatting (160). The advice is repeated by the dead Catherine to Marie-Thérèse (216), and by *IF* to the small boy in Book Three (232); remember also that the one change in Edith's perfect body was sagging buttocks (27). *I*, however, refuses this instruction, because of his "sin of pride": secretly, he wants to be the perfect superhero, "the Superman who was never Clark Kent" (116). Again, it is the broken system which forms the stem; *I*'s miserable body, the "tattered billboard" (105) for F.'s, is the one which finally achieves perfection, in the same way as Catherine's swarthy, pockmarked face turns white (210).

The culminating sexual episode in the book is of course the long scene in the Argentine hotel room (164–183). This is one of the scenes in which Cohen pulls various strands of the book together: it unites the sexual system with the pop culture world of pornographic literature, the historical world of the Jesuits and the Iroquois—not to mention Adolf Hitler—and the mechanical world of the Danish Vibrator. It provides two images—Isis and D.V.—which transcend them all. Since it is such a serious scene, it is also of course comic, an outrageous parody of all the conventions of "the orgy." The image of the Vibrator's transcendence is simultaneously absurd and profound, hilarious and awesome.

It begins in failure: Edith's confession of her inability to come, F.'s realization of his position as Moses (165–167). The sexual stimulation is that of the most debased pornography, whose banality is transcended, in Cohen's writing, only through sheer accumulation of detail, followed by the outrageous use of the Brébeuf story as sado-masochistic titillation. (E. J. Pratt, as Ondaatje aptly comments, must surely "turn in his epic grave."[29]) This stimulation reaches its climax in the use of the Danish Vibrator, and it is at this point that the system transcends itself. The scene should end (by "normal" standards!) when the machine is unplugged. But as it "learns to feed itself" (178), it becomes the D.V. (*Deo Volente,* God Willing), "ordinary eternal machinery" made in Denmark. The rest of the passage is a series of annunciations, in which love triumphs over "the Desert of the Possible" (178): the D.V.'s Assumption into the ocean (180), Edith's extraordinary gesture of sympathy towards Hitler (183), and her own revelation as Isis (183). The failure has turned to the greatest triumph Edith and F. are capable of; now they can only destroy themselves to prepare the way for *I*.

While F. and Edith are systematically exploring their sexuality, Catherine Tekakwitha is equally systematically destroying hers. Extremes meet: Catherine, in her highly conscious rejection, is fully as sexual a character as any of the others. Virginity and the mortification of the flesh are her tactics for approaching eternity; in a sense, they systematize breaking. They pursue unnatural behaviour to an extreme. Thus Catherine breaks up the ordered, rational lives of the societies around her: she introduces hysteria and disruption into the social orders of her native village, the mission, and the polite dinner table.

Cohen stresses that her "vision" could just as easily have turned "Rabelaisian" (44); the two are very close to each other, just as the birching which Catherine and Marie-Thérèse indulge in for religious purposes could just as easily be the material of sado-masochistic pornography. But Catherine Tekakwitha, "She who, advancing, arranges the shadows neatly" (44), makes a deliberate choice about the way in which her shadows will be arranged. She realizes that she must *become* Virgin, and to do so "she hurled her cunt forever into the night" (51). This is not a passive choice, an absence of action; it is decisive action, consciously taken. "I have given my fuck away,"she tells a priest, who responds — characteristically for one of Cohen's moments of high seriousness — "Don't be an Indian Giver" (86). But her action does not always meet with such approval. The norm of both societies, Indian and Christian, is marriage, and even in the mission she has to fight to establish herself as Virgin (192–193). In the vision of her body after death, "her lower body beneath the belt dissolved in the brilliance," and F. wonders, "Had she lent her other parts to you?" (216). The question is answered, in part, by the moccasined Isis of Book Three, who "was naked below the armrest," and who, like Catherine, scorns marriage (234).

It is the element of unnaturalness, or irrationality, within Catherine's system, which provides the stem out of which grow her miracles. Like F. and Edith, she pursues sexuality to a point of obsession where what is normal and reasonable has been obliterated. At this point, sexuality transcends itself, and the dead Catherine enters the "eternal machinery of the sky" (211) just as the eternal machinery of the D.V. enters F. and Edith. The final union is expressed in the sexual overtones of Catherine's prayer: "O my Lord, play with me" (207).[30]

When F. speaks of himself as Oscotarach being unable to perform the brain-removing operation on himself, he echoes *I*'s statement about having to apply to the public wards, but he also adds his own explanation: "The treehouse was too lonely for me: I had to apply to politics" (184). In politics, as in any other system, F. is supremely successful: he is elected to Parliament (to which he is going, on the night drive, to make, hilariously, his "Maiden" speech); he is accepted as a "Patriot" and revolutionary leader (121); he is "very nearly the President of our country" (239). He is similarly successful in the related field of commerce: almost without effort he buys a factory, and "The financial page talked about the brilliance of your manipulations" (43).

F. turns to politics for two reasons. The first is that, like Breavman, he always needs an audience. "The treehouse was too lonely for me": this is one of the ways in which *I* transcends his master, for *I* can and does suffer the isolation of the treehouse. By indulging his need for power, politics is a system which traps F. At the end of Book Two he is called most unwillingly back to the service of the Republic, having "almost lost everything" (225) in his isolation. Politics offers power, and power is always F.'s distraction. "Go beyond my style," he appeals to *I*, "I am nothing but a rotten hero" (164).

But the second reason that F. turns to politics is that it can perform on him the role of Oscotarach. By using politics irrationally, he can break the system and turn it into a stem. It is, for instance, his "contempt for commerce" which "enabled him to buy a factory" (46), and the factory's normal purpose is subverted by F.'s refusal to use it as anything but a gigantic playground. He intends only to "Come in, now and then. Sweep a little. Screw on the shiny tables. Play with the machines" (42). F. turns the factory, heart of the capitalist system, into a place where the "Messianic vision" of the game (29) may be realized, where Catherine Tekakwitha can again address the eternal machinery of the sky, "O my Lord, play with me."

Similarly, F. attempts to break the political structure of Canada by encouraging, in the wildest and most emotional way, the Québec revolution. He sees an historical structure of victims—"The English did to us what we did to the Indians, and the Americans did to the English what the English did to us"—and he longs to disrupt it all—"I demanded revenge for everyone. I saw cities burning, I saw movies falling into blackness" (187). (For *IF*, in Book Three, the movies do in fact fall into blackness.) Ultimately, his vision is not revolutionary but anarchist: "I want the State to doubt itself seriously" (187). In order to provoke this disruption of the system, F. plans to provide "the lubrication of a little blood" (133) by blowing up the statue of Queen Victoria.

The result of this breaking of the political system will be a new Québec in which "They walk differently now, the young men and women of Montréal" (186). It is significant, though, that the main visible difference in this vision of a future, post-revolutionary Québec is sexual: "Good fucks... have migrated from marble English banks to revolutionary cafés. There is love on Rue Ste. Catherine, patroness of spinsters" (186). (The Catherine in question is not Tekakwitha, but she could just as well be.)

But politics, or the breaking of political systems, is not fully an end in itself, even for F. For *I*, the separatiste rally (117–123) is used solely as a means of sexual stimulation, but in his failure to come he passes a test (123). His failure links him to the Québecois as losers, and so politics becomes a part of his education. In the same way, F. uses his martyrdom to serve the revolution only secondarily; primarily he uses it to advance the creation of *IF.* It is certainly possible to read the whole of *Beautiful Losers* as a political work, and to argue that the personal victimization of the central characters can be read as an allegory of Canadian society. But I am not sure that the tone of the book allows this interpretation to be primary; the tone is obsessively personal, and politics are absorbed into private vision.

Closely related to politics is the view of history as a system. The speaker at the separatiste rally attempts to see history as a liberating force for the Québecois (just as F. later hopes to see "History... jump on Canada's spine with sharp skates" [187]) but his view is limited insofar as he sees history as a force which "decrees" and "commands" (118). For the beautiful loser, history is a force to be escaped from.

"Our awareness of Historical Time," Barbour writes, "boxes us in... and keeps us from living in the Eternal Present. F.'s whole course of training... is designed to destroy *I*'s sense of Historical Time."[31] One of the attributes of the New Jew is that he "dissolves history" (161). It is history which confronts the Jesuits as the direct opposite of miracles (207), and though in this case they do choose miracles, the Jesuit historian is inadequate in that he fails to record the dying Catherine's mystical mispronunciation of the names of Jesus and Mary (209–210).

F.'s "Invocation to History in the Middle Style" (188–189) which parodies the elaborate structure of scholarly apparatus (there are footnotes to the footnotes) presents history as a means of putting consciousness to sleep. Elsewhere, F. sees history as a "sleepy tune" which "made us feel good so we played it over and over, deep into the night" (162–163). Marx described religion as the opium of the people; F. clearly casts history in that role.

The book's central character, *I,* is a historian, and he entitles his section of the novel "The History of Them All." F. sees history as that which has deformed *I*'s life—"Oh my darling, what a hunchback History and the Past have made of your body, what a pitiful hunchback" (133)—and promises to "relieve you of your final burden: the useless History under which you suffer in such confusion" (188). In order to do this, F. provides his own account of *I*'s subject, Catherine Tekakwitha. The contrast between the two accounts is startling. *I*'s is confused, meandering, constipated; F.'s is lucid, direct, flowing. *I* is one of those who "never get far beyond the Baptism" (188); F. moves effortlessly through death, ascension, miracles. *I* is continually getting bogged down in facts and details, pedantic derivations from Indian names, dates, geographical locations, citing of sources.[32] "The Church loves such details," he tells us. "I love such details" (15). F. is able to select and use details in a telling and relevant manner. In fact, F. is too accomplished a historian; as in any system, sexual or political or historical, F. is too much in control. In Book Three, *IF* returns to the details of names and derivations, this time in transcendent, iconic form (233). *I* accepts the metaphorical connection between his historical obsession and his constipation. He describes himself as "The hater of history crouched over the immaculate bowl" (38), and appeals, "Saints and friends, help me out of History and Constipation" (111). He holds the past trapped within him, blocking his life. Yet he also sees, perhaps more clearly than F., the potential stems within the historical system. In his complaint to F. about the losers — "What about us failures? What about us who can't shit properly?" — he includes "What about us Historians who have to read the dirty parts?" (124). The constipated historian is a failure, a loser, and therefore closer to sainthood, really, than the flowing historian.

It is, after all, only through history that *I* is able to approach Catherine Tekakwitha. Cohen himself has had to *use* history for this purpose. Leslie Monkman points out the degree to which Cohen's presentation of Indian life and culture is indebted to the Jesuit historian whose book was one of the few volumes eclectically chosen for Cohen's desk as he wrote the novel.

> An investigation of Cohen's sources indicates that almost all of the details of Catherine's life are taken from Edouard Lecompte's *Une Vierge Iroquoise Catherine Tekakwitha: Le Lis des bords de la Mohawk et du St-Laurent* (1656–1680). Through quotation, translation, and paraphrase, Cohen provides a full historical background for Catherine as seen by a Jesuit priest in 1927. The

picture described on the first page of the novel matches detail by detail the portrait of Catherine which serves as frontispiece to Lecompte's book. Quotations ascribed to Fathers Cholonec, Chauchetière, and Remy are also restricted to citations appearing in this volume.[33]

I must also use history to get under Catherine's "rosy blanket" (3): he achieves this aim when he is not dominated by history: when love, or a sense of the miraculous, breaks historical system into stem. Thus, Lecompte's history shows, in one "half paragraph" on Tekakwitha's spring, that he too "loved the girl," and *I* justly offers praise: "Long live History for telling us" (67–68). The spring is also closely connected, through F.'s and Edith's use of it as a narcotic, with the apocalyptic tale of the feast at Québec. *I* records, unsurprisingly, that "I find no mention of this feast in any of the standard biographers" (99). Edith's story, which ignores the limiting categories of rationality and probability, transcends what F. would call "the tyranny of Event," and thus reaches deeper into what Cohen would regard as the stem of true history.

In the closing stages of the book, history and memory have been transformed into a state of timelessness. Sequence is destroyed: the events of the "plot" can no longer be logically accounted for. F. addresses a prayer to "Thee . . . in whose flashing memory I have no past or future, whose memory never froze into the coffin of history" (215). *IF* coming down from the tree finds that "His memory represented no incident, it was all one incident, and it flowed too fast" (230): a final release from constipation. Isis insists on her present tense: it is all happening now. Is is. I change. I am the same.

The final system used for approaching Magic is that which Dave Godfrey has called "the banal." This covers pop culture generally, with special reference to pop songs and movies, and also includes the book's many references to machinery. This is a system which is already, to a great extent, broken — it contains the rejects of so-called "High Culture," and it rejoices in its own impermanence — so within the scheme of the book it is more useful than any other system. In its cultural aspects, it largely rejects the control of the discriminating intellect, concentrating instead on cheap and easily accessible emotion. This appeal also serves to ignore the individual response in favour of a mass re-

sponse, and so it is linked with the impersonal, indeed anti-
personal, forms of machinery.

Cohen's response to the images of the banal involves the
usual combination of utmost seriousness with farcical humour.
Of course much of the writing may be taken satirically, and the
accumulation of detail—as in the total reproduction of magazine
ads (107–108)—seems absurd. But it would be a mistake to see
this satire as negatively dismissing the banal. Rather, the banal
is a constant source of energy—*I* writes a lament for his outdated
"poor Top Ten that no thirteen-year-olds energize by slippery
necking on the carpet beside the hi-fi" (110)—and this energy
is constantly producing stems.

Accordingly, the initial reason F. gives for *I*'s fucking a
saint is that it will enable him to see the "akropolis rose" which
F. has created for himself by painting "a plaster reproduction
of the Akropolis" with "Tibetan Desire" nail polish (9–12).
Later, F. uses a box of fireworks as the equivalent of the flames
of Purgatory which finally drive *I* out of his basement isolation
into the treehouse, and Cohen lovingly details the contents of
the box. *I* offers an apocalyptic commentary on the comic-strip
of the Charles Axis ad, at the climax of which "Four thick black
words appear in the sky and they radiate spears of light" (70); F.
comments, "Those words are always in the sky. Sometimes you
can see them, like a daytime moon" (71). During his sexual encounter at the separatiste rally, *I* and his partner "were Plastic
Man and Plastic Woman" (120) in their contortions.

All of these are instances of the banal taking on almost
cosmic significance, within the scheme of the novel. Paradoxically, that which is cheapest, most common, most impermanent
can become the image of the absolute, as the deepest religious
beliefs can be embodied in mass-produced trinkets. "Be with
me, religious medals of all kinds," *I* prays (80), and proceeds to
expand on "all kinds" for a half-page of delirious encomium.
F.'s car has a St. Christopher's medal (91), and of course "there
is a plastic reproduction of [Catherine Tekakwitha's] little body
on the dashboard of every Montréal taxi" (5). Catherine Tekakwitha is a major figure in the popular mythology of Québec
(there are even comic books about her); it is this very popularity,
and commercial exploitation, which make her perfect for Cohen's
imagery. *I* explains,

Love cannot be hoarded. Is there a part of Jesus in every stamped-out crucifix? I think there is. Desire changes the world!. . . Peace, you manufacturers of religious trinkets! You handle sacred material!

(5)

Desire changes the world, and where is desire more obviously, more excessively to be found than in the magic worlds of pop songs and movies? At the end of *The Favourite Game,* Breavman "believed he understood the longing of the cheap tunes" coming from "everybody's neon wound." [34] *I*'s Top Ten, "cut off from the dynamic changes of jukebox stock market," still speaks of "electric echoes and longing puberty voices" (110). *I* constructs an elaborate astrological speculation on the basis of the number of words in the title "As long as you love me" (123). Painting his "akropolis rose," F. hums "The Great Pretender" (10), which could well serve as his theme-song. "With perfect taste and insight," F. listens "Ceaselessly" to The Rolling Stones (150). [35]

The ultimate statement of this theme comes, of course, in the ecstatic commentary on the song by Gavin Gate and the Goddesses (73–77). This commentary is one of Cohen's most remarkable pieces of writing even in this remarkable novel. The observation, for one thing, is very precise: he gives a marvellous transcription of the sound effects, and picks up lovely little touches like the singular "eye." The control of tone is absolute; note the perfect modulation of the sentence, "In some sad locker-room where all male lovers recreate, Gavin has heard the details of the lay." If it were satire, it would be perfect satire, but it is not. (It may of course be wish-fulfilment fantasy; as singer, Cohen has always taken care to provide himself with goddesses.) Gavin Gate (the name bearing an obvious significance) has a "strange command": he has "traveled a long path," he has "been through some ordeal and learned too much." (Note the unobtrusive "too.") The Goddesses, with their echoes of Valkyries and kamikaze squadrons, are united in suffering, and will "suck-murder" not the victim but the "victor." The song becomes a sado-masochistic orgy cum religious ritual in which the celebrants "whip themselves with electric braids," like Catherine and Marie-Thérèse. All of them "deal with sacred material" because, as Cohen says, "Oh, God! All states of love give power!" Nowhere does Cohen achieve a more cohesive image of the interdependence of love, power, religion, sexuality, and energizing emotion than through this intense contemplation of a totally banal artefact.

But even more than pop songs, movies are at the heart of the system of the banal, particularly the movies shown at the System Theatre. "I've got to get to a movie," *I* writes, "a movie will put me back in my skin" (64). Movies have a central re-integrative power, as they form and re-form new constructs of reality. Their importance is acknowledged throughout. *I* and F. break off a discussion because "we were in danger of missing the entire double feature" (19). In the depths of his misery, *I*'s ultimate threat is "I'm going to end Movies if I don't feel better very soon" (127). The cataclysmic ending of Book Two is announced by a "Close-up of Radio exhibiting a motion picture of itself" (226). Isis appears in Book Three like "the action freezing into a still on the movie screen" (234).

The kind of movies invoked are, deliberately, the most banal and commercial possible, the kind played at the System, not the art house. F. sees the "modern art-cinema house" as "a joke . . . the death of an emotion," and longs for the old, cheap movies with "hidden sex" (22). *I* sees the Mohawks as belonging to "those uncompromising black and white movies before the Western became psychological" (14).

The movies provide their own saints: "Lady Marilyn" (4), Bardot, Cagney, James Dean. These names are invoked by F. in a passage which specifically parallels an earlier passage on religious saints whose bodies remain uncorrupted in the grave (205, 126–127). The vision in the System Theatre adds Sophia Loren (Saint Sophia, Holy Wisdom?). The movie saint is associated also with F.'s vision of the new Québec: "I wanted to show Brigitte Bardot around revolutionary Montréal" (205).

Movies are the sources of knowledge and experience, all the more real if it is vicarious. "You know what pain looks like," F. tells *I*, "you've been inside newsreel Belsen" (194). Sexual exploitation and "about a thousand Hollywood Westerns" (9) are cited as the main sources of F.'s knowledge of Indians, yet it is on this basis that he is able to complete *I*'s history of Catherine Tekakwitha.

The ultimate visions of the possibilities of movies take place in the System Theatre. First (223–224), F. turns his attention away from the fixed, stable image on the screen to the not-yet-fixed, not-yet-stable projection beam. He sees it as "the first snake in the shadows of the original garden... offering our female memory the taste of—everything!"[36] This Edenic vision leads him to ask "What will happen when the newsreel escapes into the Feature?": an image of the breaking down of all the distinctions between fact and fiction, so-called reality and Magic. The two modes of perception "merged in aweful originality" and proclaim:

Sophia Loren Strips For A Flood Victim
THE FLOOD IS REAL AT LAST

The flood becomes real when a reversal occurs between the importance of Sophia Loren, who symbolizes artificiality and banality, and the importance of the newsreel, which is a vehicle of "reality." Rather than her being dignified by the newsreel, the newsreel is invaded by Magic, which alone can energize it.

This passage is the climax of F.'s insight, but since he remains a magician rather than Magic itself, he must leave it to his disciple to transcend even this insight by becoming Magic, by merging completely into that magical reality. *IF* achieves this transformation, again in the System Theatre, when the blinking of his eyes synchronizes perfectly with the blinking of the projector, 24 frames per second (235–236). He then sees nothing, the dark between the frames, and so his humanity is changed into a magical reality which is also mechanical. From here it is a short step to *IF*'s final metamorphosis into "a movie of Ray Charles" (242).

Movies are Magic produced by machinery, and the images of machinery are the last aspect of the banal to be considered. Cohen consistently presents human sexuality in mechanical terms, an association which should immediately establish that machinery is as much stem as system. *I* remembers his evenings with F. as "happy views of simple human clockwork" (13); Catherine Tekakwitha sees sexuality as an "assault of human machinery" (44), but it is an "assault" only because she does not see it in a proper context; F. listens to the "tiny swamp machinery" (165) of Edith's cunt; Mary Voolnd buzzes in sexual surprise like a pinball machine, and F.'s only regret is that she is not (yet) as eternal as a machine (191); even the "teen-age male prostitutes" are given a kind of dignity, as ultimate losers "at the very bottom of Montréal's desire apparatus" (237).

Machinery is transcended throughout. The machines in F.'s factory become toys; the Danish Vibrator becomes D.V. The mechanistic translations in the Greek-English phrase book are transformed into the rituals of prayer. The book itself was received by F. in return for an "oral favour" (56), and this reference is picked up in the transformation of the final word in Book One, the ordinary English "Thanks," into Εὐχαριστῶ, the sacred Eucharist. The malfunctions of decaying pinball machines are understood by the true initiates as "the extension of the game's complexity" (238), and the New Jew observes the final revelation while "laboring on the lever of the broken Strength Test" (242). Of course, this machine, like the Idea which Catherine Tekakwitha prays will change the world, has to be "broken."

The central image of machinery is F.'s long account of the rediscovery of the Telephone Dance in the lobby of the System Theatre (27–34). Elsewhere in the book, the Jesuit priest, as has already been shown, sees the Telephone Dance as a form of defiance against Christianity, and successfully sets out to destroy it (81–82); it is also performed by Martin Stark in *The Favourite Game*.[37] Edith and F. later perform the dance in the Argentine, this time with nipples instead of fingers; F.'s failure to hear anything leads directly to his realization that he is not going to be able to cross his Jordan (166–167).

The essence of the dance is stated by F.: "I *became* a telephone. Edith was the electrical conversation that went through me" (33). (In the same way, losing all human personality, *IF* is to *become* the movie projector.) Both Edith and F. become, in the dance, totally mechanical, depersonalized, transcended: they are "ordinary eternal machinery." This phrase is also used by the dying Catherine to describe the way she perceives the Jesuit priests (204). The common phrase not only confirms the link between Catherine and Edith but also shows that despite the Jesuits' attempt to repress the Telephone Dance they are themselves, through their acceptance of miracles, still a part of it. Finally Catherine, who in life had been "Mangled Every Hour In Mysterious Machinery" (55), at her death "entered the eternal machinery of the sky" (211). The image of transcendence is complete: all systems have been broken into stems.

The course of instruction in F.'s classroom of hysteria consists, then, of the exploration of all these systems. In each one, the stem emerges at the point where the system is broken down and it is possible for *I* to become a beautiful loser. This means that for the major part of the book F. is cast in the role of master, and in every system his control is casually, almost contemptuously demonstrated. This is F.'s great tragedy.[38] "I love your power," *I* tells him. "Teach me everything" (91). But F.'s power is what holds him back from the fulfilment of his own ideals. "I lead men too easily," he confesses: "my fatal facility" (151). In his letter, F. clearly perceives his own failure: "nothing I did was pure enough. I was never sure whether I wanted disciples or partisans. I was never sure whether I wanted Parliament or a hermitage" (162).

He offers two images which define his position in relation to *I*. The first is that of Moses: "I was the Moses of our little exodus. I would never cross. My mountain might be very high but it rises from the desert" (167). *I*, or more accurately *IF*, does have the ability to cross from the desert into the promised land, but F. cannot. The second is even more precise: "Here is a plea based on my whole experience: do not be a magician, be magic" (164). As a magician, F. still attempts to exercise control over his mystical experience; being Magic itself eliminates the very idea of control. In movie terms, F. is a director, or a projectionist; *IF*, his eyes blinking at 24 f.p.s., becomes both the projector (machinery) and what is projected; subject and object, victor and victim, Magic itself.

There are signs that F. is reaching towards his ideal. "Am I hurt enough?" he asks (150), and in his vision of the great auto wreck in which he is trying to fit the pieces back together he realizes that "I was also truly part of the disaster" (175). At the climax of Book Two, he tells Mary Voolnd "I'm almost broken, I've almost lost everything, I almost have humility!" (225) Her response is to tell him that he must lose even humility itself; finally, F. does make it, as he becomes part of the "remote human possibility," *IF*, in Book Three.

I's role as a loser is shown right from the start by his associations with the A———s, whose "brief history is characterized by

incessant defeat. The very name of the tribe, A——, is the word
for corpse in the language of all the neighbouring tribes. . . .
My interest in this pack of failures betrays my character" (5).
Edith is also an A——; for one remarkable moment, even Hitler
is seen as an A—— (183). Most of the characters are seen as
victims in one way or another: Edith brutally raped in the
(American-owned) quarry (57–61); Mary Voolnd torn to pieces
by "salivating police dog jaws" (226); even le P. Cholenec,
deprived of a vision of Catherine (216). *I* sums up their position
in his complaint to F.: "What about us with asthma? What
about us failures? What about us who can't shit properly? What
about us who have no orgies and excessive fucking to become
detached about?" (124). The point against F. is well taken, but
only gradually does *I* come to see that this condition is his glory.

For *I*, the process is long and agonizing: the "blunt tomahawk" (132) of Oscotarach. "O God," he prays, "I Love So Many
Things It Will Take Years To Take Them Away One By One"
(90). But finally he does reach the position outlined by F. in the
traditional theological definition of a saint: "disarmed and
empty, an instrument of Grace" (153).

In Book Three, Cohen presents the apocalyptic vision of
all possibilities. Everything has been lost, especially individual
personalities. The old man who descends from the tree house
(*apo kalube,* out of the cabin) is *I* emerging from his timeless
ordeal, his hands still burnt from the firecrackers (239); is F.
escaped from his asylum, his thumb blown off in the explosion
(239); is Catherine's uncle (232); is someone who has given up
eating (238), like Catherine (192, 200) and like Edith (200); is
Osiris coming out of his tamarisk; is Christ descending from his
"lonely wooden tower";[39] is *IF,* all possibilities merged. Similarly,
the woman in the car (234–235) is Catherine (wearing moccasins); is Edith (repeating the inscription of Isis); is Mary Voolnd
(wearing white); is Isis herself; is the victim of F.'s apocalyptic
car crash; is the lady from "Story," perhaps, who "contemplates
her own traffic death";[40] is the saint whom *IF* goes down on.

Since personalities have been lost, the narrative can no
longer be in *I*'s first person (Book One), nor in F.'s second person (Book Two); it is a totally impersonal third person. This
viewpoint causes problems, for Cohen does not have time to establish the tone and there is a certain ironic detachment towards

the end, as if Cohen is holding back on his apocalypse. For instance, Cohen says, "The old man had commenced his remarkable performance (which I do not intend to describe)" (241), and then goes right on to describe it.

The "performance" starts with the final disintegration of whatever tenuous physical reality the old man has left. "His presence was like the shape of an hourglass, strongest where it was smallest. And at the point where he was most absent, that's when the gasps started" (241). The loser transcends himself at the point where he loses all; the moment of greatest absence is the hourglass stem of the revelation. "The future streams through that point, going both ways" (241); it is the dissolution of historical time, the vision of "All Chances At Once" (242).

The ironical tone holds back from the "purists" for whom "this point of most absence was the feature of the evening" (242); instead, the final image is presented, consistently enough, in terms of the banal, "a movie of Ray Charles" (242) spread out across the sky like the "celestial manifestation" in Charles Axis's comic strip (70). This image may be interpreted in various "profound" ways — the epigraph to the book has Ray Charles singing a song of slavery (not even one of his own songs), and he is himself both black and blind — but I feel that Cohen is presenting us with something that is deliberately *not* "profound." For all his irony, Cohen is with the "purists"; the "point of most absence" *is* the feature of the evening, and anything that follows it has to be, to some extent, a letdown. No positive image which Cohen could have produced at this point would have been fully adequate to the situation, and any really powerful religious image would have been feeding back into a system. The image has to be banal and inadequate. One might say that here even the system of Apocalypse is broken: instead of Antichrist, anticlimax. "Thank God," someone comments, "it's only a movie" (242). And then the commercial.

The vision of *Beautiful Losers* is absolute, and in some ways it is very harsh and cruel, even inhuman. But throughout the book there still remains the concept of love, and, if this does not soften the harsh outlines of the vision as much in *Beautiful Losers* as it is to do in the songs, still it is important. In "Sisters of Mercy," love is seen as a stem; in *Beautiful Losers* love again forms the stem of all the broken systems.

Returning to the central definition of a saint, we find that the energy with which the saint makes contact is the energy of love, and if this energy leads to transcendence, so also this love leads back to the world. "His house is dangerous and finite, but he is at home in the world. He can love the shapes of human beings, the fine and twisted shapes of the heart" (96). Much of *Beautiful Losers* is savage in the excess of its images, in the hysteria which F. imposes on his pupil, in its wild and farcical sense of humour. But running through this savagery is the completely human emotion that binds *I* to his teachers, that leads him to recreate Catherine's world, and that enables him to give himself at last to all men (because, like Christ, "Something in him so loves the world") (96), realizing in a more profound sense F.'s cynical remark, "Who am I to refuse the Universe?" (6)

I is constantly surrounded by love, and he in turn brings love to others. "You are stuck with two great loves," F. tells him, "Edith's and mine" (25). At the climax of the Argentine orgy, F. and Edith exchange their pledges of love to each other and to *I*, and F. feels "a whisper of rare love... beginning in my heart" (180–181). "I know nothing about love," *I* writes (135), perhaps too modestly, but "something like love" tears from his throat the declaration "I NEED THEE, F." *I* and Edith are always able, to a greater extent than F., to love the "twisted shapes of the heart." In one of his prayers, *I* writes, "F. Suffered Horribly In His Last Days. Catherine Was Mangled Every Hour In Mysterious Machinery. Edith Cried In Pain. Be With Us This Morning Of Your Time" (55). Recalling Edith's rape, *I* hides nothing of its pain and bitterly comments, "I would like to know what kind of miracle that is, F." (61). Edith extends her lovely gesture of sympathy not only to the strange A—— on the beach (36–37) but also to the men who rape her (61) and even to Hitler himself (183).

These moments of love provide some mitigation of the harshness of the book, and some justification for Cohen's statement that it is "a redemptive novel, an exercise to redeem the soul."[41] The strongest of them comes in a beautiful comment from Catherine's uncle: "Do not weep, Kateri. We do not see well through tears, and although that which we see through tears is bright it is also bent" (113).

It is this tone, I think, which is picked up in the last paragraph of the novel (243). After the Jesuit commercial, another voice speaks: it could be *IF*, but I prefer to think of it as Cohen himself. It speaks again of "poor men" who are "broken and fled," the losers who are one letter removed from lovers. But having "come through the fire," Cohen is prepared to speak some words of comfort. The last paragraph of *Beautiful Losers* is a love poem addressed to the reader.

> Welcome to you who read me today. Welcome to you who put my heart down. Welcome to you, darling and friend, who miss me forever in your trip to the end.

In *Beautiful Losers,* Cohen pushed to their extreme limit the themes and images which had been central to his work at least since "You Have the Lovers." The novels present these images with an increasing objectivity and detachment. In *The Favourite Game,* Breavman is viewed from the detached perspective of a third-person narrative, rather than from the indulgent perspective of a first-person lyric; the result is, I have argued, an implied judgement on his human failings and shortcomings. But Breavman as a character is at least still within the range of more or less "normal" human experience. The increasing harshness of the vision in *Beautiful Losers* pushes its characters beyond that range, so that, whereas it is easy enough to admire the complexity and intellectual ferocity of the novel, it is hard for the average reader to identify with its characters. The reader is forced to stand outside the action of the novel, as a spectator; he is not allowed to participate in it. The objectivity and the extremism of Cohen's vision here reinforce each other to produce a statement which is ultimate and unique.

The fact that *Beautiful Losers* is ultimate and unique means that it is also a dead end. In his second novel, Cohen more or less exhausted one set of themes; he also exhausted, at least temporarily, the form of the novel. If he were not to relapse into complete silence, his work had to find a new direction, and a new form. Fortunately, that was exactly what he did find. In the spring of 1966, simultaneously with the publication of *Beautiful Losers,* Leonard Cohen emerged in a new role, as the composer and performer of songs.

CHAPTER FOUR

The Songs, 1968–1973

The news is sad but it's in a song so
it's not so bad.
                    (*Leonard Cohen*, The Favourite Game)

Much of Leonard Cohen's enormous popularity in the late sixties was based on his songs.[1] As his previous writings show, Cohen had always been interested in pop songs; the regular prosody of a good many of his early poems suggests that they could easily be set to music. The youth culture of the middle sixties, and especially the example of Bob Dylan, provided the context in which this interest could bear fruit, economically as well as aesthetically. A mass audience had come into existence which was prepared to take seriously a singer whose lyrics made obviously "poetic" claims; Cohen, with his images of pain and isolation, and with his mournful and sometimes cracked voice, was just right for the times.

It is possible, of course, to argue that Cohen's audience listened to his words only superficially. Frank Davey has justly described Cohen's imagery as being "of the imprecise but suggestive kind that can be easily projected into by the subjective reader."[2] The songs do continue the themes and imagery of the other work, and they are often harsher and crueler in their implications than their aura of romantic loneliness tends to suggest. But it is also true that the songs are softer, more humane, and more accessible than is *Beautiful Losers*. The vision is less absolute and impersonal; the emotions, especially love and sadness, are more to the fore.

One reason for this difference is the very fact that they are songs, not poems. There is a subtle but decisive distinction between a true song and a poem set to music. In certain works the words could stand, without too great a loss, separated from the music, whereas in a true song this separation is unthinkable. Cohen comes closest to being a true songwriter on his second album, *Songs from a Room;* at other times one can feel a distinction between his work and that of such *songwriters* (not poets) as Bob Dylan, Mick Jagger, and Jesse Winchester. But when a true song has been achieved, the listener responds to its rhythm and emotion. A favourite song, moreover, is usually listened to more often than a poem is read. It becomes familiar because the mnemonic qualities of the form induce the listener to absorb the words more deeply. You live with a song in ways that you do not live with a poem. I know most of Cohen's songs by heart, but very few of his poems.

Another reason is that the songs are presented in Cohen's own voice. Immediately the song becomes a more personal utterance than the printed page; the impersonality of *Beautiful Losers* is impossible, for the song is one person's voice addressing you from the speakers, or one person standing on the concert stage. Cohen's voice is not conventionally musical or attractive; some listeners find it an insuperable barrier. But such performers as Bob Dylan and Mick Jagger have demonstrated that in pop music beauty is not as important as expressiveness, and within its limitations, Cohen's voice is perfectly expressive for his songs.

These very limitations are another reason why the songs are softer and more personal. Cohen's singing voice is not one in which it is possible to make grand gestures; when his songs call for them, he fails utterly. Most of the time Cohen has wisely stayed within his limitations, and as a result the songs have a muted, gentle feeling to them. The limitations can even be exploited: Cohen can sound exceptionally mournful when he allows his voice to drag a little, and he can produce very deliberate effects by singing in a loud, hoarse, cracked scream (as on "Diamonds in the Mine" and "Leaving Greensleeves"). But the basic mood of the songs is quiet, gentle, and unambitious. Cohen can never pretend to be F. when he is singing.

Cohen appeared to feel that he had not found the appropriate vehicle in the rather grandiose arrangements on his first album. A note to that album says, "The songs and the arrangements were introduced. They felt some affection for one another but because of a blood feud, they were forbidden to marry. Nevertheless, the arrangements wished to throw a party. The songs preferred to retreat behind a veil of satire." In fact, the arrangements do not detract from the songs, with the possible exception of "Hey, That's No Way To Say Goodbye." Like Gavin Gate with his Goddesses, Cohen has always retained female backing vocals, and he has continued to record his songs with elaborate arrangements such as that of John Lissauer for *New Skin for the Old Ceremony.*

But perhaps the most important reason for the different mood is that Cohen regards songs as cathartic, as providing an emotional experience which is basically one of joy, no matter what the words say. This is the significance of the comment in *The Favourite Game* on Pat Boone's song: "The news was not so good," says the song, but Breavman counters, "The news is great. The news is sad but it's in a song so it's not so bad."[3] In the "Minute Prologue," which begins the *Live Songs* album, Cohen sings:

> I've been listening to all of the dissension
> I've been listening to all of the pain
> And I feel that no matter what I do for you
> It's going to come back again
> But I think that I can heal it
> But I think that I can heal it
> I'm a fool, but I think that I can heal it
> With this song

The songs themselves refer to this therapeutic function. Of the "Sisters of Mercy," Cohen says "They brought me their comfort and later they brought me this song." In "Lover, Lover, Lover" he prays:

> And may the spirit of this song
> May it rise up pure and free
> May it be a shield for you
> A shield against the Enemy

"Joy," says F. in *Beautiful Losers,* "Didn't I promise it? Didn't you believe I would deliver?"[4] If Cohen delivers joy anywhere, it is in the songs.

(i) *Songs of Leonard Cohen* (1968)

The songs of Cohen's first record present the same world of masters and saints as is present in *Beautiful Losers,* but whereas the climax of the novel is an intensification of loss and destruction, the climax of the record is reconciliation, in the song "Suzanne." ("Suzanne" is placed first on the record, because that is the traditional commercial place to put the "hit" song, but thematically it should come last, since it gathers together the themes of all the other songs.) The world of the songs is one of loneliness and parting, but the emotion is more often gentle sorrow than anguish; the feeling is muted rather than overstated.

"Hey, That's No Way To Say Goodbye" takes the classic situation of the parting of lovers and gives specific instructions about how it is *not* to be done. Instead, the song recreates the world the lovers shared together, in rich, romantic images — "I loved you in the morning / Our kisses deep and warm / Your hair upon the pillow / Like a sleepy golden storm" — and offers comfort and reassurance — "You know my love goes with you / As your love stays with me." Parting is only a natural process, "like the shoreline and the sea," and thus no cause for sorrow in the lover's eyes.

Another song of parting, "So Long, Marianne," echoes this sentiment in its chorus: "Now so long, Marianne / It's time that we began / To laugh and cry and cry and laugh / About it all again." The generalizing phrase, "It's time," asserts that tears and laughter go together, are equal alternatives. But the verses tell of the singer's loneliness and suggest the old theme that the "shelter" of security offered by the woman is a betrayal of the poet's role. (Cohen uses this kind of dialectic between verse and chorus in other songs as well, such as "The Old Revolution," "Joan of Arc," and "Lover, Lover, Lover.") The first verse pictures the singer as "some kind of gypsy boy," the archetypal wanderer, until "I let you take me home." The contemptuous tone of "let you take me" suggests the sense of betrayal in "home." But the second half of the song modulates away from this: when the singer really is alone he does not feel so happy about it. "You left when I told you I was curious / I never said that I was brave." The final impression left by the song is one of ambivalence: the singer is suspicious of what Marianne can offer him, yet he is not fully able to break away. The ambivalence is summed up in the couplet "You know that I love to live with you / But you make me forget so very much," and the chorus attempts, not altogether successfully, to provide a resolution to the conflict.

The sense of isolation is found also in "Stories of the Street," which is the only song on the album to suggest a serious concern for the social context. It pictures a world in dissolution: "The Cadillacs go creeping down / Through the night and the poison gas . . . The cities they are broke in half." The highways go nowhere; the armies that were supposed to come home are "marching still." The social system confirms itself, as Cohen suggests in lines which are both a sharp psychological insight and an acute comment on the role of consumer values in a capitalist society: "You are locked into your suffering / And your pleasures are the seal." This age gives ominous birth to an infant with "one eye filled with blueprints" — potential systems — and "One eye filled with night."

In the midst of this society, Cohen presents himself alone, in his usual "old hotel," on the brink of a flamboyant self-destruction: "one hand on my suicide / One hand on the rose." He appeals to the other "children of the dust" to deny that "these hunters who are shrieking now" are the true spokesmen of this generation, but he has no real alternative to offer. There is a brief vision of a hippy-style farm where he and a girl can "grow us grass and apples . . . And keep all the animals warm." But if that fails, as surely it will, his only resource is to immerse himself in the general destruction: "O take me to the slaughter house / I will wait there with the lamb." "Stories of the Street" is a strong vision of a decayed society, but as usual in Cohen there is no trust in any political solution, so the vision turns in on the self, and offers only self-destruction and isolation. "Lost among the subway crowds / I try to catch your eye."

This theme of isolation is continued in "Winter Lady" and "The Stranger Song," and in the case of these two songs it has been given additional force by their use in Robert Altman's film *McCabe and Mrs. Miller.* One critic has remarked that the film fits the songs so fully that "one suspects Altman of extrapolating his scenario from the songs" rather than from the novel on which it is nominally based.[5] These songs are, in a very real sense, no longer Cohen's alone; they have been absorbed into another magnificently rich and varied work of art, and it is impossible to hear them after the film without the resonances of Altman's creation.

"Winter Lady" is an extraordinarily beautiful song, offering one moment of transcendent beauty, when the lady's hair is woven "on a loom / Of smoke and gold and breathing" at the centre of a winter landscape of snow and transience. The lady is "travelling," always; she has chosen her journey, and even if she consents to "stay a while" she still knows that the singer is not her lover. The isolation between the singer and the lady is as complete and as poignant as that between Mrs. Miller and her "child of snow" who romantically "fought every man for her / Until the nights grew colder."

"The Stranger Song" is a restatement of the themes of strangerhood and shelter (and again, it makes perfect sense when applied to the film: McCabe is the archetype of those who are "reaching for the sky just to surrender"). It presents a woman, the protagonist of the song, caught in the changing and contradictory demands of "dealers / Who said they were through / With dealing every time you gave them shelter." But, as for the singer in "So Long, Marianne," "shelter" is something they are not fully happy with, since it causes their wills to "weaken with your warmth and love." So they resume the role of "stranger" and leave, only to be replaced by "another tired man" who "wants to trade the game he plays for shelter." Watching this man, the protagonist sees "a highway / That is curling up like smoke above his shoulder." This perception irresistibly produces a change of roles, for having opened this door in her mind, the protagonist discovers that "you can't close your shelter"; instead she too must "try the handle of the road" and herself assume the role of "stranger." Still she is betrayed, by those who offer to meet her "Upon the shore, beneath the bridge / That they are building on some endless river," but who in reality are "only advertising one more shelter." Since even the role of "stranger" can be used, then, as a form of "shelter," the roles are reversed once more, and the song ends where it began, with a repetition of the first verse, now more resigned and accepting.

This account of the song may be misleadingly systematic;

the main impression it gives is of a phantasmagoria of relationships in which the roles of "shelter" and "stranger" are traded
back and forth and nobody stays in one role very long. The
music gives a more unified feeling to the song than the words
by themselves could achieve, and rather than seeing a totally
coherent pattern, one is left with brilliant individual images —
"Like any dealer, he was watching for the card / That is so high
and wild / He'll never need to deal another / He was just some
Joseph looking for a manger."

The device of repeating the first verse at the end is also
used for thematic purposes (rather than for purely formal ones)
in "Master Song." The first verse sets up a typical Cohen situation: three people tied to each other by sexual and master/
pupil relationships. The singer is "sick in bed," while the "you"
who holds him "prisoner" is being instructed in her turn by a
"master." This master is himself a loser, "a numberless man in
a chair / Who had just come back from the war"; the disciple's
first reaction is to "wrap up his tired face in your hair," a gesture
reminiscent of Edith in *Beautiful Losers*.

Most of the song describes the master's course of instruction
in fantastic and surreal images, for which Cohen in the songs
shows an almost fatal facility. The images are frequently striking
— "ribbons of rain," "your love is some dust in an old man's
cuff" — but the easy rhythm and available rhymes sometimes
lead to pointless indulgence — "an ape with angel glands /
Erased the final wisps of pain / With the music of rubber bands."
The end of the song produces the expected reversal of roles:

> I loved your master perfectly
> I taught him all that he knew
> . . . .
> And I sent you to him with my guarantee
> I could teach him something new
> And I taught him how you would long for me
> No matter what he said, no matter what you do.

All the positions are neatly changed round: the master becomes
the pupil, the pupil becomes the prisoner, the prisoner becomes
the master. With these new roles in mind, the first verse is then
repeated, and all its emotional overtones and implications are
completely changed. The trick is obvious, but very well executed.

The theme of master and pupil is restated, in its harshest form, in "Teachers." The situation is the familiar one, F.'s classroom of hysteria, the protagonist being subjected to a series of koans: lessons whose purpose he does not understand. Again there is the anti-rational stress — "I met a man who lost his mind / In some lost place I had to find" — and the emphasis on self-destruction — "Have I carved enough, my Lord? / Child, you are a bone." The song has no conclusion. In the last verse the protagonist asks, "Are my lessons done?" In the version printed in *Parasites of Heaven,* the answer is "Child, you've just begun,"[6] but on the record the question is flung back at him and repeated in a fade-out ending. Again Cohen is using a song convention for thematic purposes; there is no ending, the process goes on. The tone of the song is very abrasive: the lines are short and abrupt, the tune develops momentum but no resolution, Cohen sings in a harsh, accusing voice. Of all the songs on the record, "Teachers" is the one that comes closest to *Beautiful Losers* in its uncompromising tone.

The same themes are repeated in comic form in one of the verses of "One Of Us Cannot Be Wrong."[7] This song is conscious self-parody, taking to an extreme the easy image-making of the central verses of "Master Song" and ending with an outrageous hoarse screaming of what might have been a beautiful la-la chorus. But given the tone of parody, the third verse is still an interesting version of the "saint" image:

> I heard of a saint who had loved you
> So I studied all night in his school
> He taught that the duty of lovers
> Is to tarnish the golden rule
> And just when I was sure
> That his teachings were pure
> He drowned himself in the pool
> His body is gone
> But back here on the lawn
> His spirit continues to drool.

As I commented in the Introduction, tarnishing the golden rule is the project of all Cohen's saints; there is also the familiar sexual triangle, and the self-destruction of the saint figure. Only the absurdity of the final rhyme dissolves the image into laughter.

The saint figure is more seriously used in the two songs — "Sisters of Mercy" and "Suzanne" — which pull together the themes of the album. Both are concerned with saints and disciples, with strangers and shelters, but for the harsh abrasiveness of the teaching songs they substitute the emotional warmth of the love songs. Both are songs of resolution and renewal; both perform the therapeutic function of healing dissension and pain.

"Sisters of Mercy" presents the saint figure (plural this time, and with religious associations in the name) as bringing comfort to the singer at an extreme point of his existence, a point where "I thought that I just can't go on." Their mercy is not for him alone, and about sharing them he has no hesitation — "I hope you run into them soon" — or jealousy — "We weren't lovers like that / And besides it would still be all right." The "you" addressed (the inevitable third party) is someone who "must leave everything that you cannot control," from the social trappings of "family" right through to "your soul," the deepest sense of self. In other words, here we have again the isolated "stranger," the "travelling lady," with "one hand on my suicide." When that isolation is not redeemed by "feeling holy," then "your loneliness says that you've sinned." It is at this point of desolation that the sisters of mercy enter.

The "comfort" they bring is associated, as I have already pointed out, with the therapeutic value of song. Unlike the dubious comfort offered by Marianne, or the various fake "shelters" of "The Stranger Song," this gift is presented by Cohen without reservations. (Significantly, "Sisters of Mercy" is the one song that does not work in *McCabe and Mrs. Miller*. Altman tries to use it ironically, and the song will not support that intention.) Indeed, in the most beautiful lines of the song, Cohen's image for their gift is the central image from *Beautiful Losers* of love and renewal: "If your life is a leaf / That the seasons tear off and condemn / They will bind you with love / That is graceful and green as a stem."

This process of renewal and reintegration, sketched briefly in "Sisters of Mercy," is developed in full in "Suzanne." Suzanne is cast in the saint's role, which is reinforced by the structural parallel to (almost identification with) Jesus.[8] The "you" of the song (generalized, sex unspecified) is in the position of disciple.

"Suzanne takes you down," the first words of the song, immediately suggest that the experience of encountering the saint will be one of descent, into a reality which is in some ways darker and more uncertain than "normal" life. This direction is reinforced by the images of the "river" (flowing, changing, never at rest), "half crazy" (the anti-rational stress again — though anyone who is half crazy is also half sane), and the exotic "tea and oranges / That come all the way from China."[9] The disciple enters this world hesitantly and uncertainly, meaning "To tell her / That you have no love to give her." But the saint forestalls this response: instead, "she gets you on her wavelength," a phrase which depicts a moment of instinctive empathy in an image which combines the suggestions of a radio (the medium of pop songs, the "machinery" of *Beautiful Losers*) with the literal waves of Suzanne's river. It is in fact the river itself, not Suzanne, which gives the answer "That you've always been her lover," dissolving time sequence. The unity of the saint, her disciple, and her element is now complete.

The repeated chorus of the song stands slightly back from the intensity of the verses, as a kind of commentary. It expresses the disciple's desire for unity, and this unity is embodied in the almost interchangeable use of the personal pronouns "she, he, you," and in the touching of body and mind, which also switches easily between "*you*'ve touched *her* perfect body with *your* mind" and "*she*'s touched *your* perfect body with *her* mind." (My emphasis.) The project is one of travelling blind, not knowing where you are going, and this demands "trust" from all parties: "you know that she will trust you," "you think maybe you'll trust him," "you know you can trust her."

The river/wave image is picked up in the second verse in the image of Jesus watching from "the lonely wooden tower" of his cross; his own experience on the cross is one of suffering and death, and it is only through such an experience that others can approach him. Knowing, then, that "only drowning men could see him," he attempts to extend his charity by decreeing that "All men shall be sailors then." But again we have the image of the breaking of a religious system: the grace of Suzanne and Jesus stems not from their power but from their powerlessness. Jesus himself is "'broken" by "your wisdom"; that is, by the so-called wisdom of his followers, who have codified grace into a system. He himself still dies "forsaken" and "almost human," but (like the inhabitants of the room in "You Have the Lovers") not quite. In fact, it is only because Jesus is "broken" that the possibility of trusting him exists.

Up to this point, the song has pursued the theme of the destruction of the saints, but in its third verse it presents, perhaps more convincingly than anywhere else in Cohen, the transcendence of that destruction. The song returns to Suzanne, who has now absorbed the religious dimension to become "our lady of the harbour." The phrase recalls the titles of the Virgin Mary; "harbour" not only presents that area of a port city which is most broken and desperate but also forms the culmination of all the images of "shelter." As "the sun pours down like honey" around her, Suzanne offers her comfort, and this song. In her function as teacher (but much more gently, lovingly than the other teachers of the album), "she shows you where to look / Among the garbage and the flowers."[10] And there we find the children "leaning out for love."

This is a slightly ambiguous image. Does the fact that "they will lean that way forever" imply that they are *never* going to be satisfied in their search, or that they will *always* be receiving love, like flowers leaning to the sunlight? Does Suzanne's "mirror" offer only their own sterile reflection, or is it the door to magic, the opening into love? Given the general tone of the song, the emotional mood of the music, and the recurrence of the chorus in its most positive form, I think we have to understand the positive side of these ambiguities. If so, "Suzanne" becomes a song of triumph, a song in which all the loneliness and pain of the beautiful loser is transmuted into joy. If any song can, as Cohen "foolishly" believes, heal the pain and the dissension, then that song is "Suzanne."

(ii) *Songs from a Room* (1969)

Songs from a Room is Cohen's most accomplished album. It contains some of his best songs, and the musical arrangements are ideally suited to his voice. One possible exception is "Bird on the Wire," in which the tune demands a richer, more full-voiced treatment than Cohen is able to give it.[11] But this very failure underlines the success of the other songs, which call for a gentle, understated treatment. Even one song not by Cohen himself, "The Partisan," responds brilliantly to his subdued singing of it. The arrangements are much simpler than on the first album, apart from one flourish on "A Bunch Of Lonesome Heroes"; even the female backing vocals are used only for the French choruses of "The Partisan." Most of the time Cohen is working perfectly within his limitations, and the quiet mournfulness of his voice establishes the emotional mood for the album.

The songs are also much shorter than on the first album and less pyrotechnical in their imagery. They do not show off Cohen's ability to pile phrases on top of each other; rather, they are concise, economical, and condensed. At times this condensation makes them cryptic and elusive, but at the same time it moves them closer to true songs. These words need their music; without it, they are tenuous and incomplete.

The songs are all about losers, about the lonely, the deserted, the betrayed, the sacrificed, the forgotten, but instead of approaching the idea of losing with the kind of fierce exultation apparent in *Beautiful Losers,* Cohen here treats it with compassion, with sadness, with empathy, and with love. The songs on this album do not feature the masters and the saints; they are with the losers, and Cohen sees himself as one of them. There is no implied arrogance; he too is "a broken man" trying in his way to be free. This is the slaughterhouse, and he is waiting with the lamb.

The emotional mood of the album is best expressed in the chorus of "The Old Revolution": "Into this furnace I ask you now to venture / You whom I cannot betray." These lines might be taken to be addressed by Cohen to his audience: the "furnace" is the total vision expressed in all his work. Here its harshness and its cruelty are recognized, but rather than *demanding* that we *enter,* as he does in *Beautiful Losers,* Cohen *asks* us to *venture,* and he pledges his own commitment. He does not stand back from the furnace; he is part of it too.

This theme is continually expressed in the verses of the song. The singer tells us "I finally broke into the prison / I found my place in the chain." Participating in the destruction, and no longer able to rejoice in it as when he was "very young," now Cohen "can't pretend I still feel very much like singing." Breaking down all of his systems ("To all of my architects let me be traitor"), he confesses that "I myself gave the order / To sweep and to search and to destroy." If there is suffering and misery, he is not merely part of it, he is responsible.

The suffering is seen not in the intensely personal manner of earlier works but in a more general, social setting: the song uses the imagery of armies, war and revolution. The revolution is the "old" one: the one that is always going on, in one form or another; the revolution of the poor against the rich, or of the body against its mortality. The "brave young men" wait to fight for an ideal, but they are betrayed; the signal will be lit by "some killer" (Cohen himself, as his confession tells us) "for pay." The cause is doomed, and their bodies can only be carried away.

Out of this suffering, Cohen turns to the "you" of the song: other victims, who have "started to stutter," who are fed by false ideals ("You who are kings for the sake of your children's story"), and who are now "broken by power." All he can tell them is that the social order has collapsed — "The hand of your beggar is burdened down with money" — and that he shares the disaster with them — "The hand of your lover is clay." All he can give them is the pledge that he himself will no longer betray them as they venture into destruction. "The Old Revolution" is a magnificent song — along with "Suzanne," probably Cohen's best — and it points to what is most essential in this album: a sense of suffering shared in compassion and sorrow rather than intensified and celebrated.

In the same way, "Story of Isaac" takes up the image of the sacrificial victim and cautions against its glorification. The first two verses present the early part of the story in concise and vivid images ("The trees they got much smaller / The lake a lady's mirror") which depict the gradual falling away of the normal social world as father and son approach the isolation of the sacrificial mountaintop. As Cohen reaches the climax of the story he breaks off his narrative and becomes directly didactic. "You who build these altars now / To sacrifice these children / You must not do it any more." The reason, very significantly within Cohen's work, is that "A scheme is not a vision." Abraham's action was inspired by total faith, and his faith was rewarded by Grace; his hand trembles not with fear but with "the beauty of the word." (In the version on *Live Songs,* Cohen stresses the word "beauty" by repeating it.) But for those who have never known such faith, who "never have been tempted / By a demon or a god," there are no visions but only schemes or systems, and systems are deadly; they make men "stand above" their children with "hatchets blunt and bloody."

In this context, Cohen finds himself forced into the position of the soldier: at best, "I will kill you if I must / I will help you if I can," or at worst, "I will help you if I must / I will kill you if I can."[12] The image of the soldier is very important in Cohen's songs (he later named his backup group "The Army"), but the soldier is never seen as the aggressive victor. Rather, he is usually on the losing side, often betrayed in his ideals, an expendable part of a system he does not understand. In the closing lines, Cohen asks for "mercy on our uniform," and ends the song with the sudden, chilling image of the peacock spreading its fan. Again, the live album clarifies the intention here: the word "mercy" is repeated, and the fan is described as "deadly."

The soldier image is stated most strongly in a song which is not in fact by Cohen himself: "The Partisan," by Anna Marly. It presents a resistance fighter in an unspecified war, fighting a guerilla action against an invading army.[13] In some ways, he is a typical Cohen figure, a loser who has given up everything: "I took my gun and vanished . . . I have changed my name so often / I've lost my wife and children . . . There were three of us this morning / I'm the only one this evening." His fate is summed up in the phrase "The frontiers are my prison." This is the aspect of the song which Cohen's singing emphasizes: although the ending is hopeful — "Freedom soon will come / Men will come from the shadows" — Cohen's voice remains subdued, resigned to fate. His partisan is bound to his suffering and to his loneliness; the song treats this with sympathy but no false hope. It is a lament, not a revolutionary call to arms.

Soldiers also appear in one of the most puzzling songs on the record, "A Bunch of Lonesome Heroes." It is puzzling partly because the compression of the words obscures certain connections (it is not clear, for instance, what relation the lines beginning "Put out your cigarette, my love" bear to the rest of the song), and partly because the tone seems more ironical than in any other song on the album. "A bunch of lonesome heroes" seems like a standard Cohen image, though the word "bunch" is unusually flippant, but the first line complicates the response by adding the adjective "quarrelsome." The soldiers are sitting smoking, isolated from each other by the night "very dark and thick between them," and each one carrying "his ordinary load." One of them proposes to tell his story "before I turn into gold"; the image comes from the "The Cuckold's Song,"[14] where, it will be remembered, the first stage of turning into gold is to turn into clay.

But the isolation continues — "no-one really could hear him" — and Cohen makes the comment "I guess that these heroes must always live there / Where you and I have only been." The tone sounds ironic, directed against the concept of heroism, and again identifying Cohen with those who are not heroes, but the soldiers in the songs are never conventional "heroes," and the irony's target is not clear. Now follow the lines beginning "Put out your cigarette, my love," demanding "to hear what it is you've done that was so wrong." Perhaps they are addressed to the soldier who is smoking, but the context does not prepare for this. Nor is there any answer to the question; Cohen turns instead to dedicate the song to "the crickets . . . the army . . . your children . . . all who do not need me." Then the song closes by repeating the young soldier's appeal to tell his story. The individual images in the song are very striking, but they do not hang together. Musically, it feels like the other soldier songs, but an examination of the words only raises more questions than it can answer. The song remains intriguing but inconclusive.

In "The Butcher," the imagery moves from a general to a more personal suffering. The song starts with the slaughtering of a lamb, recalling "Stories of the Street," but when Cohen accuses the butcher he replies, "I am what I am / And you, you are my only son." As in "The Old Revolution," Cohen sees himself as sharing the responsibility and guilt on a personal level, and it is on this level that he seeks an answer. The second verse describes a drug experience which provides only a limited and insufficient relief; the third verse responds with bitter irony to the hopefulness of "some flowers growing up / Where the lamb fell down"; the fourth verse appeals "Do not leave me now / I'm broken down." Again, "The Butcher" is an understated song; the misery is there, but it is muted, and the song ends in an appeal for help and sympathy.

This sense of desolation is continued in "You Know Who I

Am," another of the album's enigmatic songs. The verses describe a negative and hopeless relationship: "I cannot follow you my love / You cannot follow me / I am the distance you put between / All of the moments that we will be." The demands the singer makes are uncertain and contradictory: sometimes he regards the woman mechanistically—"I need you to carry my children in"—and sometimes savagely—"I need you to kill a child." But he also comes to her as "one broken man" whom her love can "repair"—except that she needs to be taught how to do it by him. The verses, then, are confused, despairing and abrasive, and the chorus does not resolve any of this. "You know who I am," the singer claims, but the implications are never clear to the listener. "You've stared at the sun," the line immediately following, could imply that the singer *is* the sun, but it also suggests a dazzled and partially blinded vision. The only redeeming note is that the singer claims to be "the one / Who loves changing from nothing to one," which is at least a positive direction.

Like "A Bunch of Lonesome Heroes," this is a song which never fully emerges from obscurity. But it is clearly very deeply felt: it is repeated on *Live Songs* with a magnificently ominous musical setting, and is the most powerful piece on that album. The later version makes one change in the words: on the repetition of the first verse, it substitutes for the last two lines: "I am not life, I am not death / I am not slave or free." This negative sense of non-being, of almost complete dissolution, dominates the song.

It is from the position of being "broken down" that "Bird on the Wire" begins. The images are again those of desolation and loneliness, and the song confesses guilt: "I have torn everyone who reached out for me." There is an attempt to justify the loneliness as "my way to be free," but this is tempered by the realization of the hurting involved: "But I swear by this song / And by all that I have done wrong / I will make it all up to thee." The live version accentuates this guilt: where the original says, "If I, if I have been untrue / I hope you know it was never to you," the self-justification of that second line is replaced by the further confession, "It was just that I thought a lover had to be some kind of liar too." Nevertheless, "Bird on the Wire" does point to a marginally more hopeful and positive resolution.

The defeatist advice of the "Beggar leaning on his wooden crutch" is countered by the more hopeful statement of the "pretty woman leaning in her darkened door." And for all its loneliness and confession, "Bird on the Wire" *is* a love song; the final repetition of "I have tried in my way to be free" is firm and hopeful.

The remaining songs on the album express a sense of love and renewal, but not in the grand, almost cosmic terms of "Suzanne." As befits this album, they are still gentle, muted, tentative, and tinged with sadness.

"Tonight Will Be Fine" has a jaunty and happy tune; it sounds like a love song, but the optimism is clearly limited. "Tonight will be fine" all right, but only "For a while."[15] The first verse speaks, albeit whimsically, of a division between the lovers; the second stresses the bare, lonely room; the third distances the experience by speaking only of memory and by shifting from the second to the third person in talking about the woman. "If I've got to remember" suggests the same desperate attempt to escape history as is found in *Beautiful Losers*. Still, within these limitations, something is offered — "If I've got to remember / That's a fine memory" — and the song attempts to hold on to it. The final chorus avoids the screaming deliberate ugliness of "One of Us Cannot Be Wrong," so it is the happiness of the tune which is left as the final impression of the song and of the record.

"Lady Midnight" starts in division and desperation, but it moves away. The singer is "looking for someone who had lines in her face": an ambiguous image, in that the lines could be the lines of sorrow or the lines of a song. When he finds her, "she scorned me and she told me / I was dead and I could never return." But the song works through this mourning, transcending the "darkness" in which "Stars eat your body and the wind makes you cold." The song refuses to rest in misery and self-pity — "'If we cry now,' she said, 'it will just be ignored'" — and instead asserts a joyful conclusion:

So I walked through the morning, the sweet early morning,
I could hear my lady calling, "You've won me, you've won me, my lord.
You've won me, you've won me, my lord.
Yes, you've won me, you've won me, my lord."

The assertion is made more convincingly in the music than in the words, but it is there.

The most beautiful of these songs, and one which is simultaneously joyful and sorrowful, is "Seems So Long Ago, Nancy." Nancy is the one figure from the songs on this album who might be seen as a saint. She is associated with love and with death, and she brings comfort to others: as Cohen looks back, he sees her performing the saint's role of intermediary. "I think she fell in love for us / In nineteen sixty-one." The specificity of the date carries an emotionally evocative charge and suggests that this is a very personal song.

The first image associates Nancy with the magic world of movies—"Looking at the late late show / Through a semi-precious stone"—but the stone is only semi-precious, and she is, always, alone. The group of friends who surround her are not "strong": they depend on her, but she has to live without their support. "She never said she'd wait for us / Although she was alone." Unknowingly, they fail her, and Cohen once again is implicated in the guilt for her suffering. But, through the grace and generosity of her love, she is able, like Suzanne, to bring them comfort and love: "Nancy wore green stockings"—a line which Cohen sings with great tenderness—"And she slept with everyone."

The source of her love is that, like the singer of the album's other songs, she participates in the destruction surrounding her: Nancy is dead, a suicide. This is never stated fully explicitly in the song, but the lines "A forty-five beside her head / An open telephone" certainly suggest it, and this interpretation is reinforced by the poem in *Parasites of Heaven,* "Nancy lies in London grass,"[16] and is made quite unmistakeable in the live version of the song, which substitutes "The morning had not come" for the first line of the first verse, and then "The morning would not come" for the first of the third. The "House of Mystery" in which "none of us would meet her" may now be identified not only with her love but also with her death. In one respect, the song is an elegy for Nancy, a sad and beautiful tribute to her strength and to her fragility, to her loving and to her dying. But the final verse transcends mourning: "now you look around you / See her everywhere." In the moments of desolation, the "hollow of the night / When you are cold and numb,"

Nancy's love is still there. The singer is now prepared to join her, in death, in love, in the House of Mystery where death and love are combined, and "She's happy that you've come."

In the same way as "Suzanne" unites and renews all the themes of the first album, "Nancy" is the culmination of the second. All its desperate and lonely characters are comforted by her; all its misery and destruction are joined in her death, and yet the song can still end with the word "happy." It is a song in which Cohen extends the full force of his love and compassion; as such, it (and the whole album) seem to me to offer the deepest and most humane vision in the whole of Cohen's work. The love in this song is the guarantee that Cohen will indeed not betray those who venture with him into the furnace.

(iii) *Songs of Love and Hate* (1971)

After the beauty and emotional depth of *Songs from a Room*, Cohen's third album is something of a disappointment. At best it is a divided and uneven collection; a couple of songs continue the themes and attitudes of the previous album, but the majority are throwbacks in style to an earlier period. Three of the eight songs are in fact old enough to be rejects from the first album: "Dress Rehearsal Rag" was one of the first Cohen songs to be recorded,[17] "Avalanche" appeared in *Parasites of Heaven* in 1966, and "Love Calls You by Your Name" is copyrighted 1967.[18] The arrangements are once more elaborate: "Avalanche" announces itself in a plethora of ominous strings, Cohen sings in his most pretentious voice, and the female backing vocals appear on almost every track. The songs are long, abandoning the concision of the second album to return to overly facile strings of images.

Thus a good half of the album is negligible, even though the songs have interesting premises. "Love Calls You by Your Name" presents a series of images of love entering at decisive moments "between" things: the balanced knife-edges of experience. But the impact is dissipated in such indulgent images as "You say they chained you to your fingernails / And you climbed the halls of fame," whatever that means. The song finally gets lost in its own elaborate rhyme-scheme.

"Sing Another Song, Boys" presents a characteristic Cohen

image of two hopeless lovers "wondering why they cannot have each other," but the imagery of the narrative is foolish and pointless. At the end Cohen, as if realizing this, breaks off — "let's sing another song, boys / This one has grown old and bitter" — and the sour singing of the final chorus provides a good illustration of what he means.

"Diamonds in the Mine" is presumably intended as a joke: the chorus parodies all sorts of pop and country-and-western songs, and Cohen sings it in his most outrageous growl. The third verse might be taken as a bitter attack on the feminist movement and its advocacy of abortion, but it is difficult to decide how seriously anything in this song could be meant. As a parody it is mildly amusing, and that's all there is to it.

"Avalanche" is a reasonable poem, but the musical setting overloads it. It presents the familiar images of the saint going through destruction, the master and the pupil changing roles. The song begins:

> I stepped into an avalanche
> It covered up my soul
> When I am not this hunchback that you see
> I sleep beneath the golden hill
> You who wish to conquer pain
> You must learn, learn to serve me well

The images of destruction continue, asserting that the suffering master is "at the center, the center of the world." As the song progresses, the interchangeability of the saint's and the disciple's experience is developed — "The crumbs of love that you offer me / They're the crumbs I've left behind / Your pain is no credential here / It's just a shadow, shadow of my wound" — so it is no surprise that by the end of the song the reversal of roles is complete — "I have begun to long for you" — and the identity of the two personalities established — "It is your turn, beloved / It is your flesh that I wear."

"Dress Rehearsal Rag" is another old song, this time focusing on the figure of the loser: a broken-down man in a cheap hotel room confronting his failure in the shaving mirror. The song describes the situation in relentless detail: "Don't drink from that cup / It's all caked and cracked around the rim / That's not the electric light, my friend / That is your vision that is growing dim." Memories of a former happiness only serve to increase the torment; the ironic transformation of the soap-lathered face into Santa Claus only results in instructions "where to hit" with the heroin needle or the suicide razor; the chorus devastatingly restates "It's come to this / Yes it's come to this / And wasn't it a long way down?" Cohen's singing is harsh and abrasive: on the final chorus he heavily underlines the puns implicit in "stand-in *stunt* man" and "dress re*hearsa*l rag."

"Avalanche" and "Dress Rehearsal Rag" are certainly much better songs than the previous three, but on this album they seem curiously dated. What all these songs most obviously lack is the emotional mood of love, compassion, and shared suffering evident in *Songs from a Room*. "Avalanche" is the master/pupil game at its harshest; "Dress Rehearsal Rag" is sung more in contempt and derision than in sympathy. But that softer mood is present, partly, in "Last Year's Man," and in the two great songs of the album, "Famous Blue Raincoat" and "Joan of Arc."

Structurally, "Last Year's Man" begins and ends with a picture of its protagonist in his attic room; the three verses in between, which have only tenuous connections with each other, may perhaps be taken as his reflections. The protagonist is again a loser, perhaps a failed artist, and the lonely room in which he sits is the isolation of his impaired consciousness. He is an anachronism, last year's man. Rain falls on him through the skylight, which is broken like "a drum I'll never mend," an expressive power irrecoverably lost. He is, however, a man of broken systems: the "corners of the blueprint" are "ruined," because they have "rolled / Far past the *stems* of thumbtacks" (my emphasis). From these stems, and the shadows that they throw, something is still possible.

The first verse uses the soldier imagery of *Songs from a Room* and unites it with the figure of Joan of Arc, which is later expanded in a full song. "I met a lady, she was playing / With her soldiers in the dark / Oh one by one she had to tell them / That her name was Joan of Arc." Again, the soldiers are betrayed into destruction, fighting on the losing side. They become "wounded boys," and all that Joan can do is "lie beside" them. The emotional tone of this verse is very close to "The Old Revolution."

But the next two verses take off in an extravaganza of sexual and biblical imagery which seems deliberately extreme even by Cohen's standards. "Great Babylon was naked / Ah, she stood there trembling for me / And Bethlehem inflamed us both / Like the shy one at some orgy."[19] These rather strained images culminate in the statement "And we read from pleasant bibles / That are bound in blood and skin / That the wilderness is gathering / All its children back again." The verses are a sketch of that wilderness and its children: the wounded soldiers of Joan, the frenzied participants in Babylon's orgy, the women who wait for Jesus or for Cain. The song then returns to "last year's man." Cohen presents the potentiality still inherent in his loneliness: "But everything will happen / If he only gives the word / The lovers will rise up / And the mountains touch the ground." (The last two lines are emphasized by the chorus.) Despite this hopefulness, however, the song ends on the image, once more, of the broken skylight and the rain. Although the word could be given, it has not been given yet.

"Famous Blue Raincoat" is much more successful, and more obviously personal. It takes the form of a conversational, almost chatty letter, beginning with the date and place of writing, and signing off "Sincerely, L. Cohen."[20] The letter is addressed to a "you" whose sex is, unsurprisingly, unspecified. (One image, "with a rose in your teeth," suggests female, via the Carmen stereotype; but "you" is also addressed as "my brother.") Other characters are "my woman" and, not necessarily the same person, "Jane." The song takes place against a network of personal relationships which are never made fully explicit.

"You" is regarded with a certain amount of awe, and is seen in the role of the saint. He or she has built a house "deep in the desert" and is "living for nothing now." There are also associations from a kind of pop mythology: the "blue raincoat" is "famous," and he or she perpetually visits train stations. But the loser image is also present: the raincoat is "torn at the shoulder," and "You came home without Lilli Marlene." He or she is venerated like a saint, with relics — "Yes, and Jane / Came / By with a lock of your hair" — but Cohen feels it necessary to ask how absolute the saint's experience has been — "Did you ever go clear?"

Under the impact of this personality, the woman possessively described as "my woman" becomes "nobody's wife." In this respect the saint is to Cohen "my brother, my killer." Yet there is no conflict here; should the saint ever return, "for Jane or for me," Cohen knows that the part of himself that was "your enemy" is sleeping, and "his woman is free." In their complex relations, the lovers have moved beyond the simple jealousies of possessiveness. The song closes with a beautiful gesture of confession and gratitude. "Thanks for the trouble you took," it begins, then neatly turns and literalizes that conventional phrase by adding "from her eyes." Gratitude is due because, as Cohen "sincerely" confesses, "I thought it was there for good / So I never tried."

The character of "you" in this song remains, in the last resort, too undefined: the image is not as strong or as individual as those of Suzanne and Nancy. But Cohen's own emotion — the gentle loneliness of the beginning, the lovely gesture of friendship and thanks at the end — is beautifully stated, and the final "Sincerely" is surely meant genuinely and not ironically. The tune, soft and reflective, fits the mood perfectly, and the song also features one of Cohen's most successful uses of backing voices.

The most interesting song on this album is "Joan of Arc." The image of Joan of Arc seems ideally suited for Cohen — a martyred saint, whose career carries strange sexual overtones — but the song does not celebrate her destruction. For the most part, the tone is distantly, almost bitterly, ironic. Joan is presented as someone who wants to get out of her role — "I want the kind of work I had before" — an ordinary, even foolish girl, who needs a man "to get her through this very smoky night." When she is seduced by "Fire," she is appallingly naive — "Then Fire, make your body cold / I'm gonna give you mine to hold" — and only at the last moment does she realize "If he was Fire, oh then she must be wood." Their union is not a glorious celebration: Fire claims only her "dust," and what he hangs "high above the wedding guests" is only "the ashes of her wedding dress."

The irony is directed against the whole concept of martyrdom, the beautiful loser, which the novel had so fiercely celebrated. Furthermore, the irony is specifically directed against the idea, not against Joan herself, because running through the song is a feeling of compassion for her. In *The Energy of Slaves,* Cohen writes "I am the ghost of Joan of Arc."[21] In the poem, he is again using the image ironically (as a threat, in fact), but again he feels the tragedy of Joan, "bitter / in the consequence of voices." In the song, this sympathy is expressed mainly in the chorus, a mournful la-la-la which runs in constant juxtaposition to the ironic verses.

The ambivalence of the total response is summed up in the last four lines (which are spoken as well as sung). The first two carefully balance the two elements of Joan's experience — "I saw her wince, I saw her cry / I saw the glory in her eye" — and the second two express Cohen's reaction — "Myself, I long for love and light / But must it come so cruel, and oh so bright?" These lines are a definitive measure of the difference in attitude between the novels and the songs. If *Beautiful Losers* had asked such a question at all, it would certainly have answered "Yes, it must come so cruel, it must come so bright." The song answers only

La la la La la la La la la la la la.

(iv) *Live Songs* (1973)

At first sight, *Live Songs* is a very odd album which looks as if it had been flung together more to satisfy a contractual require-ment than for any aesthetic reason. Of the ten songs on the al-bum, only two are new Cohen work. Of the remaining eight, five are previously recorded songs, one is a musical setting of a poem from *Flowers for Hitler* (1964), one is a (rather dull) instrumental, "Improvisation," and the other, "Passing Thru," is not by Cohen at all, even though the record blithely credits it to him. (It was in fact written by Richard Blakeslee, and has been recorded by Pete Seeger, among others.)

The front cover uses the same photograph as had already appeared on *The Energy of Slaves.* Whereas on the book it served the purpose of helping to define a "new" image, its use on this essentially retrospective album seems pointless. The back cover reproduces a piece of writing by one Daphne Rich-ardson (1939–1972). It is a poorly written piece of pretentious "mysticism"; whatever the writer's sincerity, she is entirely unable to express her perceptions in words of any precision or freshness. The only interesting phrase, "mad mystic hammering," is taken from Bob Dylan.[22]

But allowing for these oddities, *Live Songs* is in the end a rather interesting album which is a good deal more consistent and satisfying, as a unit, than *Songs of Love and Hate*. The first interesting point is Cohen's choice of songs to repeat. This is obviously not a "greatest hits" album but one where the selection has been made with a thematic point in mind. In the first place, all the repeated songs — "You Know Who I Am," "Bird on the Wire," "Nancy," "Story of Isaac," and "Tonight Will Be Fine" — are from *Songs from a Room*; the first and third albums are completely unrepresented. Secondly, the other pieces on the album — the two new songs, the poem "Queen Victoria," and even "Passing Thru" — all fit the mood and thematic stance of the repeated songs. If Cohen was under commercial pressure to produce a "live" recording, he used the opportunity to pass a judgement on his own work and to reassert the position of the second album.

In discussing *Songs from a Room*, I have already commented on some of the changes Cohen makes in the repeated songs. By and large, these changes are aimed at making the songs more explicit: the final images of "Story of Isaac" are elucidated, the confessional tone of "Bird on the Wire" is strengthened, the suicide references in "Nancy" are expanded. "You Know Who I Am" is given a brilliantly ominous arrangement with bass and organ; "Tonight Will Be Fine" becomes a jaunty country-and-western song with fiddles. Two new verses are added to "Tonight Will Be Fine," but they contribute very little to the song; indeed, by getting away from the single-room setting, they detract from it.

"Passing Thru" is a song of political and philosophical commentary, in a homespun manner. Cohen allows himself a cynical aside — "Oh the fool!" — on Roosevelt's idealism, but basically he seems to have chosen the song for its assertion that "we're all brothers and we're only passing through" and its advice to "Talk of love not hate."

The poem "Queen Victoria" fits in well with the general theme of the losers and the outcasts with their "incomparable sense of loss." As I mentioned in my previous discussion,[23] the poem is one where the harshness of Cohen's vision is mitigated by his real sympathy for the much-maligned character he is writing about. The musical setting is absolutely simple, and the text of the poem is sung intact except for one small cut.[24]

I have already quoted in full the "Minute Prologue," which states Cohen's view of the therapeutic function of his songs with an explicitness characteristic of the album. The other new "song" is "Please Don't Pass Me By," which is subtitled "A Disgrace." This is a long (almost fourteen minutes), rambling, semi-improvised piece which at times sounds like an evangelistic meeting, with Cohen preaching salvation to the crowds. The "disgrace" lies in the completeness with which Cohen lays himself bare, abandons the disguises of a symbolic style, and cajoles his audience into sharing his suffering. The style is certainly not graceful, and one feels a little uncomfortable about the degree to which the effects are consciously worked for, but by and large it must be taken as one of Cohen's most remarkable statements.

It starts with Cohen telling how he saw a blind man in New York wearing a placard which read:

> Please don't pass me by
> I am blind but you can see
> I've been blinded totally
> Please don't pass me by

These words become the chorus, sung in gospel style, which is repeated throughout Cohen's monologue, becoming more and more frenzied as time goes by. An especially strong emphasis is put on the word "totally."

Cohen starts by telling of seeing other "curious mutilations of the human form" until it seems as if "the whole city was singing" this appeal. At first he tries to think of it as something sung by "them, the other, someone else," but "as I moved along I knew it was me, and I was singing it myself." This is the first major theme of the song: that Cohen himself is part of the suffering he sees. This alternates with the second theme, which is the attempt to involve the audience, "deep in your velvet seats," in the same experience. The address to the audience is direct, hortatory, uncompromising. "I wanted to hurt you," Cohen tells them, and warns that they too will some day be singing the same song. "You'll be on your knees, and I want you to know the words when the time comes."

The song provides several lists of those for whom it is being sung, the losers unredeemed by beauty, the outcasts with whom Cohen is asserting his identity.

> I sing this for the Jews and the Gypsies
> and the smoke that they made
> And I sing this for the children of England
> their faces so crazed
> And I sing this for a Saviour
> with no one to save
> Hey won't you be naked for me
> Hey won't you be naked for me

Even more explicitly:

I sing this song for you blonde beasts
I sing this song for you Venuses upon your shells on the foam of the sea
I sing this for the freaks
and for the cripples
and for the hunchbacks
and for the burned
and for the burning
and for the maimed
and for the broken
and for the torn
and all of those that get talked about
at the coffee table
at the meeting
at the demonstration
on the street
in your music
in my songs
I mean the real ones who are burning
I mean the real ones who are burning

The song continues with its exhortation of the audience: "You're going to get down on your knees," Cohen tells them, hypnotically repeating the phrase eight times. Then he turns to his own position, listing the things he has: his songs, his poems, his books, the Army (i.e. his group), "your applause," "some money." But still, he says, "I'm out there on the corner" with the freaks, the hunted, the maimed, the torn, the down.

The song works to its climax as Cohen tries to go even farther. "Take away my dignity," he appeals:

> Take my dignity
> Take my form
> Take my style
> Take my honour
> Take my courage
> Take my time

Finally, he appeals to his audience to "go home with someone else. Don't be the person that you came with. . . . I'm not going to be, I can't stand him! I can't stand who I am!" As a gesture of destruction against his own style, against his own cult persona, this is far more effective than anything in *Flowers for Hitler*. The roughness and embarrassing abrasiveness of the song are doing the very things it appeals for. But throughout this breakdown, this disgrace, the chorus continues its appeal for sympathy, for the suffering to be not transcended but simply shared. "Please don't pass me by." The statement was perhaps made with greater subtlety and grace on *Songs from a Room,* but scarcely with greater power.

This rather favourable view of *Live Songs* is a product of hindsight. When the album was first released, its retrospective nature and its lack of much new material seemed a kind of epitaph on Cohen's career as a songwriter. The "disgrace" of "Please Don't Pass Me By" could be taken as a confession that Cohen was all burned out, he had nothing left to say. In the five years after *Songs from a Room,* Cohen the songwriter produced practically nothing (except "Famous Blue Raincoat" and "Joan of Arc") of any value. It was therefore all the more remarkable that, at the end of 1974, he returned to the form with the energy, subtlety, inventiveness, and mastery evident in *New Skin for the Old Ceremony.*

CHAPTER FIVE

Postscripts and Preludes

*"It may not always look like it, but I know
what I'm doing."*
(*Leonard Cohen,* The Toronto Star,
January 22nd, 1975)

The decade stretching from *The Spice Box of Earth* in 1961 to
Songs from a Room in 1969 marks the most prolific and confident period of Leonard Cohen's career. The 1970s, in contrast,
have been marked by a sporadic and hesitant production of
works which do not yet fall into any significant pattern.

In a recent poem,[1] one of Cohen's many exercises in self-
denigration, he writes, "Lost my voice in New York City / never
heard it again after sixty-seven." The "voice" that Cohen lost
was the confident, self-assured voice of his early writing, and its
"loss" has been reflected in an increasing hesitancy about publishing anything at all, and, in the work that has appeared, in
an apparent obsession with the pose of the anti-poet. Of all the
work to appear in the seventies, only *New Skin for the Old
Ceremony* (1974) stands out as a really satisfying and complete
accomplishment.

Cohen has continued to perform and record his songs, but
even here the tone of uncertainty persists. *Songs of Love and
Hate* (1971) was, I have argued,[2] at best uneven, and *Live
Songs* (1973) was interesting mainly in a retrospective sense and
for the grand self-destructive gesture of "Please Don't Pass Me
By." *The Greatest Hits* album of 1975 contained no new songs
at all, though the album-cover notes offered intriguing asides

on the old ones. Cohen was still performing occasionally, with great vigour — I heard him at the Olympia in Paris, in June 1976, where he drew no less than a dozen encores from a wildly enthusiastic audience — but his program consisted mainly of old songs. Then in 1977, he issued *Death of a Ladies' Man,* which the production by Phil Spector turned into yet another self-destructive gesture as Cohen surrendered artistic control to a musical arrangement totally opposed to the values of his songs.

In terms of published works, the decade since the *Selected Poems* of 1968 can show only one volume, *The Energy of Slaves* (1972), and that volume is largely dedicated to the assertion that "I can't write a poem anymore."[3] In a later interview (1975), Cohen had a more interesting comment on *The Energy of Slaves*: "It was like dipping all the parts into tetrachloride to clean them — I wanted to get back into my own baroque from a clean position."[4]

Some indication of what this new "baroque" might consist of was given in the same interview:

> I'm writing a lot of things, but they're all going into one massive book — novelistic passages, poems, journal entries. It's called *The Woman Being Born.* The poems are invocations to create the woman. . . . I want it to be like a reference book, something with a friendly presence that you can keep by the bedside and dip into anywhere. It'll even have appendices of things like love letters and journal material from other ages. It's the kind of book I've always wanted to have on my shelf, to consult from time to time like the *I Ching.* I don't expect everyone to love it. But it will document a certain kind of sensibility.[5]

Then in the spring of 1977, McClelland and Stewart announced the publication of a new book, to be called *Death of a Lady's Man.* (All the early references to it have "lady's" as singular; when the record eventually appeared, "ladies' " was in the plural.) Publication was delayed to the fall, and then Cohen withdrew the MS for further revision. I wrote to Cohen, asking him about the relationship between *Death of a Lady's Man* and *The Woman Being Born,* and he replied, in July 1977, "*Death of a Lady's Man* derives from a longer book called *My Life in Art,* which I finished last year and decided not to publish. *The Woman Being Born* was the title of another manuscript and also an alternative title for both *My Life in Art* and *Death of a Lady's Man.*"[6] Furthermore, "Death of a Lady's / Ladies' Man" is also the title for the new album, though only the title song comes from the book MS.

It is clear, then, that a large body of interlocking material is still coming together. I speculate that Cohen has not yet found the form with which to fix and focus his new writing in the way that the fictional situation (however tenuous) of *Beautiful Losers* provided a form for its concerns. The idea of the *I Ching* as a formal model is interesting but contains the obvious danger of complete open-endedness.

This danger is apparent in the early drafts of *Death of a Lady's Man,* which one critic has described, unkindly but not entirely inaptly, as "prose poems that are confessional about nothing in particular."[7] The draft which I have seen contains many flashes of brilliance—especially the "Advice to Some Actors" on how to read poetry—but as a whole it suffers from a lack of specific reference. All the impassioned pleas to dozens of different and nebulous women, the anguished confessions, the cascades of surrealist imagery, need a context—otherwise the writing just goes round in circles, trapped inside its patterns of images. *Death of a Lady's Man* is, as far as I can tell at the moment, a more positive book than *The Energy of Slaves,* less obsessed with the anti-poet stance, back in some measure to the old "baroque." But Cohen's continual delays and revisions indicate that he too finds something deeply unsatisfactory about it.

This very hesitance and uncertainty may in fact be the most important aspect of Cohen's work in the seventies. In contrast to the continuous and confident publishing of the sixties, we have one book of anti-poems, five years of silence, and then this heterogeneous collection of MSS that are continually being revised. Whereas in the sixties Cohen was asserting his vision with uncompromising certitude, the seventies have seen him questioning and undercutting his own role as poet, to the point where withdrawing a MS from publication becomes a more significant gesture than publishing it.

On the other hand, it is always possible that Cohen will be able to put together a single cohesive volume which will define the concerns of a second phase of his work as centrally and as completely as *Beautiful Losers* did the first. Until we can see the final form of the new MSS, any judgements on the work of the seventies (such as this chapter) must of necessity be provisional and premature.

(i) *The Energy of Slaves* (1972)

A new face stares out from the back cover.[8] Brushcut, up against the wall, smoking a famous cigarillo, lots of hair on his fore-arms: another mask of Leonard Cohen. "You can call me Len or Lennie now," he invites us (112). It's all over. "The poems don't love us anymore" (117).

These attributes of the book's presentation — the choice of cover photograph, the lines which just sit up and beg to be quoted in negative reviews — point towards the most important aspect of *The Energy of Slaves*: its overall stance or tone. The lack of individual titles on most of the poems also encourages a response to the book as a whole, as one long sequence of poems. The scope of the book is larger than the individual poem, and it can accommodate good poems as well as some blatantly bad ones. The book is dominated by an emotional tone and stance which override the reader's response to any one part of it.

That tone is basically one of disgust, especially self-disgust. The poems are headed by the silhouettes of razor blades: some are sharp and some are dull, but they are all aimed at Cohen's own wrists. The book is an assault on his own image as "the sweetest singer I could imagine" (88): it is deliberately ugly, offensive, bitter, anti-romantic.

Some critics have simply taken Cohen at his word, and agreed with him when he says, "I have no talent left / I can't write a poem anymore" (112). But this is too easy a response, for *The Energy of Slaves* is a carefully crafted book; Cohen has too good an ear not to be aware of the prosaic sound of some of the poems and the crassness of others. When, for instance, he presents one of his women as a dumb TV-addict — "I loved to creep up behind her / when she was engrossed in Star Trek / and kiss her little ass-hole" (85) — and ends the poem with the self-consciously arch line "(I do not think she minded my pranks)," the tone makes it impossible to take the poem at face-value. Cohen is simply not that stupid. The poem has to be directed against his own sexist image, with an irony so understated that it emerges only in the deliberate crassness of the language. Whatever the poem does or does not say about the woman, it is surely inviting our disgust at the poet.

One of the strongest attacks on *The Energy of Slaves* comes from Tom Wayman, in a review article in *Canadian Literature*.[9] In extremely forceful and witty terms, Wayman attacks the book's views on women ("discussed in terms of their usefulness to the poet for sticking something into the holes that they have and are") and politics ("some whimpering that is either for or against the vague idea of revolution.") Much of what he says is undeniably true, but I think he fails to give Cohen the benefit of the doubt, namely, that Cohen himself is aware of these shortcomings. Wayman's arguments are in a sense irrelevant, in that they miss the point that *The Energy of Slaves* is not primarily about women and politics but about Cohen himself, and about Cohen's disgust with his own sexual and political position.

A poem such as the following —

> I did not know
> until you walked away
> you had the perfect ass
> Forgive me
> for not falling in love
> with your face or your conversation
> (21)

— is offensive, and obviously a bad poem. Why then does Cohen include it? Part of the reason is that Cohen is once again trying on the mask of anti-poet. "Take my dignity," he is appealing again. "Take my style."[10] As in *Flowers for Hitler*, he is attempting to destroy the image of the "golden-boy poet" and move into "the dung pile of the front-line writer"; again he is openly inviting the response, "this is derivative, this is slight, his power has failed."[11] "I am now broken down," he claims (65), "no leader of the borning world, no saint for those in pain, no singer, no musician, no master of anything, no friend to my friends, no lover to those who love me." It would be difficult to envisage a more concise and comprehensive rejection of his old roles. He would like to destroy his fame; he would like it to be true that "nobody's gonna notice / if I never write again" (88).

Much of the book is therefore an attempt to reject his past. The language is plain and direct: no lush exotic images, no flights of surrealism. The rhythms of many of the poems are flat and prosaic. In "The progress of my style" (52), he remembers his style's old "beauty," but claims that now, "I can't get off on it / I have no altar for my song." His own fame is the subject of sour humour. A "drunk" poet with "some notion of poetry," he "wonders what / he will write next," and can come up only with a few lame and inconclusive phrases: "Three nights at the Hilton / a girl with round buttocks / suntanned and cheerful, fourteen, Athens" (99). More playful, but no less ironic, is the infamous

> the 15-year-old girls
> I wanted when I was 15
> I have them now
> it is very pleasant
> it is never too late
> I advise you all
> to become rich and famous
> (97)

Here the disgust is modified, but only slightly, by the open enjoyment of the humour.

None of this, however, escapes from the paradox of the so-called anti-poem. The more Cohen protests that he cannot write poems any more, the less he is to be believed. Either the poems are deliberately bad (which is a form of aesthetic control), or else, like "The poems don't love us anymore" (117), they are rhetorically impressive. Either way, they work only to persuade us that Cohen's self-disgust is simply an inverse form of his egotism, and that the self is still the obsessive subject of his true poetry.

The paradox is best shown in one striking and beautiful poem:

> I was lost
> when I met you on the road
> to Larissa
> the straight road between the cedars

> You thought
> I was a man of roads
> and you loved me for being such a man
> I was not such a man
>
> I was lost
> when I met you on the road
> to Larissa
>
> (50)

The disavowal of the role of "man of roads" is all very well, but, though the poet professes to be "lost," he still knows where the road is going. Perhaps more honest is the one poem in the collection which still speaks of poetry as a function of divinity and beauty: "I make this song for thee / Lord of the World / who has everything in the world / except this song" (40).[12]

However, if we refuse to take Cohen completely seriously when he says, "I am no longer at my best practising / the craft of verse" (24), we must take seriously the tone of self-disgust, for in whatever form it is the central statement of the book. The "anti-poet" is only one aspect of a more general nausea. The poem quoted above continues, "I do better / in the cloak-room with Sara / But even in this alternate realm / I am no longer at my best."

Wayman is perfectly right to say that the women in *The Energy of Slaves* are dehumanized and boring. But Cohen presents himself, in his own relations to them, as no less dehumanized and boring. There are no poems about women in this book which have the emotional depth of the songs: no portraits of a Nancy, or a Suzanne. Suzanne is, in fact, explicitly dismissed:

> I blame it on me and Suzanne
> the death of poetry
> and the fucking torture that preceded it
>
> The whole world told me
> to shut up and go home
> and Suzanne took me down
> to her place by the river
>
> (107)

Again, the tone is one of bitterness and self-disgust. "O darling," one poem begins, and immediately adds, "(as we used to say)"

(111). "Why don't you come over to my table / with no pants on," he sneers to another woman; "I'm sick of surprising you" (82). Sex has become a boring game played by banal people; the tone here is one almost of loathing.

In this mood of self-disgust, Cohen presents himself as consumed by an obsessive jealousy (27), an emotion almost entirely alien to the rest of his work. He sees himself reduced to animalistic terms: his prayers have been debased to "Let me have her" (106) or "give her to me and let me be for a moment in this miserable and bewildering wretchedness, a happy animal" (65). Attraction to a woman's "hurt" imprisons him in animality: "You throw me food / and change my dirt" (89). The lightest version of this mood that he is capable of is this amusing prose piece:

> — I don't know what to call it, he said.
> — Call it your friend.
> — My friend.
> She held it, not as tightly as he wanted.
> — God, it looks so archaic, she said.
>
> (38)

But even here a certain sour disgust underlies the humour. The attempt to view sexuality in the human terms of "friend" (a word continuously used in *Beautiful Losers*) now seems "archaic."

Attempting, then, to reject his roles as saint and master, poet and lover, Cohen seeks once more to align himself with the losers, with the slaves. The most interesting aspect of the book is the degree to which Cohen attempts to present his slaves in political terms. Cohen has never put any faith in political systems; the political feeling here is an aspect of Cohen's personal disgust rather than a genuine commitment to any revolutionary cause.

Wayman attacks the political poems for their vagueness and rhetorical generalization and attributes this flaccidity to Cohen's remoteness from any particular political party or action movement. "Once outside of one's own head," he writes, "where you are free to be vaguely 'revolutionary,' any thinker moving into the real world of people and their problems in present-day North America soon finds he or she has to tighten up mentally in both concepts and language. The sort of sloppy, generally anti-establishment sentiments Cohen's poems here sag into reek of the world of radical chic." [13] This is an accurate enough criticism, from the point of view of the kind of political poetry which Wayman himself so brilliantly writes, but again it is somewhat beside the point of what Cohen is trying to do. The book is not really concerned with actual political issues *out there*: it is describing a cathartic revulsion within Cohen's own consciousness.

"Welcome to these lines," the book opens. "There is a war on" (9). The war is seen both on the personal level and on the political level — the two in fact are as intimately connected as sex and religion were in previous works — and on both levels Cohen tries to stand with the slaves:

> To the men and women
> who own men and women
>
> those of us meant to be lovers
> we will not pardon you
> for wasting our bodies and time
> (66)

But the slaves are no longer content to be slaves: the war is on, the revolution has arrived. "You have many things on your mind," Cohen warns; "We think only of revenge" (58). In another poem he sees himself as "the angel of revenge" and dreams of torture: "This machine is rubber and metal / it fits over your body and you die slowly" (53). Cohen recognizes the link between his attempt to write the poetry of slaves and his attempt to renounce the role of poet. In the poem beginning "The poems don't love us anymore" (117), he claims that his work has "gone back into the world / to be with the ones / who labour with their total bodies." The rhetoric is at its most direct and impressive in the poem "Any system you contrive without us / will be brought down" (121), a statement of great power and dignity.

But the paradoxes remain. Do these poems really establish Cohen's right to make that kind of statement? What is the point, for instance, of renouncing the roles of master and saint if all you do is reappoint yourself "the angel of revenge"? Wayman's criticisms point to a continuing vagueness in the definition of the "we" who are slaves, especially the puzzling distinction between "slaves" and "employees" (95). Cohen himself sees the poems, in some unspecified manner, as a "way to betray / the revolution" (122), again indicating that the "revolution" in question is essentially an internal, personal one. "Slave" is not so much an objective political fact as a role in Cohen's private psychodrama.

The Energy of Slaves is a fascinating but limited book. It is fascinating to see Cohen struggling against the images he has made for himself, to see an accomplished poet beating his head against the brick wall of the "anti-poem," and to see an apolitical sensibility attempting to express its disease in political terms. But it is also limited, for one can only take so much self-disgust, one can only put up with so many bad poems unsuccessfully attempting to establish the notion that Leonard Cohen is a bad poet. The emotional force of the book is strong, but its range is narrow. One reads it with interest, but puts it aside with relief.

(ii) *New Skin for the Old Ceremony* (1974)

New Skin for the Old Ceremony[14] is Cohen's masterpiece of the seventies. It is immediately obvious that in it Cohen has again abandoned the anti-poet pretences of *The Energy of Slaves*. These songs are full of imaginative detail, a careful use of images, and control over varied moods and stances. Even the music is fuller, richer, and more expressive than in the immediately preceding albums. (Much of the credit for this must go to John Lissauer, whose arrangements are varied, imaginative, and well suited both to the songs and to Cohen's voice: everything, in fact, which Phil Spector's production of *Death of a Ladies' Man* is not.)

"Variety" is perhaps the key word for the album, for it is difficult to pin down any one central mood or thematic concern. If the album has a fault, it is that it is too scattered: the songs do not emotionally reinforce each other as those on *Songs from a Room* do. The variety of themes seems at times like a review of all Cohen's old attitudes; the songs are by turns tender and cynical, public and private, lucid and enigmatic. Even within an individual song, the mood will change (see especially "Field Commander Cohen") or remain unresolved. The record may not have the strength of a unified tone, but it certainly has the tension and energy of a continuously unpredictable one.

The album opens with a song which is rooted in the self-disgust of *The Energy of Slaves,* but which shows, by the exuberant inventiveness of its humour, the degree to which Cohen has advanced beyond this attitude. The chorus—"And is this what you wanted / To live in a house that is haunted / By the ghosts of you and me?"—comes in fact from *The Energy of Slaves,* where it acts as the inconclusive end to a confused poem.[15] Here, the lines are used as a sarcastic commentary on a relationship which is, in the verses, expressed in delightful and hilarious comedy. Cohen takes the basic idea—exalting the woman, debasing himself—and plays with it in a consciously outrageous way which is reminiscent of the most scandalous humour in *Beautiful Losers.* From "You were the promise at dawn / I was the morning after," he progresses to the comedy of "You were Marlon Brando / I was Steve McQueen. . . . You were the Whore at the Feast of Babylon / I was Rin Tin Tin." And yet the humour is never allowed to dissipate the seriousness of the situation. The third verse brings a characteristic reversal; it is Cohen the loser who is actually operating on a deeper level than the accomplished woman: "You defied your solitude / I came through alone." The song is able to use both the self-disgust and the humour as elements in a complex balance of emotion and tone.

The album continues with "Chelsea Hotel #2," a beautiful and deeply moving tribute to Janis Joplin. As Cohen explained to an audience in Paris, he and Joplin "fell into each other's arms by a process of elimination—which is the process everything happens by."[16] The specific reference returns the song to a level of emotional depth and complexity not reached by Cohen since "It Seems So Long Ago, Nancy." The setting starts out as one of bitter cynicism: the unrewarding sexuality which "was called love / For the workers in song / Probably still is for those of them left." Cohen presents himself and Joplin as losers, "oppressed by the figures of beauty," consoled only by the fix and by the knowledge that "We are ugly but we have the music." Janis, however, has broken out of the limited circle of dependence—"Oh but you got away / Didn't you babe"—and Cohen sings the song as a tribute to her. The ending—"I don't even think of you that often"—is an elaborately unnecessary disclaimer, a defence against sentimentality, which is belied by the intensity of emotion in the song.

The harshness of Cohen's voice and the compelling forward drive of the tune make "Lover Lover Lover" an urgent, almost a desperate statement. The singer feels himself imprisoned by his past, by his body and by his name, and longs for the chance to "start again" with "a spirit that is calm." But the past (his father, to whom this plea is addressed) returns the responsibility to him—"It was you who covered up my face"—and insists that he has the choice of using his body (and, by extension, the whole personal/historical situation in which he is inevitably placed) "for a weapon" or "to make some woman smile." Counterpointed to this dialogue is the singer's equally urgent appeal to his "lover" (the word repeated seven times) to "come back to me." In one sense, the song reaches no resolution, since the chorus's appeal is still being repeated at the end, but the final verse (which I have previously quoted)[17] suggests the therapeutic value of the song in resolving these tensions.

"Field Commander Cohen" is perhaps the most difficult song on the album, in that its changes of mood and style do not seem to fit together into any coherent pattern. It starts with an ironic look back at Cohen's surrealist phase. The reference to Fidel Castro evokes "The Only Tourist in Havana," and much of the language of *Flowers for Hitler* is parodied in "Silver bullet suicides, and / Messianic ocean tides, and / Racial roller-coaster rides / And other forms of boredom advertised as poetry." The song proceeds to a slightly jaundiced look at Cohen as a "favourite singing millionaire / The patron saint of envy / And the grocer of despair / Working for the Yankee Dollar." (There is a possible pun here between "grocer" and "grosser.") But juxtaposed to this depiction is the chorus, "I know you need your sleep now / I know your life's been hard / But many men are falling / Where you promised to stand guard." The "you" of the song is never precisely identified (a lover? Cohen's past selves?). The final verse appeals to him or her to "be your sweetest self a while" until the "other selves" take over in a vision of dark possibilities where "Every taste is on the tongue / Till love is pierced and love is hung." The song then fades out on the words "Oh, my love . . ." The effect is striking but confused: it is not at all clear how the song progresses from the flippancy of its opening to the disturbing emotion of its close.

"Why Don't You Try" finds Cohen in the slightly unusual role of an advocate for women's liberation. The song attempts to persuade a woman to break away from her dependence on a man, asking "Do you need his label for your baby?" The appeal is not wholly altruistic: Cohen himself would like to "take you to the ceremony," but he admits that he is no longer sure whether he remembers the way. Moreover, it seems unlikely that the circle will be broken: the couple, Jack and Jill, are too determined to "join their misery" for anyone to "put a loophole in their way." All this is presented in a beautiful and mellow tune, which (especially the woodwind solo at the end) produces a rather odd contrast to the mood of the words. The tune is more suited to the cheerful pragmatism of "this life is filled with many sweet companions / Many satisfying one-night-stands" than it is to the picture of the couple locked inside their self-perpetuating misery.

The second side of the record opens with "There Is a War," the album's most direct echo of *The Energy of Slaves* ("Welcome to these lines / There is a war on." [18]). The song uses the same generalized political vocabulary as the book: Cohen is not talking about any particular war but rather, in the broadest terms, about the war between the rich and poor, between men and women, between left and right, between black and white, between odd and even ("Let's all get even," he puns), and, most interestingly, "between the ones who say there is a war / And the ones who say that there isn't." The war, then, is essentially internal, a state of mind; it is in that sense that Cohen appeals, in mock-commercial terms, "Why don't you come on back to the war?"

The war is presented in a more unavoidably political context in "A Singer Must Die," a bitterly ironical song about the repression of artistic expression in the totalitarian state. Cohen adopts the role of the frightened and surrendering singer who is prepared to accept that "Your vision is right / My vision is wrong / I'm sorry for smudging / The air with my song." But the mournful voice underplays the irony, suggesting a sense of complicity, thus making the song more complex than a straightforward political statement. The singer's failure is linked to the woman he wishes he could "forgive," but with whom he is trapped "night after night after night." A variety of elements—his own sense of having really betrayed something as well as his simple fear of "Their knee in your balls / Their fist in your face"— leads him to his final statement: "long live the state / By whoever it's made / Sir, I didn't see nothing / I was just getting home late." One wonders how seriously Cohen intends this song as a criticism of his own political position; after all, few recent governments have insisted in more unambiguous terms than the Greek junta did that "A singer must die / For the lie in his voice."

The next song illustrates one small incident in the "war," this time on the personal level. "I Tried To Leave You" is about a man who wishes he could break away from a love affair but is continually drawn back into it. The final sentiment, however, is not bitterness. The first line of the last verse—"Goodnight, my darling, I hope you're satisfied"—could certainly be taken ironically, but the irony is countered by "The bed is kinda narrow, but my arms are open wide," which prepares for the moving simplicity of the final line, "And here's a man still working for your smile." For a moment Cohen succeeds in establishing and celebrating a working class of lovers.

"Who By Fire" is a brilliantly unsettling *memento mori.* The verses simply list possible ways of dying—(those) who (die) by fire, by water, and so on—while the chorus turns the pronoun "who" into an interrogative, asking "And who / Shall I say / Is calling?" The polite question evokes an image of a highly formal Death presenting his visiting card. The ominous mood is marvellously sustained by the backing vocals and the jerky strings arrangement.

By contrast, "Take This Longing" is one of Cohen's gentlest and most gorgeous love songs. It sets out the normal requirement of Cohen's lovers, that they be losers too—"your beauty," which is "broken down," is "lost to you yourself"—but the mood is one of great tenderness within the sorrow. The images are among Cohen's most elaborate but successful: "Hungry as an archway / Through which the troops have passed / I stand in ruins behind you / With your winter cloak, your broken sandal strap." The lovers come to each other with everything stripped away—"Let me judge your love affair / In this very room where I have sentenced mine to death"—but the song asserts that they can give each other comfort. "Untie for me your high blue gown," Cohen appeals, and, in some of the most lovely lines he has ever sung: "Take this longing from my tongue / All the useless things my hands have done / Let me see your beauty broken down / Like you would do for one you love."

This would be a beautiful note on which to end the album, but Cohen, characteristically, does not. Instead he sings the outrageous parody "Leaving Greensleeves" in his most cracked and ugly voice. "I sang my song, I told my lies / To lie between your matchless thighs." The words are angry, scornful, and cynical. Their anger, though, is directed mainly against false images of the lover and of the woman's beauty. The chorus in fact sees Greensleeves herself as a loser, deserted not only by her lovers but also by the artificial image of beauty which the classic song imprisons her in. "Greensleeves, you're all alone / The leaves have fallen, the men have gone / Greensleeves, there's no one home / Not even the Lady Greensleeves." The images have gone, and there is nothing left to do but sing in celebration of the desolation. While Cohen sings these lines in harsh desperation, the chorus sings them in a softer form, with lovely elaborations and grace notes to the tune. At the end of the song, the two modes—the chorus's romantic harmony and Cohen's anti-romantic discord—merge into a paradoxical and wholly characteristic unity.

(iii) *Death of a Ladies' Man* (1977)

The appearance of *Death of a Ladies' Man* [19] was accompanied by a series of interviews which revealed Cohen's great ambivalence about his collaboration with Phil Spector. "There's nothing I like about it," he told Janet Maslin for *The New York Times*;[20] "there are four seconds on the record that I think are music." He speaks of Spector's production as a "catastrophe" which allows no air for the songs to breathe; he admits that, because of the arrangements, "I wasn't able to convey the meaning of the songs," and the record "foundered in the realms of experiment and eccentricity."

On the other hand, and in the same interview, he claims

that the record may be a classic. "Like a lot of classics—somehow they're too dense, too boring. But they have some enduring power, and you know there's something excellent and strong about them. You just don't like them, that's all." To another interviewer[21] he praised the record's energy: "Play the record loud and the gift of energy is quite tangible. It's not a quiet record to sit by the record player with and lick your wounds. It's lusty and it's vital and it's right out there."

Maslin's article ends with a humorous balance of this ambivalent reaction to Spector: "'If the world hates it, I want it known that it's all his doing,' said Mr. Cohen, quite merrily. 'If the world loves it, 50–50.'"

This ambivalence is easy enough to understand. In many ways, *Death of a Ladies' Man* is the record that Cohen always wanted to make: considering all the references to 1950s pop music in *The Favourite Game,* and considering the detailed description of just such an overblown arrangement in the Gavin Gate and the Goddesses section of *Beautiful Losers,* who better than Phil Spector to realize Cohen's ideals of pop music? "This record," he told Maslin, "is in the area of extremism," and then added, in what for Leonard Cohen is hilarious understatement, "Sometimes that has its own appeal."

The problem, however, is that the whole drive and direction of Cohen's songs have been away from extremism. In introducing my discussion of the songs[22] I said that the limitations of Cohen's own voice imposed a different style on him, and that he could never sound like F. when he was singing. In *Death of a Ladies' Man,* that is exactly what he is trying to do. The result is, to say the least, bizarre, and one's first reaction is to laugh at the sheer incongruity between the fragility of Cohen's voice and the massive "wall of sound" with which Spector surrounds it.

Spector's style may be what Cohen always wanted, and sooner or later he had to try, but fundamentally it is wrong: wrong for the voice, wrong for the songs (most of them), and, in the last analysis, not particularly interesting in itself. It is certainly excessive—never use a single guitar when you can use twelve guitars, an organ, three drummers, strings, two saxophones, and a female choir—but it is also banal. (Cohen, of course, may have enjoyed it for precisely that reason.) But what is the point of having Bob Dylan and Alan (sic) Ginsberg singing back-up vocal (!) if you can't even make out their voices in the general din?

The style does work well on "Memories," a song in which both words and music are engaged in an open parody of 1950s teenage romance. As Cohen performs a *reductio ad absurdum* on the desires of the high-school gym dance—"Won't you let me see / Your naked body?"—Spector piles the crescendoes on top of each other until they cannot help but collapse under their own weight. There are some indications in Cohen's writing and singing—"In solemn moments such as this I have put my trust"—that he was trying to make the pop banality transcend itself, but Spector's production keeps it firmly on the level of parody. As the song interminably fades out, an old pop tune appears in the background, with one voice asking "Do you remember Frankie Laine?" and another answering "Yes I do, yes I do, yes I do. . . ."

Because of the element of parody, "Memories" is a song in which the music helps the words. The only other song in which this happens is "Iodine," where the bluesy, abrasive arrangement is just right for the words, even when it totally drowns them out. But for all the other songs, the music is at best neutral and at worst positively harmful, as in the simpering chorus of "I Left a Woman Waiting," or in the pointlessly long-drawn-out endings of "Paper-Thin Hotel" and "Death of a Ladies' Man" itself.

One's reaction to Phil Spector, then, may well be as ambivalent as Cohen's own. But what about one's reaction to Leonard Cohen? The first thing to notice is how much old material is being recycled. David Pyette describes "Death of a Ladies' Man" as "the only [song] for which Cohen had the lyrics down before meeting Spector,"[23] but this is simply not true; three out of the other seven songs have appeared, in whole or in part, in previous Cohen books.

"True Love Leaves No Traces" uses two out of the three verses of "As the mist leaves no scar," first published in *The Spice-Box of Earth* sixteen years earlier.[24] The additional verses contain some pleasant images—"Like arrows with no target / Like shackles made of snow"—but they do nothing to advance the old theme of the absence of scars, the lack of lasting commitment. The tune is quite catchy, but the tempo drags, and the song is a nullity.

"Fingerprints" appeared, in a slightly longer version, in *Parasites of Heaven* in 1966.[25] I described it above[26] as a not completely successful "restatement, in comic terms, of the scar motif of *The Favourite Game*." Here, it is given a lively country-and-western treatment which emphasizes its whimsy rather than its seriousness.

Finally, "I Left a Woman Waiting" is adapted from a poem in *The Energy of Slaves*.[27] But whereas the poem ends, "cruelly," on the very strong lines "Whatever happened to my eyes / happened to your beauty," the song softens and dissipates the impact by proceeding to a soppily romantic conclusion, in which the lovers are "Free as running water." This dissipation of intensity is exactly paralleled in the music, where the line "Whatever happened to my eyes" is spoken gravely and seriously, whereas "happened to your beauty" becomes part of a stupid, simpering chorus which destroys whatever impact the words had left.

Among the new songs, "Don't Go Home with Your Hard-On" is at least enjoyable, as a good dirty joke. To take it too seriously, as an expression of disgust at female sexuality, would be a mistake. It's lively and it's loud, and Dylan and Ginsberg are somewhere there in the background.

"Paper-Thin Hotel" is another statement of the theme of love as not involving lasting commitments or possessive jealousies. The singer is glad to hear that "love is out of my control." The tone is deliberately crude and clumsy — "the grunt of unity when he came in" — and the song belabours its point rather badly.

"Iodine" deals with another familiar Cohen theme, the close connection between beauty and pain, and provides memorable expression for it: "You let me love you till I was a failure / Your beauty on my bruise like iodine." As I have said before, the music is just right, and the result is one of the best songs on the album.

Even so, the overall impression from these songs is decidedly retrospective. Lines lifted from sixteen-year old poems; a parody of 1950s adolescence; a re-run of such old motifs as scars and detachment: what does it all lead up to? The answer, of course, is "Death of a Ladies' Man" itself, the one major new piece of writing on the album. Despite Spector's pretentious arrangement, and the awful repeated ending, the words of this song give an important indication of new directions for Leonard Cohen.

It begins as an encounter between two lovers who are locked in a characteristic interchangeability of powerlessness: "The man she wanted all her life / was hanging by a thread." As the song develops, however, it is clear that the man's tenuous position is caused by his inability to come to grips with a fundamental change in the woman's conception of herself. The Ladies' Man meets Women's Lib.

The phrase "ladies' man" is itself ambiguous. Used to mean a roué, a philanderer, it reflects the values of an earlier age in announcing that the casually impersonal attitude of, say, the young Breavman, is dead—is no longer intellectually or emotionally tenable. But used as a possessive—a man who belongs to a lady, or ladies—it indicates an equally outmoded fear, on the part of the macho male, of the "liberated" woman's aggressiveness.

The "ladies' man," in the old sense, is now the subject of ridicule. "His style was obsolete" and the woman now mocks "his cocky dance." All the "virtues" of his old position are now "burning / in the smoky holocaust"; he offers her the traditional values of sex and "protection / for the issue of her womb," but they are no longer relevant. The plight is the general one of the macho male overtaken by the profound shift in women's consciousness over the last twenty years, but it is also of course a personal reflection on Cohen himself, as may be indicated by such details as the "blonde madonna" and the "monastery wine." When the woman says, "The art of longing's over / and it's never coming back," she is delivering an epitaph on the major part of Cohen's career.

This aspect of the song—its presentation of the ladies' man's "death"—is its most powerful and disturbing feature. The presentation of the lady herself is less certain. She starts out in a traditional attitude of submission, kneeling by his feet, admiring his arms; then, as he begins to falter, she takes on the "virtues" that he has lost, becoming master and teacher. When he offers her sex, she rejects it, mutilating her own sexuality on "a sharpened metal spoon," denying the "bloody rituals" of her own fertility. She then moves through a period of mockery to end up, rather oddly, "living with a boy / who gives her soul an empty room / and gives her body joy." This kind of freedom seems to be possible only with a boy, who may be seen either as belonging to a generation untainted by older assumptions, or as less powerful, more easily dominated. This portrayal verges on the clichés of male chauvinism—the "castrating female," the sexless bitch—and it does not have the same force and conviction as the picture of the man's bewilderment.

The man himself is left, at the end of the song, trying to understand what has happened. "The last time that I saw him / he was trying hard to get / a woman's education / but he's not a woman yet." There is a certain amount of equivocation here, indicated by Cohen's sudden introduction of the "I," which relegates the character "he" to a secondary position. Many men, over the last decade, have had to take "a woman's education," but the aim is surely not to become a woman: it is to redefine what it means to be a man.

The song, it seems to me, has run into an impasse; the problem is genuine enough, but the resolution has still to be found. This inconclusiveness is recognized in the final verse:

> So the great affair is over
>   but whoever would have guessed
> it would leave us all so vacant
>   and so deeply unimpressed.
> It's like our visit to the moon
>   or to that other star:
> I guess you go for nothing
>   if you really want to go that far.

In some ways, this conclusion is merely evasive, declaring as "vacant" a relationship whose issues are anything but. The last lines can be seen as a retreat to old romantic poses: Cohen seeks the poetic inspiration of the moon, or else the self-destruction of the beautiful loser, the Icarian plunge into the sun ("that other star"). Neither course will do much good for the death of a ladies' man.

But if this verse is an unsatisfactory ending for this particular song, it is nevertheless of great interest as a statement at this present stage of Cohen's career. We may be tempted to see it, superficially, as a dismissal of the whole collaboration with Phil Spector, which does indeed "leave us . . . deeply unimpressed"; but more seriously, it testifies to the risks that Cohen is taking not just with this album but with the whole body of material of which *Death of a Ladies' Man* is only a small part. It may well be that he will in the end prove to have gone for nothing — but it has always been the glory of Leonard Cohen that he really wants to go that far.

Reference Notes

Chapter One

1. Allen Ginsberg, *Howl and other poems* (San Francisco: City Lights Books, 1956), p.9.

2. Jeff Nuttall, *Bomb Culture* (New York: Delacorte Press, 1968), pp. 12–13.

3. Sandra Djwa, "After the wipe-out, a renewal," *The Ubyssey,* February 3, 1967, 8. This interview is also the source for the epigraph to this chapter.

4. Michael Gnarowski, "Introduction," *Leonard Cohen: the Artist and His Critics* (Toronto: McGraw-Hill-Ryerson, 1976), p. 2.

5. Sandra Djwa, "Leonard Cohen: Black Romantic," *Canadian Literature,* 34 (Autumn, 1967), 32–42. Reprinted in *Poets and Critics: Essays from Canadian Literature 1966–1974,* ed., George Woodcock (Toronto: Oxford University Press, 1974). pp. 179–190. All page references are to the original appearance of this article.

6. John Glassco, *The Fatal Woman* (Toronto: Anansi, 1974), p. 34.

7. Donald Cameron, ed., *Conversations with Canadian Novelists* (Toronto: Macmillan, 1973), I, 36.

8. Cameron, I, 85.

9. Michael Harris, "Leonard Cohen: The Poet as Hero," *Saturday Night* (June, 1969), 30.

10. Dennis Lee, reply to Robin Matthews, *Saturday Night* (September, 1972), 33.

11. Dennis Lee, "Running and Dwelling: Homage to Al Purdy," *Saturday Night* (July, 1972), 14.

12. Cf. Kroetsch's description of Canadians as "fascinated with problems of equilibrium."

13. The term was introduced by Northrop Frye in his "Conclusion" to the *Literary History of Canada,* and its use was extended by D. G. Jones in *Butterfly on Rock.*

14. D. G. Jones, *Butterfly on Rock* (University of Toronto Press, 1970), pp. 7-8.

15. Stephen Scobie, "Scenes from the Lives of the Saints: a hagiology of Canadian literature," paper delivered to the Canadian Conference of Writers and Critics, University of Calgary, February, 1973; published in *The Lakehead University Review,* VII, 1 (Summer, 1974), 3-20.

16. See Stephen Scobie, "Magic, Not Magicians: *Beautiful Losers* and *Story of O,*" *Canadian Literature,* 45 (Summer, 1970), 56-60.

17. *Beautiful Losers,* p. 76. (See Chapter Three, footnote 18, for bibliographical details.)

18. Susan Sontag, "The Pornographic Imagination," *Styles of Radical Will* (New York: Farrar Strauss Giroux, 1969), p. 69.

19. Margaret Atwood, *Survival* (Toronto: Anansi, 1972), p. 39.

20. *Beautiful Losers,* p. 153.

21. Archibald Lampman, "In November," *The Poems of Archibald Lampman* (University of Toronto Press, 1974), p. 158.

22. For this phrase I must acknowledge my indebtedness to one of my professors at the University of St. Andrews, Nigel Alexander, who used to apply it to Dr. Kinsey and the Elizabethans.

23. Dagmar de Venster, "Leonard Cohen's Women," *Mother Was Not A Person,* ed., Margret Andersen (Montreal: Content Publishing/Black Rose Books, 1972), pp. 96-97.

24. Irving Layton, "The Birth of Tragedy," *Collected Poems* (Toronto: McClelland and Stewart, 1965), p. 64.

25. A. M. Klein, "Portrait of the Poet as Landscape," *The Rocking Chair and Other Poems* (Toronto: Ryerson, 1948), pp. 50-56.

26. Djwa, "After the wipe-out, a renewal."

Chapter Two

1. *Let Us Compare Mythologies* was first published by Contact Press in Toronto in 1956, as No. 1 in the McGill Poetry Series. It was reprinted by McClelland and Stewart in 1966. Since the first edition is very rare, I have used the 1966 edition as my basic text. Unless otherwise noted, all page references in Chapter Two, section (i) are to this edition.

2. Djwa, "Leonard Cohen: Black Romantic," 37.

3. The address may also be a literary allusion: Mountain is only one block over from Crescent, the site of the boarding house in which Morley Callaghan's Peggy Sanderson meets a very similar fate in *The Loved and the Lost* (1951).

4. Michael Ondaatje, *Leonard Cohen* (Toronto: McClelland and Stewart, 1970), p. 10.

5. Djwa, "Leonard Cohen: Black Romantic," 36.

6. T. S. Eliot, "Journey of the Magi," *Collected Poems* (London: Faber and Faber, 1963), p. 109.

7. Leonard Cohen, *The Spice-Box of Earth* (Toronto: McClelland and Stewart, 1961). Unless otherwise noted, all page references in Chapter Two, section (ii) are to this edition.

8. Ondaatje, p. 21.

9. Ondaatje, p. 16.

10. Ondaatje, p. 19.

11. Cohen has twice selected "For Anne" as his favourite among his own poems. See John Robert Colombo, ed., *How Do I Love Thee* (Edmonton: M. G. Hurtig, 1970), pp. xi, 101–102.

12. See Chapter Three, footnote 6.

13. Ondaatje, p. 21.

14. Gary Geddes and Phyllis Bruce, eds., *15 Canadian Poets* (Toronto: Oxford University Press, 1970), p. 82; John Newlove, ed., *Canadian Poetry: The Modern Era* (Toronto: McClelland and Stewart, 1977), p. 67.

15. Irving Layton, Foreword to *Balls for a One-Armed Juggler* (Toronto: McClelland and Stewart, 1963).

16. Leonard Cohen, *Flowers for Hitler* (Toronto: McClelland and Stewart, 1964). Unless otherwise noted, all page references in Chapter Two, section (iii) are to this edition.

17. This paragraph appears on the back cover of the original edition. It was omitted from later paperback re-issues of the book (as was Frank Neufeld's cover drawing.) The re-issues claim, "Here for the first time in a paper edition is *Flowers for Hitler*," but the first edition did have a paperback printing, which cost less than the re-issues.

18. Ondaatje, p. 43.

19. See footnote 15, above.

20. John Glassco, *Memoirs of Montparnasse* (Toronto: Oxford University Press, 1970), p. 27.

21. Ondaatje, pp. 35–36.

22. Djwa, "Leonard Cohen: Black Romantic," 40.

23. See below, pp. 113-115.

24. The version of this poem printed in *Selected Poems* (pp. 126–128) adds the explanatory line "Hitler and his ladies" after "Braun, Raubal and him."

25. See Alan Bullock, *Hitler, A Study in Tyranny* (London, 1952), pp. 358–359, and Joachim Fest, *Hitler* (New York, 1974), pp. 321-323.

26. Gail Fox, "Poetry and the Writer," a talk sponsored by the Canada Council and the League of Canadian Poets, 1974.

27. Djwa, "Leonard Cohen: Black Romantic," 35.

28. Ondaatje, pp. 43–44.

29. See Ondaatje, p. 63.

30. Ondaatje, p. 39.

31. Ondaatje, pp. 41–42.

32. Leonard Cohen, *Parasites of Heaven* (Toronto: McClelland and Stewart, 1966). Unless otherwise noted, all page references in Chapter Two, section (iv) are to this edition.

33. Ondaatje, p. 57.

34. Leonard Cohen, "New Poems," *Selected Poems 1956–1968* (Toronto: McClelland and Stewart, 1968). Unless otherwise noted, all page references in Chapter Two, section (v) are to this edition.

35. Ondaatje, p. 60.

Chapter Three

1. See Ondaatje, p. 43.

2. George Robertson, "Love and Loss," *Canadian Literature,* 19 (Winter, 1964), 69–70.

3. Leonard Cohen, *The Favourite Game* (London: Secker and Warburg, 1963). This is the first edition; the McClelland and Stewart paperback edition (1970) is an offset edition, and so has exactly the same pagination. There is an American edition, *The Favorite Game* (New York: The Viking Press, 1963), reprinted by Avon in paperback in 1965. (Note the spellings "favourite"/ "favorite.") I have used the British/Canadian edition as my text. Unless otherwise noted, all page references in Chapter Three, section (i) are to this edition.

4. This line appears on the front cover of the Avon paperback edition.

5. Patricia Morley, *The Immoral Moralists* (Toronto: Clarke Irwin, 1972), p. 73.

6. The British/Canadian edition prints the complete text of "As the mist leaves no scar" as an epigraph, after the dedication "To my mother." The American editions have no epigraph, and the dedication reads "To _____, as promised."

7. Claude Lévi-Strauss, *The Savage Mind* (London: Weidenfeld and Nicholson, 1962), pp. 23–24.

8. Morley, p. 77.

9. Michael Ondaatje also "loves the pictures of Henri Rousseau." For a fuller treatment of the affinities between Cohen, Ondaatje,

and Rousseau, see my article in *Canadian Literature,* 76 (Spring, 1978), 6–21. "His Legend a Jungle Sleep: Michael Ondaatje and Henri Rousseau."

10. Keats's phrase has since been used by another great contemporary songwriter, Bob Dylan, on his album *Planet Waves.*

11. Ondaatje, p. 26.

12. See Ondaatje, pp. 26–28.

13. Rowland J. Smith, Introduction to the McClelland and Stewart edition, unpaginated.

14. See, for example, the incident (pp. 208–209) when Tamara is with someone else when Breavman wants her.

15. Morley, p. 77.

16. Ondaatje, p. 33.

17. Compare the figure of Bernard in Virginia Woolf's *The Waves,* who envies Louis his ability to remain isolated and perfect: Louis is able to produce the hard "steel rings" of poetry, whereas Bernard can only produce the evanescent "smoke rings" of conversation.

18. Leonard Cohen, *Beautiful Losers* (Toronto: McClelland and Stewart, 1966). Unless otherwise noted, all page references in Chapter Three, section (ii) are to this edition. There is also a paperback edition (Bantam, 1967).

19. Douglas Barbour, "Down With History: some notes towards an understanding of *Beautiful Losers,*" *Open Letter,* Second Series, No. 8 (Summer, 1974), 48.

20. Professor R. T. Harrison has observed, in conversation, that the elevator also "goes down on" Edith: a gruesome but not uncharacteristic implied pun.

21. F. M. Macri, *"Beautiful Losers* and the Canadian Experience," *The Journal of Commonwealth Literature,* VIII, 1 (June, 1973), 93.

22. Linda Hutcheon, *"Beautiful Losers:* All the Polarities," *Canadian Literature,* 59 (Winter, 1974), p. 53. This is a very interesting article, but one with which I am in fundamental disagreement.

23. See Chapter One, footnote 9.

24. Leslie Monkman (see below, footnote 33) attempts to draw a parallel between the stages of the approach to Oscotarach's hut and various episodes in the novel, but the parallels he offers are rather tenuous. He is also wrong in identifying the "piercing needle" (p. 17), as F.'s: the speaker of that passage is *I*.

25. See Barbour's article for a full discussion of the word "apocalyptic."

26. Hutcheon, p. 44. I disagree with the use of the word "parody" here.

27. Barbour, pp. 53–54.

28. Phyllis Webb, "Breaking," *The Sea Is Also A Garden* (Toronto: Ryerson Press, 1962), unpaginated.

29. Ondaatje, p. 50.

30. It will be seen from the whole course of my discussion of *Beautiful Losers* that I am in deep disagreement with the view of the novel put forward by Dennis Lee in *Savage Fields: An Essay in Literature and Cosmology* (Toronto: Anansi, 1977). My detailed criticisms of Lee's reading will be found in a review of *Savage Fields* for *Canadian Literature;* here I can only indicate very briefly some of my major points of disagreement. (See also footnote 38.)

    The account of Catherine's sexuality given above will, I hope, serve as a refutation of Lee's notion that Catherine's "rejection" of sexuality was "an act of blasphemy," or "a fall" (*Savage Fields,* pp. 64–65). The problem does not lie with Catherine but with that aspect of society—whether it be Indian or Christian, Jesuit or Canadian, seventeenth- or twentieth-century—which refuses to accept the totality, and hence the disruptiveness, of Catherine's commitment. Far from being a symptom of the disease, Catherine is one of the possible cures.

31. Barbour, p. 49.

32. See, for instance, pages 13, 15, 37, 44, 67, 78–80 and 83–84.

33. Leslie Monkman, "*Beautiful Losers:* Mohawk Myth and Jesuit Legend," *Journal of Canadian Fiction,* III, 3 (1974), 57.

34. *The Favourite Game,* pp. 222–223.

35. See Barbour, p. 51. In 1965, when Cohen was completing *Beautiful Losers,* the big Rolling Stones hit was "I Can't Get No Satisfaction"—a sentiment entirely apposite to the book. It would also

be nice to see an implied pun in the "dancing boulders" through which the pilgrim must himself dance on his way to the hut of Oscotarach (pp. 114, 183).

36. The Bantam paperback edition here has "?" instead of "!"

37. *The Favourite Game*, p. 191.

38. This view of F. is another of my major points of disagreement with Dennis Lee's *Savage Fields*. Lee argues that the destruction of F.'s personality in Book Two "undercuts" the validity of the world view presented in Book One (*Savage Fields,* p. 83.) I argue the exact opposite: that the stripping away of all aspects of F.'s mastery in Book Two is the necessary process by which alone he can enter the ecstatic reality of Book Three. Lee's reading leads him to see *Beautiful Losers* as a fractured failure in which Book Three makes no sense; I would argue that my view allows us to see *Beautiful Losers* as a successful unity crowned by Book Three. My view accounts for the structure of the novel as it actually stands; Lee seems to want Cohen to have written a different novel, and, not finding it, Lee is forced to dismiss the novel that Cohen did write.

39. "Suzanne," *Songs of Leonard Cohen.* (See below, Chapter Four, footnote 1.)

40. *Let Us Compare Mythologies,* p. 63.

41. Djwa, "After the wipe-out, a renewal."

Chapter Four

1. Leonard Cohen has issued, so far, seven records:
Songs of Leonard Cohen (1968). Columbia, CS 9533.
Songs from a Room (1969). Columbia, CS 9767.
Songs of Love and Hate (1971). Columbia, C 30103.
Live Songs (1973). Columbia, KC 31724.
New Skin for the Old Ceremony (1974). Columbia, KC 33167.
The Best of Leonard Cohen (1975). Columbia, ES 90334.
Death of a Ladies' Man (1977). Columbia, PES 90436.
There is no single authoritative text for the songs. A lyrics sheet was included with the first album, and lyrics are printed on the cover of *Death of a Ladies' Man,* but none of the other albums included a text. Various collections of words and sheet music have been published, of which the most comprehensive is *Leonard Cohen Folk* (New York: Charles Hansen, n.d.) These texts, how-

ever, frequently diverge from the words actually sung on the records. Therefore, all my quotations in Chapter Four, and in Chapter Five sections (ii) and (iii), are direct transcriptions from the records themselves. The lineation and punctuation are, consequently, in many cases mine: most often, the rhyme makes the lineation obvious, and I have kept the punctuation to a minimum.

2. Frank Davey, *From There to Here* (Erin: Press Porcepic, 1974), p. 69.

3. *The Favourite Game,* p. 97.

4. *Beautiful Losers,* p. 224.

5. Jan Dawson, "McCabe and Mrs. Miller," *Sight and Sound,* Vol. 40, No. 4 (Autumn, 1971), 221.

6. *Parasites of Heaven,* p. 57.

7. This title is perhaps an echo of Bob Dylan's "Sooner or Later One Of Us Must Know."

8. The Name—Suzanne—and the structure of verses—Suzanne, Jesus, Suzanne—are repeated in James Taylor's "Fire and Rain."

9. "Tea" could also be understood as drug terminology for marijuana.

10. Cf. *Beautiful Losers,* p. 8.

11. See, for example, the Judy Collins version on *Who Knows Where The Time Goes* (Elektra: EKS 74033). There are also fine versions of this song by Joe Cocker and Rita Coolidge.

12. There is an interesting variant on the words of this song in the version sung by Judy Collins (on *Who Knows Where The Time Goes*). Instead of the lines "I will help you if I must / I will kill you if I can," she sings "And may I never learn to scorn / The body out of chaos born / The woman and the man." These lines make even more explicit the rejection of "schemes" and systems which have no place for the individual.

13. Unspecified, that is, in the English version. The song is originally a French Resistance song from World War II, and the French lyrics identify the invading army as German. The translation makes the song more general. For further details, see Jacques Vassal, *Leonard Cohen* (Paris: Albin Michel, 1974), pp. 47–48.

14. *The Spice-Box of Earth,* pp. 42–43.

15. The French translation by Graeme Allwright omits this phrase

(ending only "Et je sais / Que demain, que demain, que demain / Sera bien"), and thus changes completely the meaning of the song. Allwright's translations, which are generally much better than this one, are available on *Graeme Allwright chante Leonard Cohen* (Mercury: 6.325.600).

16. *Parasites of Heaven*, p. 33.

17. By Judy Collins, on *In My Life* (Elektra: EKS 7320).

18. Vassal says that "Famous Blue Raincoat" is also an old song, written as far back as the late fifties, when Cohen was at Columbia. See Vassal, p. 15.

19. It may be remembered that Catherine Tekakwitha is also called "Perfectly Shy": see *Beautiful Losers*, p. 207.

20. Curiously, this line is printed in *Leonard Cohen Folk* (p. 63) as "Sincerely, your crime."

21. *The Energy of Slaves*, p. 32. See Chapter Five, footnote 8.

22. Bob Dylan, "Chimes of Freedom," *Writings and Drawings* (New York: Knopf, 1973), p. 126.

23. See above, p. 60.

24. The lines "the slim unlovely virgin anyone would lay / the white figure floating among German beards" are compressed into the single line "the slim unlovely virgin floating among German beards." See *Flowers for Hitler*, p. 88.

Chapter Five

1. This quotation comes from the unpublished manuscript "Death of a Lady's Man," a copy of which was generously provided for me by the author.

2. See above, pages 144-149.

3. *The Energy of Slaves*, p. 112. See below, footnote 8.

4. Roy MacSkimming, " 'New' Leonard Cohen opens up his thoughts," *The Toronto Star*, January 22, 1975, E16. This interview is also the source of the epigraph to this chapter.

5. MacSkimming, p. E16.

6. Letter to the author, July 28, 1977.

7. Anonymous comment, quoted in Sandra Martin, "Don't be impatient: Leonard Cohen will let you see his new poems. Eventually." *Saturday Night* (November, 1977), 30–35.

8. Leonard Cohen, *The Energy of Slaves* (Toronto: McClelland and Stewart, 1972). Unless otherwise noted, all page references in Chapter Five, section (i) are to this edition.

9. Tom Wayman, "Cohen's Women," *Canadian Literature,* 60 (Spring, 1974), 89–93.

10. "Please Don't Pass Me By," *Live Songs.*

11. Cover statement on the original edition of *Flowers for Hitler.*

12. Interestingly, the Swedish edition of *The Energy of Slaves— Puckelryggens Sånger* (Stockholm, 1972)—prints this poem on the back cover:

   Jag gör den här sången åt dig
   Världens Herre
   som har allt som finns i världen
   utom den här sången.

13. Wayman, p. 92.

14. See Chapter Four, footnote 1.

15. *The Energy of Slaves,* p. 39.

16. These words are quoted from memory from an introduction Cohen gave to the song at a concert in Paris in June, 1976. The dedication to Joplin is not explicit in the song, and Cohen coyly avoids it in his notes on the song for the back cover of *The Best of Leonard Cohen.* Jacques Vassal suggests that an early version of the song was written as far back as the fifties (see Vassal, pp. 15, 156). Nevertheless, I have always felt, from my first hearing of the song, that it was about Janis Joplin, and I was pleased to hear this conclusion confirmed by Cohen himself.

17. See above, p. 171.

18. *The Energy of Slaves,* p. 9.

19. See Chapter Four, footnote 1.

20. Janet Maslin, "'There's Nothing I Like About It—But It May Be a Classic,'" *The New York Times,* November 6, 1977, pp. 18, 40.

21. David Pyette, "The mellowing of a ladies' man," *The Montreal Star,* November 26, 1977, pp. D1, D7.

22. See above, pp. 127-128.

23. Pyette, p. D1.

24. *The Spice-Box of Earth,* p. 56.

25. *Parasites of Heaven,* pp. 72–73.

26. See above, p. 64.

27. *The Energy of Slaves,* p. 35.

Selected Bibliography

1. Books

Gnarowski, Michael, ed. *Leonard Cohen: the Artist and his Critics.*
Toronto: McGraw-Hill Ryerson, 1976. Includes bibliography.

Lee, Dennis. *Savage Fields: an Essay in Literature and Cosmology.*
Toronto: Anansi, 1977.

Matos, Manuel Cadafaz de. *Leonard Cohen: Redescoberta da Vida
e uma Alegoria a Eros.* Lisbon: Livros E (co) logiar a Terra, 1975.

Morley, Patricia A. *The Immoral Moralists: Hugh MacLennan and
Leonard Cohen.* Toronto: Clarke Irwin, 1972.

Ondaatje, Michael. *Leonard Cohen.* Toronto: McClelland and
Stewart, 1970. Includes bibliography.

Vassal, Jacques. *Leonard Cohen.* Paris: Albin Michel, 1974.

2. Articles and Reviews

Anonymous. "Black Romanticism." *Time,* September 13, 1968, 92,
96, 98. Included in Gnarowski.

Anonymous. "In Haste." *Times Literary Supplement,* July 24, 1969,
828. Included in Gnarowski.

Anonymous, "Automotively Erotic." *Times Literary Supplement,* April 23, 1970, 445.

Barbour, Douglas. Review of *Selected Poems. Dalhousie Review,* XLVIII (Winter, 1968), 567–568. Included in Gnarowski.

Barbour, Douglas. "Down with History: some notes towards an understanding of *Beautiful Losers.*" *Open Letter,* Second Series, No. 8 (Summer, 1974), 48–60. Included in Gnarowski.

Batten, Jack, Michael Harris, and Don Owen. "Leonard Cohen: The Poet As Hero." *Saturday Night* (June, 1969), 23–32. The Michael Harris interview is included in Gnarowski.

Bensky, Lawrence M. "What Happened To Tekakwitha." *The New York Times Book Review,* May 8, 1966, 30. Included in Gnarowski.

Bissett, Bill "!!!!!" *Alphabet,* 13 (June, 1967), 94-95.

Bloomstone, F.A. "The Poetry of Leonard Cohen and Margaret Atwood." *McGill Reporter,* Vol. 1, No. 14 (January 20, 1969), 7.

Bowering, George. "Inside Leonard Cohen." *Canadian Literature,* 33 (Summer, 1967), 71-72. Included in Gnarowski.

Bromige, David. "The Lean and the Luscious." *Canadian Literature,* 10 (Autumn, 1961), 87-88. Included in Gnarowski.

Buitenhuis, Peter. "Two Solitudes Revisited: Hugh MacLennan and Leonard Cohen." *The Literary Half-Yearly,* VII, 2 (July, 1972), 19-32.

Chambers, D.D.C. "[Leonard Cohen.]" In *Contemporary Poets of the English Language,* ed. Rosalie Murphy. Chicago/London: St. James Press, 1970. Pp. 209-210.

Colombo, John Robert. "Cohen: The Operative." *The Globe and Mail Magazine* (December 10, 1966), 22.

Davey, Frank. "Leonard Cohen and Bob Dylan: Poetry and the Popular Song." *Alphabet,* 17 (December, 1970), 12-29. Included in Gnarowski.

Davey, Frank. "Leonard Cohen." *From There To Here.* Erin: Press Porcepic, 1974. Pp. 68-73. Includes bibliography.

De Venster, Dagmar. "Leonard Cohen's Women." In *Mother Was Not a Person,* ed. Margret Andersen. Montreal: Content publishing/Black Rose Books, 1972. Pp. 96-97.

Djwa, Sandra. "After the wipe-out, a renewal." *The Ubyssey*, February 3, 1967, 8.

Djwa, Sandra. "Leonard Cohen: Black Romantic." *Canadian Literature*, 34 (Autumn, 1967), 32-42. Reprinted in *Poets and Critics: Essays from Canadian Literature*, ed. George Woodcock. Toronto: Oxford University Press, 1974. Pp. 179-190. Included in Gnarowski.

Donaldson, Allan. Review of *Let Us Compare Mythologies*. *The Fiddlehead*, 30 (November, 1956), 30-31. Included in Gnarowski.

Duffy, Dennis. "Beautiful Beginners." *Tamarack Review*, 40 (Summer, 1966), 75-79. Included in Gnarowski.

F.D. (Frank Davey). "Leonard Cohen." In *Supplement to the Oxford Companion to Canadian History and Literature*, ed. William Toye. Toronto: Oxford University Press, 1973. P. 45.

Garebian, Keith. "Desire as Art: Leonard Cohen's *The Favourite Game*." *The Golden Dog*, 4 (November, 1974), 29-34.

Geddes, Gary, "Leonard Cohen." *20th Century Poetry and Poetics*. Toronto: Oxford University Press, 1969. Pp. 577-578.

Geddes, Gary. "Leonard Cohen." *Fifteen Canadian Poets*. Toronto: Oxford University Press, 1970. Pp. 272-274.

Goldstein, Richard. "Beautiful Creep." *The Village Voice*, December 28, 1967, 18, 20, 27. Included in Gnarowski.

Gose, E.B. "Of Beauty and Unmeaning." *Canadian Literature*, 29 (Summer, 1966), 61-63.

Grant, Judith Skelton, "Leonard Cohen's Poems-Songs." *Studies in Canadian Literature*, II, 1 (Winter, 1977). Pp. 102-107.

Hafferkamp, J. "Ladies and Gents, Leonard Cohen." *Rolling Stone*, 75 (February 4, 1971), 26-28.

Holden, Stephen, "A haunting by Spector." *Rolling Stone,* 257 (January 26, 1978), 17.

Hutcheon, Linda. "*Beautiful Losers*: All the Polarities." *Canadian Literature*, 59 (Winter, 1974), 42-56. Reprinted in *The Canadian Novel in the Twentieth Century*, ed. George Woodcock. Toronto: McClelland and Stewart, 1975. Pp. 298-311.

Jackson, M. "Leonard Cohen: He's Bored, Bitter, and out of Love." *The Toronto Star*, November 25, 1972, 64.

Jones, D. G. "In Search of America." *Boundary 2*, III, 1 (Fall, 1974), 227-246.

Kleiman, Ed. "Blossom Show." *Alphabet*, 9 (November, 1964), 78. Included in Gnarowski.

Klinck, Carl F., and Reginald E. Watters. Bibliography of Leonard Cohen. *Canadian Anthology*, Third Edition. Toronto: Gage, 1974. Pp. 662-663.

Lumsden, Susan. "Leonard Cohen Wants the Unconditional Leadership of the World." *Weekend Magazine*, XX, 37, 22-24. Included in Gnarowski.

Macri, F. M. "*Beautiful Losers* and the Canadian Experience." *The Journal of Commonwealth Literature*, VIII, 1 (June, 1973), 88-96.

MacSkimming, Roy. " 'New' Leonard Cohen opens up his thoughts." *The Toronto Star*, January 22, 1975, E16.

Mandel, Eli. Review of *The Spice-Box of Earth*. *Canadian Forum*, 41 (September, 1961), 140-141.

Mandel, Eli. "Cohen's life as a Slave." *Another Time*. Erin: Press Porcepic, 1977. Pp. 124-136.

Marchand, Philip. "Beautiful Survivor: On Tour with Leonard Cohen." *Miss Chatelaine* (March, 1975), 63, 97-101.

Martin, Sandra. "Don't be impatient: Leonard Cohen will let you see his new poems. Eventually." *Saturday Night* (November, 1977) 30-35.

Maslin, Janet. " 'There's Nothing I Like About It — But It May Be a Classic.' " *The New York Times*, November 6, 1977, 18, 40.

Monkman, Leslie. "*Beautiful Losers*: Mohawk Myth and Jesuit Legend." *Journal of Canadian Fiction*, III, 3 (1974), 57-59.

Morley, Patricia. "The Knowledge of Strangerhood: 'The Monuments Were Made Of Worms.' " *Journal of Canadian Fiction*, 1 (Summer, 1972), 56-60. Included in Gnarowski.

Pacey, Desmond. Review of *Let Us Compare Mythologies*. *Queen's Quarterly*, 63 (Autumn, 1956), 438-439.

Pacey, Desmond. "The Phenomenon of Leonard Cohen." *Canadian Literature*, 34 (Autumn, 1967), 5-23. Included in Gnarowski.

Purdy, Al. "Leonard Cohen: a Personal Look." *Canadian Literature*, 23 (Winter, 1965), 7-16.

Pyette, David. "The mellowing of a ladies' man." *The Montreal Star*, November 26, 1977, D1, D7.

Robertson, George. "Love and Loss." *Canadian Literature*, 19 (Winter, 1964), 69-70.

Rodriguez, Juan. "Poet's Progress—to Sainthood and Back." *The Montreal Star*, June 31, 1969, 3-4.

Saltzman, Paul. "Famous Last Words from Leonard Cohen." *Maclean's*, Vol. 85. No. 6 (June, 1972), 6, 77-80.

Scobie, Stephen, "Magic, Not Magicians: *Beautiful Losers* and *Story of O.*" *Canadian Literature*, 45 (Summer, 1970), 56-60. Included in Gnarowski.

Scobie, Stephen. "Scenes from the Lives of the Saints: a hagiology of Canadian Literature." *The Lakehead University Review*, VII, 1 (Summer, 1974), 3-20.

Scobie, Stephen. Review of *The Energy of Slaves*. *The Humanities Association Review*, XXIV, 3 (Summer, 1973), 240-243.

Smith, Rowland J. Introduction to *The Favorite Game*. Toronto: McClelland and Stewart, 1970.

Snider, Burr. "Leonard Cohen: Zooey Glass in Europe." *Gypsy*, I, 1, 10-14. Included in Gnarowski.

Stern, Daniel. "Picaros in Montreal." *Saturday Review*, 46 (October, 1963), 42.

Waddington, M. "Bankrupt Ideas and Chaotic Style." *The Globe and Mail Magazine*, April 30, 1966, 17.

Wain, John. "Making It New." *The New York Review of Books*, VI, 17 (April 28, 1966), 17-19. Included in Gnarowski.

Wayman, Tom. "Cohen's Women." *Canadian Literature*, 60 (Spring, 1974), 89-93.

Wiebe, Rudy. *The Blue Mountains of China*. Toronto: McClelland and Stewart, 1970. Pp. 183-184.

Williams, Stephen. "The confessions of Leonard Cohen." *Toronto Life* (February, 1978), 48-49, 59-62.

Wilson, Milton. Review of *Let Us Compare Mythologies*. *Canadian Forum*, 36 (March, 1957), 282-284. Included in Gnarowski.

Wilson, Milton. Review of *The Spice-Box of Earth*. *University of Toronto Quarterly*, 31 (July, 1962), 432-437.

Wilson, Milton. Review of *Flowers for Hitler*. *University of Toronto Quarterly*, XXXIV, 4 (July, 1965), 352-354. Included in Gnarowski.

Woodcock, George. "The Song of the Sirens: Reflections on Leonard Cohen." *Odysseus Ever Returning*. Toronto: McClelland and Stewart, 1970. Pp. 92-110. Included in Gnarowski.